THE FLAVOUR OF SPICE

Journeys, Recipes, Stories

Marryam H. Reshii

hachette INDIA

First published in India in 2017 by Hachette India
(Registered name: Hachette Book Publishing India Pvt. Ltd)
An Hachette UK company
www.hachetteindia.com

This edition published in 2021

SRD

Hardback edition ISBN 978-93-5009-908-7
Paperback edition ISBN 978-93-5009-571-3
Ebook edition ISBN 978-93-5009-909-4

Hachette Book Publishing India Pvt. Ltd
4th & 5th Floors, Corporate Centre,
Plot No. 94, Sector 44, Gurugram – 122003, India

Typeset in Chaparral Pro by SÜRYA, New Delhi

Printed and bound in India by
Manipal Technologies Limited, Manipal

FSC
www.fsc.org
MIX
Paper from responsible sources
FSC™ C104740

THE FLAVOUR OF SPICE

Marryam H. Reshii has written about food for the past three decades for a number of publications, including the *Times of India*. She is the curator of the prestigious *Times Food Guide* for Delhi and the author of several works on Kashmir, restaurants, chefs and recipes. She thinks of her life as divided into two phases – before she discovered spices and after (although it is impossible to say whether Marryam discovered spices or they discovered her).

Praise for *The Flavour of Spice*

'Celebrating spices in all its glory, noted food writer Marryam H. Reshii in her book, *The Flavour of Spice* embarks upon a delightful journey tracing their history as far back as possible.' – NDTV

'*The Flavour of Spice* celebrates spices and talks about the many ways in which they shape our cuisine. This book is a result of Marryam H. Reshii's pursuit to comprehend the nuances of these indispensable ingredients.' – Food Lovers TV

'*The Flavour of Spice* needs a volume II very, very soon.' – *Deccan Chronicle*

'Flavour guaranteed' – *The Hindu*

'If you are interested in knowing more about spices, this is the book for you.' – Anil Mulchandani, food writer and *Times of India* restaurant critic

'A brilliantly pieced together book, which showcases recipes collected over the years, the medicinal benefits that spices have been treasured for, the very sources they come from and the cuisines of those lands, and how we're all faintly related in our food cultures sometimes.' – Manu Chandra, chef and owner of Toast and Tonic, Fatty Bao and Monkey Bar

'Nurtured over years, brilliantly researched, hugely knowledgeable, yet written with humour and accessible to the common reader, this book really raises the bar for food writing in India.' – Sumana Mukherjee, food writer and critic

'A captivating narrative backed by serious academic research, folklore, and warm stories interspersed with recipes (from chefs, from her home, from friends' homes), makes *The Flavour of Spice* a book that appeals to everyone, whether you want to cook from it or read it in the study.' – Saee Koranne-Khandekar, author of *Crumbs* and *Pangat, a Feast*

To Hafeez, the love of my life

Contents

INTRODUCTION

My love affair with spices started at the unlikeliest of places: the funeral of a close friend's brother. I was at the friend's place, helping out with the unending stream of visitors who had come to pay their last respects, when she turned to me and said that lunch – a humble khichdi – was being served in the next room. Then, with an apologetic grimace, she added, 'Only thing, it doesn't have any spices. Because we are in mourning.' That's when I had my epiphany: Indian food is so inextricably interwoven with spices that not only is one unthinkable without the other but the sign of being in mourning is to abjure spices. Until then, I had been more or less indifferent about the world of spices and their exact role in our cuisine. But once my interest was piqued, there was no turning back.

A millennium ago, the term 'Indian spices' didn't mean what it does today. For instance, chillies – which in the eyes of the world are most commonly associated with Indian food – only came to our shores approximately 450 years ago. Not to mention spices like coriander and fenugreek, which came from Egypt and Greece respectively, as well as nigella seeds, mustard seeds, cloves, cinnamon, nutmeg and mace. India has taken all of these and a host of others and incorporated them in supremely sophisticated ways into its regional cuisines, even going on to become the largest producer and consumer of spices in the world. Not for us the use of a single spice as a top-note in a coulis on a plate of panna cotta. Every single dish, from main courses like the

Dogri khatta meat to desserts like payasam and halwa, is bathed in a medley of spice, to the extent that it is the spice that defines a dish rather than the main ingredient. Not even accompaniments like yogurt have escaped the touch of spice, often flavoured with dark-roasted cumin, black cardamom or asafoetida, as any street-food seller will tell you. You'll even find them in every Indian sweet shop, in the golden yellow of the laddoos made with sesame and khoya and flavoured with a touch of saffron, or in the scent of green cardamom that permeates the milk-based confections.

Indian cooking plays with spices in a manner that is unparalleled anywhere else in the world. Some spices are roasted before being used, others are pounded finely or coarsely depending on the recipe. Spices are used for tempering right at the end of cooking, or at the very beginning. They can be dry-ground or pulverized with other ingredients like coconut. They can be flashed in smoking-hot oil for just a second or sautéed for half-an-hour over low simmering heat.

In fact, spices are so integral to our culture that they've moved out of our kitchens and into every aspect of our daily lives. Go to the chemist to buy a winter tonic and you'll be given a jar of Chyawanprash. The gooey brown paste tastes like an oriental Christmas cake, laden as it is with quite as many aromatic spices as a plum pudding: cinnamon, cloves, cardamom and long pepper. Also at the chemist's are several spices lurking on shelves, disguised as other products. If you want to rid yourself of acne, use a well-known brand of cream that contains turmeric. If you dream of becoming a few shades fairer, there are several products that contain saffron to fulfil your desire. Want sparkling pearly whites? Use a toothpaste that has clove oil in it.

On your way back to the car from the chemist's, stop for a paan; it will probably contain a silver-coated green cardamom and will be pierced with a clove to keep it firmly folded. Your car, being brand new, has a swastik sign on the bonnet. It has been made with a slurry of turmeric and water and signifies good luck – the golden yellow of the turmeric in itself an auspicious colour. Check into a spa today and it's likely that the body scrub being used contains black pepper, turmeric and fennel. At home, too, you can treat your spice rack as an instant-remedy counter. If you suffer from a cold, cough or indigestion, there is no need to look beyond your kitchen.

Considering how all-pervasive spices are, it is rather surprising how little is known about them. Ask the average grocer anywhere in the country where the cumin he is selling comes from and he'll answer with a bored shrug. Ask a spice seller where the large, carmine chilli at his store comes from and unhesitatingly he'll reply 'Kashmir'. Actually it doesn't, because what is called 'Kashmiri' in the market is usually grown from seeds that, at some point, originated in Kashmir, but have been grown for years, if not decades, in Karnataka and Andhra Pradesh.

It has always surprised me that schoolchildren are taught about the crops that grow in each state but never learn about spices, although some spices are extremely important crops in the states where they are cultivated. Even state maps resolutely avoid the smallest mention of spices. They list every agricultural crop, from pulses to grains to flowers and vegetables, but none of them touches upon spices. I find this utterly confounding. (Or, perhaps, looked at from another perspective, it is fitting, since spices are like secret ingredients that are added to lentils, lamb or rice, turning them into dishes fit for kings.) One thing is for sure: There's little literature from within the country about our spices and their provenance, and that which does exist tends to be written with all the passion of a textbook.

So how is it that India has co-opted spices that came from all over the world and integrated them so seamlessly with the host of regional cuisines that exist within its borders? At what point in history did this trade take place? How did the spices that we see on our plates today come to be grown in India? I have been intrigued by these questions for years, and the more I have delved into the spice story, the more fascinated I have become.

One aspect in particular that I have found no apparent answer to is the provenance of a spice versus its use. Take Kashmir, for instance. It might be the only place where saffron grows in India, but Kashmiri cuisine uses insignificant amounts of saffron, whereas the predominantly vegetarian states of Gujarat and Rajasthan use the spice generously in their fare. Or take West Bengal. It is one of the largest users of poppy seeds in the country, which grows nowhere near its borders. Just how did spices travel from one corner of the country to the other? How was it that turmeric from Tamil Nadu and fennel from the fields of Uttar Pradesh (UP) made their way to the very north, to Kashmir?

And so began my quest to find answers to these innumerable questions. For many years now, learning about spices, travelling to spice markets and plantations, and worrying chefs, food technologists and indeed any hapless individual from the trade who comes my way for any nuggets of information they may have, has been the mission of my life. On the way, I've collected information, stories and recipes, some of which I've shared in this book.

Although I abhor one-size-fits-all terms like 'seed spices' and 'tree spices' because they are maddeningly inconclusive, they do have their uses, especially when you're writing a book! So, for the sake of convenience, I've divided the book into three sections. The first is the 'big four' – chilli, turmeric, cumin and coriander, the four spices that you are most likely to find in any household across the country, whether they are called mirchi, haldi, zeera, dhaniya or by any other vernacular name. Next I've grouped together spices like black pepper, cardamom and cinnamon into a section called the aromatics (in my opinion, a far more accurate term than 'tree spices', their official classification). I've also included in this section asafoetida and kalpasi (I have used the Tamil name throughout since the English term, black stone flower, is a less than accurate descriptor) because they are avowedly not seed spices but are known for their aromas, even though I am aware that they do not quite fit into a conventional list of aromatics. And finally, seed spices like poppy, nigella and mustard, used in specific cuisines in different parts of the country, round off the last of the three sections. Saunth, or dried ginger, while technically neither an aromatic nor a seed spice, I've included in the seed spices section because its usage, judicious and only in certain parts of the country, matches the usage of other spices in this section.

Before you begin, I must warn you that this book is by no means exhaustive, since my own journey into the many enigmas of the spice world is far from over. I still have a wish list as long as my arm. I still haven't visited the original islands in Indonesia where cloves and nutmeg were first discovered. I haven't been to Romania, the northernmost outpost of coriander growing that I know of. Come to think of it, I still have to meet a few million home-cooks from all over our own country, who could tell me how they use spices in their unique ways. It is a subject that is so vast that it is impossible to find all the answers in a single lifetime. Because that is the beauty of spice: It is not a static subject, but one that changes constantly from one part of India to the next, and from one period in history to another. In each era, in each incarnation, it changes our palates, and our lives, in irrevocable ways, and I hope this book can carry a small part of that magic to you.

THE BIG FOUR

CHILLI

Ask any ten people from across the world what they correlate with Indian food, and at least nine of them will reply with a single word: 'Chillies'. It will not be far off the mark either, even though it was, in historical terms, only last week that the marriage between Indian food and chillies was solemnised.

This hottest of spices has been around since 7500 BCE, pre-dating the Indus Civilization by five millennia. The earliest accounts that we have of chillies being used in cuisine are from around 5000 BCE in Mexico: Astonishing when you consider that chilli reached Indian shores a mere 450 years ago, that too, when the Portuguese brought it with them to Goa, in what must rank as a supreme twist of irony. It seems scarcely believable that it was the Europeans who introduced Indians to an ingredient that has since been subsumed into Indian cookery so thoroughly that today India is the world's largest producer, consumer and exporter of chillies, of which 75 per cent come from Andhra Pradesh alone.

Considering what an integral spice chillies are to Indian cuisine, it is mystifying how the records that exist are maddeningly imprecise; all we know for sure is that the Portuguese brought chillies to Goa, presumably from Brazil. In her fascinating book, *Curry: A Tale of Cooks and Conquerors*, Lizzie Collingham notes that within 30 years of Vasco da Gama arriving at Goa (in 1498 BCE), three varieties of chillies had started being grown around Goa.

They were known as Pernambucco peppers, suggesting that their place of origin was Brazil, a Portuguese colony at the time. Their use grew rapidly southwards, supplanting the far more expensive black pepper and pipli (long pepper). According to Collingham, the use of chillies spread to Delhi and Agra only with the Marathas towards the end of the Mughal period. It is scarcely believable that even 250 years after the Portuguese introduced chillies to India, North India was still without this spice.

So integral is chilli to our cuisine that the most damning indictment of a meal in India is the sentence: *Namak mirchi kam hai* (There's not much salt or chillies in this dish). It puts the cook down completely. It also tells us about the elemental place of chillies in the Indian diet. Nobody quibbles over the amount of turmeric or cumin in a dish. But add too few chillies and the dish is bland and boring.

But where did the chilli originate? Scientists believe that Bolivia is the cradle of chillies and have postulated an interesting theory about its flavour versus its hotness. Every plant in the wild needs the propagation of its seeds to multiply. In the case of chillies, it's mostly done by birds. On the other hand, destructive insects also perceive the chilli as delicious and bore through its flesh, but do not play a part in seed dispersal. So nature seems to have devised a way for chilli plants to be hot enough for birds to find attractive, but too hot for insects to handle. Scientists discovered this when they looked at chilli plants growing wild all over Bolivia: Those that existed in relatively cold, temperate areas did not have to be protected from insects and were mild while those in hot, humid areas needed all the protection they could get from insects, and so were hot.

Today, the world has moved a long way from wild chilli plants. It is believed that Mexico was the first country where chilli plants were cultivated. It certainly makes sense. Though every country of South America grows chillies, none have the spectacular range of Mexican chillies, where it is believed to have been introduced over 6,000 years ago by Native American communities called the Pueblo. And indeed, the use of chillies in mole sauces in Mexican cuisine is more nuanced than anywhere else in the world.

Now grown in many places in Asia, Africa, South and Central America, as well as Europe and Australia, chillies are carefully hybridized for colour, hotness and thinness (or thickness) of skin. Out of the approximately 200 varieties of chillies grown in India, 36 grow in Andhra Pradesh, India's largest chilli-growing belt. Ever heard of wonder hot, teja or byadagi? No? You might still have tasted any, or all, of them at some point in your life because these are just some of the varieties of chillies that grow in Andhra Pradesh.

Although chillies are grown in many parts of Andhra, the catchment area is certainly Guntur, with its rich black cotton soil that is conducive to chilli farming. So it makes sense that I start my journey into the world of chillies here.

In Guntur, the government-controlled market yard for chillies (that, by its very nature, does not take into account chillies from other regions in Andhra Pradesh, much less those from Rajasthan and Tamil Nadu, India's other chilli-growing regions) has an area of 50 acres that allows 2,000 farmers to sell upto 60,000 quintals of fiery red chillies a day to customers that range from aggregators to branded spice merchants. You'll often see huge trucks around the area, with goods securely wrapped in layers of tarpaulin, plying miles and miles from India's chilli capital to destinations across the country. You'll know what they're carrying as soon as you get the familiar pungent whiff, right in the middle of a highway. I remember on my drive back from Guntur, through Vijaywada to Hyderabad, the air-conditioning of the taxi I had hired had coughed weakly and faded away. There had been no other option but to roll down the windows. After a while on the road, I developed a sort of sixth sense about the giant trucks that overtook us ever so often. They were laden to the gills with chillies, which had presumably been packed into sacks and then covered with at least one layer of water-proofing and then tied firmly down with ropes. But even through all the layers, they still exuded a pungency that burnt my eyes and seared my throat, making me hurriedly roll up the windows.

Around the area, you'll also see fields of chilli plants, vast courtyards where different types of chillies are being sorted expertly by women, who appear to suffer no ill-effects after sifting through chillies for upto eight hours a day, and four-storeyed cold storage facilities that have a holding capacity of up to 50 lakh sacks, each containing 50 kilos. Freshly harvested chillies typically have a moisture capacity of 80 per cent, which makes them highly susceptible to spoilage. Keeping them in cold storage till the farmer gets the right price is a practice that works well for everybody concerned: The farmer gets his price, the cold storage owner gets his rent and the customer gets chillies that have taken anywhere between two to eight days to dry out, depending on the temperatures at that time. Guntur has, in its immediate vicinity, no fewer than 600 cold storage facilities.

You don't have to have endless acres of land to stand up and be counted as a chilli farmer in Guntur. In fact, all you need is 10–12 acres and the biggies in Guntur have around 20 acres. Unlike many other spice crops, farmers here don't have to hedge their bets by planting more than one crop. It is just chillies that do it for them because demand always outstrips supply in this famous chilli growing belt. The more pressing problem for them is the variety of chilli to plant. The endemic variety, Guntur Sannam, is beautiful to look at, but agriculturalists deride it since it's very susceptible to pests. LCA 334 is one of the latest varieties, having been developed by Guntur's agricultural scientists. (All chillies – indeed all agricultural products – are often hybridized, and as nobody has the time to think up evocative names, the way they do for race horses, crops are saddled with singularly impersonal names.) LCA 334 has the great advantage of not needing much fertilizer and being far more pest-resistant than older varieties.

Of course, it helps to have pest-resistant chillies, but the other variable that affects the crop profoundly is the weather. If it rains in the final couple of months of their cultivation cycle, the crop is ruined, causing half of the produce to turn white. The nimble-fingered women of Guntur usually remove impurities from bags of chillies in no time at all, their fingers long past the sensitivity that affects us lesser mortals, but spoilt crops confound even these experts. These white chillies (as they are known in the trade) are usually kept aside and sold to some unscrupulous trader who probably mixes one bag of white with several of red, since the price of white chillies is one-fifth that of the highest grade of the popular red chillies. No large brand name will buy white chillies (or so one hopes), since there's only one way to make them look red, and that is by adding artificial colour. Rajesh Kumar, a Hyderabad-based agricultural technologist who has taught me a lot about this particular spice, tells me of a simple test you can perform in your kitchen to tell whether there are artificial chemicals in your chilli powder: Just add ether to a measure of chilli powder, pour the surface layer into another container and add a few drops of hydrochloric acid. If the colour turns pink, it means that the chillies have been tampered with.

Why does Andhra Pradesh in general, and Guntur in particular, do so well by growing chillies? In part, it is because of mother nature, who has endowed the centre of the state with swathes of the rich, black soil that retains the moisture that chilli plants need. In part, it is because of the patient nature of the Andhra farmers, who painstakingly pluck chillies several times a year. You cannot harvest chillies once a year and relax for the rest: they are more demanding than that. They are sown in May, transplanted in July, and the first crop comes within a month, and it is always green. The first couple of crops of green chillies have to be plucked while they are green as the first two pluckings of a new plant are always scant. It is after the third plucking, that is after November, when the fruit – as it is known in the agricultural trade – begins to form in abundance and when it turns red after being left on the plant.

Some farmers elect to grow only green chillies – the kind that all of us get free of cost at the neighbourhood vegetable vendor. This sort of farmer has to have a *lot* of patience, because his fruit has to be picked three times a week or else it will turn red. Rajesh Kumar tells me that this kind of farmer has to start differently as well because green chillies usually come in a different set of species from red ones. Let me rephrase: *All* green chillies eventually grow red however, it would be rather eccentric for a farmer to grow the tomato chilli, a variety that gives a beautiful red colour, but hardly any pungency, and then decide to pluck it three times a week so that his entire crop is picked green. Instead, he would choose varieties that are best eaten green.

The species of chilli decides the kind of cuisine it will eventually be used in. There are chillies with thin skins and those with thick ones. When chilli powder is the ultimate objective, thin-skinned chillies are essential. In general, the skin of the Andhra Pradesh chilli is thin so that disintegration in a cooked dish, podi or chutney is instantaneous. On the other hand, when you are making a coarse powder, such as the kind that fast food outlets serve in pouches and place in jars on the tables, thick-skinned chillies work best. They also work better for tempering, especially in food down south, where a huge range of dishes is tempered with broken red chillies, mustard seeds and maybe a teaspoonful of urad dal (pulses) and/or curry leaves.

Some particularly interesting and photogenic chillies include the fat, round chillies of Tamil Nadu called gundu, the byadagi (or bedgi) chillies that are long and crinkly and the lesser-known kundapuri chillies, both from Karnataka, Goa's famous aldona chilli, the tiny bird's eye chilli of Assam and Nagaland, the glossy scarlet dallae khursani of Sikkim, which looks like innocuous cherries, to name only a few.

There are also chillies that don't turn red at all. Andhra Pradesh has one such. It is called Gollapadu, after the village near Rajahmundry around which it grows in such tiny quantities that exporting, or even trading, it is out of the question. Expert Andhra Pradesh pickle-makers, usually those from women's cooperatives, hunt down the Gollapadu for those pickles where a red colour is not desirable.

The other is the yellow chilli that grows in very small quantities in pockets of the country. Manali is one place where they actually have a slight flavour, besides being just plain hot. Traditionally, in Ladakh, the only chilli eaten was the Manali chilli after it is gently fried and then coarsely pounded. It is put on the table of every household in Ladakh and added, according to personal preference, by each family member. Thukpas, momos and even Ladakhi sausages made of lamb are all spiced with Manali chilli.

In its powdered form, yellow chilli is also used in surprisingly large quantities by the Muslim community of North India. In Old Delhi, the no-nonsense stalls of fried chicken and fried fish that line the roads all over Urdu Bazar opposite the Jama Masjid, all use yellow chilli rather than the common red chilli powder in conjuction with curd (dahi) and gram flour (besan) to marinate meats and fish. As a result, it's quite easy to score a packet of yellow chilli in this part of town as compared to other parts of the city, where you're often met with a blank stare.

But one can hardly blame the local shopkeeper as it is often hard to tell one type of chilli apart from another, so much so that even seasoned spice merchants can be fooled. One example of this is the elusive 'Kashmiri chilli'. Chillies of this variety are fragrant and mild, and when you eat them uncooked in summer, you just know that they are slated to metamorphose into a most superior product: full of flavour without being too spicy. They are also coveted because of their 'bleeding' nature as their signature fiery colour 'seeps' into the dish. But what is often masqueraded as 'true'

Kashmiri chilli at your local grocer's is rarely, if ever, the original Kashmiri strain. The local crop of Kashmiri chillies, grown in Pampore and Noor Bagh, is too tiny to go around the state, let alone the whole country. It is the chillies from Himachal, often grown in the valley and hybridized with the original strain, that are found in grocery stores. Most often, this hybridization is performed by agriculturists. Sometimes, however, accidental hybridization has also taken place because the two varieties are grown in proximity to each other, and the features of one have begun to show up in the features of another. That is the reason why the original strain called Kashmiri chillies has now been altered, perhaps irrevocably.

When Chef Alejandro Estrada Vela came from Mexico City to The Lalit hotel for a Mexican food festival, he told me a story that had me in splits. Apparently, he took a walk around some of the city's markets to familiarize himself with local ingredients. At INA Market, where the who's-who of Delhi does its shopping, maids and chauffeurs in tow, Vela chanced upon a spice shop selling whole red chillies, and asked to taste the hottest one. The shopkeepers sat up bright-eyed and bushy-tailed. If they could reduce a foreigner to a snivelling wreck, it would brighten up their day! They gave him a Reshampatti, popular in Gujarat and Maharashtra for pickle making. 'Not hot,' grumbled Vela. They gave him a Guntur Sannam, the variety native to Guntur. No response. With increasingly falling faces, they kept feeding him every chilli they had in stock, but Vela just kept munching them down like they were carrots. Finally, in disgust, Vela took out a couple of habaneros from his pocket. 'Do you have anything like this?' he asked. The shopkeepers reached out eagerly, not knowing that they were about to partake of the world's second spiciest chilli. Vela's face was impassive as they bit into the Mexican bombshells and their heads almost exploded. I pity the shopkeepers in this story, because the Mexican habanero measures between 100,000 to 350,000 units on the Scoville scale, which is used to measure the hotness of the alkaloid enzyme that gives chillies their pungency. It starts from 0 in the case of capsicum which is, botanically, a chilli pepper, and can go over 10 lakh Scoville Heat Units (SHU) for hybrids developed as 'the world's hottest chilli', like Infinity chilli and the Naga Viper pepper.

There is a continuum on the chilli scale. And everyone's tolerance to the enzyme is different. One man's outer tolerance level barely registers as spicy at all on the next person. And even though as Indians we pride ourselves on our spice-tolerance levels, most of us are not accustomed to eating very spicy chillies, except for maybe people in North-East India, who habitually ingest one of the world's hottest chillies: The bhut jolokia, or the ghost chilli. The first time I tasted it, albeit in a watered-down version, what struck me most was the manner in which the spice hit me. It was rather like getting an electric shock, even though the owner of the Naga restaurant where I tasted it assured me that for the sake of customers who were unused to the real thing, she had diluted the proportions greatly. You are, apparently, not even supposed to eat the chilli itself, but soak it in oil for a few days, and then use the oil. Even that has to be used judiciously. The Naga restaurant-owner told me that their version of the dish uses three chillies in oil to spice five kilos of meat for Delhites. Customers hailing from Nagaland would be served far spicier food than that!

Sikkim's dallae khursani is a close second when it comes to packing a mean punch. Almost indistinguishable from cherries, they are as small and as round, though not, let it be said, as sweet. Perhaps because of their thick skin, these beauties cannot be dried, so they have to be eaten fresh. They are fantastically spicy and available branded in shops in tourist areas or unbranded at local vegetable wholesale markets where they are sold in huge plastic vats and ladled out in multiples of 100 grams. The Sikkimese eat them with every meal, either fresh or after cooking them into a deadly chutney.

However, compared to two of China's regional cuisines – Sichuan and Hunan – the predominant chunk of Indian cuisine isn't even particularly spicy. Try eating the Sichuan speciality Chongqing chicken, in which tiny pieces of chicken are fried in chilli-flavoured oil and dunked into a bed of angry red chillies. A person from the province of Sichuan knows that all 250 grams of the chopped chillies used in the dish have to be eaten; I have never even tried to do more than peck at the chicken nuggets. In fact, what we are served in Chinese restaurants in India in bowls placed at the table is not the chilli paste used in China, but a version that is much milder, and contains no dried seafood in deference to Indian vegetarian sensibilities. All across the Chinese speaking world, however, you will be served, at your table, an eye-wateringly spicy pounded chilli paste with dried shrimp for a double whammy of savoury and spicy.

But because we, somewhat mistakenly, constantly associate spicy chillies with Indian food, I am often surprised when I encounter the fiery red devils in other countries. Europe is not the prime example of spicy food, so it is surprising to find that the southern toe of Italy, Calabria, is famous throughout the country for its chillies. If, at an Italian delicatessen, you spot a couple of types of speckled red *salume*, you will know that it is Calabrian without having to ask. Many varieties of chillies grow in Calabria with the smallest looking like bird's eye chillies. Packed in brine, they make great gifts for friends who enjoy spicy food. The best part is that just one or two of these tiny chillies are hot enough for a lover of pungent food.

The Mercado Central of Valencia, in Southern Spain, a spectacular indoor market built entirely of iron girders and covered with glass, has a section for meats, hams, Agua de Valencia, seafood, vegetables and chillies! But such is the mildness of these chillies that you won't cough or sneeze even if you are standing right next to where the chillies are hung in display.

On the other hand, walk down the local market behind the Shangri La Hotel in Bangkok and you will find a modest, pedestrian-only lane selling ingredients and spice pastes for curries. Because the chillies, as well as the rest of the spices, have been freshly ground, you will sneeze away till you cover your nose with a damp kerchief. As it is all made for locals, there are no wrappers and the balls of chillies, cilantro, turmeric and cumin are like powerful bombs, ready to explode on someone's palate, unless tamped down with enough coconut milk. Every Thai restaurant has phrik nam pla, sliced fresh chillies in fish sauce, on the table, the way Indian restaurants have green chutney and vinegared onions. Only take a bite if you know what you are doing because they pack a mean punch.

I never expected to see chillies in Pike Place, Seattle, that too, in colours ranging from yellow to purple. But there they were, in decorative wreaths, waiting to be bought by anyone who welcomes a touch of pungence in their food. With low temperatures and low humidity levels, fresh chillies can stay fresh for a couple of weeks, brightening up a corner of a kitchen, with one or two going into the cooking pot.

Another difference I've noticed in my travels is how chillies are used in India – as also China and South-East Asia – and in other parts of the world. Here, we mostly use it to spice our food; flavour is not the primary motivation. If you don't have Karnataka's kundapuri chillies, you would happily use Kashmir's pampori ones. In fact, no recipe book that I have ever come across has ever made the distinction between one type of chilli and the other which, in my opinion, is a shame. Chilli growers, suppliers and vendors, too, categorize chillies solely on the basis of their hotness quotient. But in a place like Mexico, however, things are very different. They have over 200 varieties of chillies, each of which has a specific flavour and a well-defined place in each dish. Some are smoked, some are sun-dried, some are sweet and mild, while some are deadly spicy. You cannot substitute anchos for poblanos in Mexican cuisine, and expect to get away with it! And yet, we do just that in most Indian cuisines. Not only are all Indian chillies different, with various distinct attributes, different countries and regions pick them for uses based on their specifications. Rajesh Kumar, whom I've mentioned before, runs his own business as an aggregator of the spice. That means that when major importers of chillies (and other agricultural products) come looking for, say, two lakh tonnes of a particular product, Rajesh Kumar gets varying amounts from a clutch of different sources and ships it off. He usually exports chillies to US, UK, Canada, UAE, Saudi Arabia and Kuwait. He says that the most fascinating aspect of his business is to figure out what the buyers want from the same spice, and why. For example, in India, all Surya-, Swastik- and Priya-brand pickles require chillies that will retain their red colour for a long time. If consumers feel their pickle is turning brown rapidly, they will move on to another brand, even though it has been proved that colour does not have any correlation to taste. In addition, South India requires its chilli powder to be less red than North India, even within the same brand. One of the ways to do this is to blend the same three varieties of chillies all over the country, but in different proportions, so that the one with the most colour-giving properties dominates in the north, but recedes in the south. The other way to do it is to put more seeds in the south and less in the north.

Other buyers want specific attributes not just a specific colour. UK requires that its chillies be plaited in long braids so as to be used along with braids of onions and garlic that hang in the kitchen. They are plucked from the braid, one at a time, as and when required. That's probably why they go for Guntur chillies since they have around 11 per cent moisture and therefore, can easily be plaited together. Rajasthani chillies, on the other hand, are too brittle for that, since they have only 3 per cent moisture. The Arab countries, that Kumar exports to, require stalks to be left on the chillies. They are very specific about this, and they are the only market to have this specification. Chefs in Arab countries de-stalk chillies and crush them between their palms at the time of using them, usually on spit-grilled meat which has been basted with olive oil. Because of the stalk, all the seeds are still inside the chilli and, when the meat is roasted, they catch the flame and turn it blue. If the meat is being grilled outdoors at night, or in front of diners, the whole effect is quite dramatic. Without the seeds, half the drama is lost. Hence, the importance of the stalk.

Here in India, you can count on the fingers of one hand the savoury dishes in each community that do not use this spice. You'll find them easily enough with some one or the other pointing out, 'Don't bother with this one. It has no chillies. The gravy is white.' The idea being that white, of course, is the most unattractive colour when it comes to Indian food. But this too is hardly a universal fact. Kerala's meen moilee is pale yellow, as are Goa's fish caldine, Bengal's doi maach, the Bohra dabba gosht and Kashmir's mutton yakhni.

Like turmeric and saffron, chillies, too, are often credited with a value that transcends the mere culinary and I'm not talking about the occasional newspaper reports that tells us how certain prisoners escaped from jail by throwing chilli powder into the eyes of their captors. Red chillies, in Indian culture, reportedly remove the effects of the 'evil eye'. Astrologer Paresh Arya, whom I spoke to about this, says that since red is the colour of the planet Mars, and the day of the week associated with Mars is Tuesday, that is the most propitious day for removing the evil eye with chillies by burning them. The only criterion is that they should have their stalks intact, for some mysterious reason that nobody can explain.

In some parts of the country, green chillies do a similar job. Seven green chillies suspended horizontally from a string with a lime at the base – an image that is so iconic in the country that it has acquired a cultural status that transcends state borders – is called nazar kawatch. All over India, wholesale vegetable markets will have a corner devoted to ladies busily making these miniature totems to sell to owners of small shops.

Is it because chillies burn that the connection with evil eye has been formed? After all, burning is associated with fire, which in turn, is a symbol of purity, of cleansing out the evil. It's hard to be certain, but it's a likely explanation. Try burning chillies in a clay brazier and the smoke will singe your eyes and throat. In fact, when the market yard at Guntur suffered from a devastating fire in 2008, the firemen complained that they could not get close enough because the fumes, caused by so many burning chillies, were suffocating and made them nearly blind. It is the reason why chillies are often the last spice to be added to a dish. Typically, you would sauté onions, ginger and garlic, followed by powdered coriander seeds, zeera and haldi and finally add powdered red chillies, but only after the pan has been taken off the heat. Try sautéing chillies on a high flame and you'll be left with a burnt mass that will sting your eyes and be inedible in the bargain.

For a spice that had its inception in South America, and was introduced to Asia by Europeans, the chilli has had a long, glorious and rather unexpected history. But even more wondrous is how we Indians have, in less than 450 years, embraced this spice so completely that it is now indistinguishable from Indian cuisine.

NADIYAH AKRAM'S POL-SAMBOL (COCONUT RELISH)

For Nadiyah Akram, my friend from Sri Lanka, cooking is a lightning fast activity, with whatever ingredients are at hand, in the midst of her busy lifestyle.

INGREDIENTS

- 1 cup fresh coconut, scraped
- 3 tsp chilli powder (or to taste)
- 1 tsp chilli flakes (or to taste)
- 1 tsp canned tuna fish flakes
- 2–3 tbsp lime juice (or to taste)
- ½ cup shallots, finely chopped
- 1 green chilli, finely chopped
- Salt, to taste

METHOD

- Grind the scraped coconut, chilli flakes and powder, tuna fish and lime juice together in a mortar and pestle until the coconut has become completely red.
- Add other ingredients and mix well.

Note: This is best eaten with roti, bread or string hoppers. Also great in a sandwich! You can add chopped tomatoes to the mix if desired.

ATUL SIKAND'S JUNGLI MAAS

For a building contractor who only picked up cooking when he went to the UK to attend university, Atul Sikand was born to be in the kitchen. He runs a highly successful recipe group on Facebook called *Sikandalous Cuisine*, where members share recipes. Sikand only needs to glance at them to tell whether they will work or need tweaking.

Jungli maas was originally a meat prepared by the Rajput community when they were travelling or out on hunting trips. As there was little access to ingredients during travel, the meat was cooked using non-perishable ingredients such as ghee, salt and red chillies.

INGREDIENTS

- 500 g mutton, cubed
- 4 tbsp ghee
- 15–20 red chillies, preferably from Mathania
- ½ cup water
- Rock salt or pahari namak, to taste

METHOD

- Heat the ghee, add the meat and sauté well for 10–15 minutes.
- When the meat has browned well, add salt and dried red chillies.
- Cover and let it simmer. Half-way through, say about 25 minutes later, add the water in stages and gently let the meat simmer till succulent and tender – the idea is to keep the balance between the ghee and the water. There shouldn't be too much water at any time, nor should the meat fry.

Note: Don't let the quantity of chillies intimidate you: This dish remains medium hot and is absolutely melt-in-the-mouth delicious.

KAVERI PONNAPA'S PRAWN PERI-PERI

Food blogger Kaveri Ponnapa's recipe uses three kinds of chillies. It is from the Mozambique coast and is a throwback to the Portuguese voyages of world discovery.

STEP I: *Peri-peri Butter*

INGREDIENTS

- 500 g unsalted butter, softened.
- 4–5 dried bird's eye chillies (or more according to taste)
- 6 cloves garlic
- 1 tbsp paprika
- Red chilli powder, to taste
- Juice of 3–4 limes (or to taste)
- Sea salt, to taste

METHOD

- Pound the chillies and garlic together in a mortar and pestle.
- Mix with the softened butter, along with paprika, red chilli powder, salt and lime juice.
- Chill, until required.

STEP II: *The Prawns*

INGREDIENTS

- 1 kg jumbo prawns, cleaned, with shells and heads left on
- Lime juice, to taste
- Peri-peri butter
- Fresh coriander leaves, chopped
- Lime wedges, to serve

METHOD

- Using a sharp knife, slice through the backs of the prawn shells keeping the shells intact and, remove the vein.

- Wash in lightly salted water, drain and pat dry.
- Place the prawns in a glass or stainless steel bowl, drizzle with lime juice, and cover with the peri-peri butter. Marinate for about 5–10 minutes.
- Preheat the grill to 200°C.
- Place the prawns on a baking tray under the hot grill for 5–7 minutes, basting with the melted butter, turning once if necessary, taking care not to overcook. They should be very tender with plenty of liquid, spiced butter.
- Sprinkle with chopped coriander leaves and serve.

Note: Saffron rice can be served with this dish.

Cumin

One of my earliest memories as a child is of receiving 10 paise every morning as pocket money from my parents. Even in the 1960s, while it was far from being a king's ransom, it was quite adequate. It got me my favourite zeera golis, among other things. I can't remember how much they cost, but it was obviously less than 10 paise. They came in a cardboard box, half the size of a matchbox, with a red print on it. I used to suck at the churan-like sweet-sour-salty coating and savour the zeera that, even at the age of nine, struck me as sharp and astringent.

Sharp and astringent it is, and also peppery, with citrus overtones according to people who use this spice. And there are many users. Zeera is used not only in virtually every corner of India, but in wide swathes all over Asia, Mexico and North Africa. Lebanese shish taouk, Thai green curry, Indonesian and Malaysian rendang all use this humble spice, which is native to the Mediterranean basin. And it has been around for centuries: In fact, there is evidence that cumin was in use in parts of the world over 5,000 years ago. Cumin seeds excavated at a site in Syria have been dated to 2000 BCE. Evidence of the use of cumin, found in the New Kingdom of Egypt, dates back to the period between the 16th–11th century BCE. Even the Bible mentions cumin, as well as mustard seeds and coriander. The book of Isaiah in the Old Testament, chapter 28, verse 27 imparts the information that 'Certainly caraway seed is not threshed with a sledge, nor is the wheel of a cart rolled over cumin seed. Certainly caraway seed is beaten with a stick, and cumin seed with a flail.'

From Egypt, where cumin is believed to have originated, it spread to other parts of the Middle East, where it is prevalent to this day, being served in its powdered form as seasoning next to salt at every dining table. It is believed that cumin first spread to Iran and from there to India and the Far East in one direction, while the Spanish took it with them to the Americas, having been converted themselves to its cause by the Moors. Yet, there's no denying that India is the largest, most significant producer and exporter of this most elemental of spices. The lion's share of cumin comes from Rajasthan and Gujarat, and though some other states produce it too, the quantities are too insignificant to contribute to national figures.

There's a fair amount of confusion in the etymology of the various kinds of cumin. All European languages refer to it using the root word cumin, for example, cominho in Portuguese, komino in Basque, kimino in Greek and so on. However, all the Asian and Central-Asian languages – Georgian, Hindi, Thai, Uighur – use variations on the root word *zeera*. The only exception is the Arabic word kamoun, that has more in common with Europe.

Due to translation errors, it is often interpreted as aniseed, fennel (saunf), caraway or even nigella seeds (kalonji). That's because kalonji, the teardrop-shaped black spice that is sprinkled over naans in restaurants, is called kalo jeere in Bengali while Germans call cumin kreuzkümmel, kümmel being the name for caraway, another quite different, spice. Even the Chinese call cumin 'little fennel', leading to confusion all around!

In the course of my research for this book, I bought cumin from wherever in the world I happened to be. Hapless friends were bribed and blackmailed to procure a tablespoon of cumin from friends/relatives/buyers/customers/suppliers who happened to be visiting Delhi from anywhere between Mexico to China. In a few months, ingenuity and luck had increased my stash to a sizeable amount. They all seemed different, yet had one common characteristic when I looked at them under a magnifying glass: black ridges running down their length. When I counted them, each cumin seed had exactly nine ridges, no matter where in the world they originated from. There were no other commonalities. The sample from Uzbekistan was tiny and fat, almost like carom (ajwain), except that it had the flavour of cumin and had the characteristic ridges. The Moroccan sample was faintly curved and far darker than almost any other sample I had, except for the Iranian variety which was the darkest, most shapely and fragrant. The Indian sample was the strongest in flavour and the Chinese sample had the lightest colour.

When I looked at a single cumin seed under a microscope, I could make out tiny bristles. These are what differentiate cumin from other, similar spices like fennel and caraway. There are a lot of differences between the wild caraway that grows in Ladakh and the Gujarati/Rajasthani cumin. Ladakhi caraway is rounder and much darker in colour, because it is a completely different spice, albeit one that has been historically confused with cumin, both in Northern Europe and in India.

I looked for a laboratory that could analyze the composition of each sample and tell me about it. A couple of samples looked like black cumin. Was that really what they were? Or were they simply a mutation from regular cumin? Why was one sample fragrant and another intense? Why was one mild and another strong? But, unfortunately, no laboratory that I contacted had the equipment to carry out such a study. 'Give us the samples,' they all entreated, 'and we'll tell you what adulterations and pesticides have been used.' There was no point in telling them that I simply was not interested in adulterations. I imagine that this stems from the fact that in our country, adulterants occupy our mind space more than pure knowledge for its own sake. When I mentioned this to Delhi-based food technologist Iram Rao, she was not surprised in the least. In the absence of government rulings, there is no standard curve for components.

Frankly, I was shocked. Traders buy spices in great volumes from other countries, keeping a close watch on international cumin prices, which rise to a crescendo near the time of harvest. Websites give information on weather conditions in and around the fields of other cumin-producing countries. However, soil and climatic conditions impact the flavour profile of spices a great deal, as indeed, they do all agricultural products. So if one is importing a substantial quantity, the least an importer can do is to match flavour profiles as accurately as possible, and the only way of doing that is to test for components and their percentages. The owner of G Waterfront, an upmarket Indian restaurant in Shanghai, told me that he imports cumin from India rather than use the far more economical Chinese cumin. The reason being that the latter is not only much lighter than its Indian counterpart, it has a pronounced lemony note and lacks the earthy pungence of Indian cumin.

Speaking of components, all spices contain volatile oils. Roasting or sautéing serves the purpose of bringing these to the surface. While most spices benefit from being roasted (turmeric doesn't), cumin is absolutely transformed when roasted. I've always felt that the half hour or so a week that I spend roasting my cumin and coriander seeds is well worth the trouble. This is one chore I am happy to do myself. I add one drop of ghee to the cumin and roast it gently. After it changes colour and releases a glorious fragrance, I grind it in the food processor. It makes a huge difference to any dish. When I have the time, I even pound whole cumin seeds in my limestone mortar and pestle, and then add them to whatever I'm cooking. Even on days when I hardly have more than a minute to do this job, the coarsely ground cumin releases so much flavour that it makes the whole exercise worthwhile.

Black cumin is the default variety that grows all over the Kashmir valley, though the higher the altitude, the better, and more fragrant the spice. It even grows in rather unexpected places, for example, along the runway at Srinagar airport. It is tended to assiduously by the maintenance men of the Airport Authority of India, who then sell it at the downtown market on their day off. Once I got to know about this, every time I was on a flight from Srinagar to Delhi, I'd keep my eyes peeled on the strips of wild grass that grow on either side of the runway!

Kala zeera, or black cumin, is also called shah zeera. But Gernot Katzer, the author of the definitive spice pages on the internet, suggests that 'shah' may be a mispronunciation of 'siyah', the word for black in Persian. With a far more flowery flavour, as compared to the stronger, more robust but less refined product that we all use in our kitchens, black cumin grows wild in Himachal Pradesh and in Kashmir. Within Kashmir, there is a huge difference between the cultivated product of say HMT (around the now extinct watch factory), on the outskirts of Srinagar, and the wild product of the Gurez valley. The former is fairly fragrant. But put it next to what suppliers bring to Srinagar from Gurez, and it suddenly seems a rather sorry specimen. When professional cooks, or wazas, make lists of things for their customers to buy, they invariably specify that they want shah zeera from Gurez. And because wazas are notorious for wanting only the best (and, in the process, wringing their customers' pockets dry), one can presume that Gurezi cumin is indeed the finest. By comparison, what grows in HMT sells for one-sixth of the price.

Does black cumin make the journey to the plains well? Well, yes and no. I buy a couple of month's supply at a time either during my visits to Kashmir or ask for it when family comes visiting from Kashmir. As this happens to be a continuous process through the year, I have never had to stock more than 100 grams of it at a time. It survives well in a tiny, air-tight steel jar which I keep especially for black cumin. On the other hand, every time I have had occasion to ask for it in a grocery store in Agra or Delhi, I have been handed some musty-smelling substance – that I would not otherwise touch with a bargepole – usually from the back of a store where no more than a few hundred grams of it are lying in a giant grubby plastic jar that would comfortably fit over two kilograms of the spice.

So is it poor planning on the part of shopkeepers or the too-short shelf-life of the spice? I haven't quite figured out that one myself. However, what I do know is that when I first visited Srinagar as a newly-wed in the early 1990s, you couldn't find regular cumin in the valley at all, only black cumin. Because regular cumin is hardly used in Kashmiri cuisine, nobody ever needed it. Now, with several thousand people from the plains living in the valley, you can find lads selling piles of common Indian spices in each of the main markets: Lal Chowk, Maisuma, Kokur Bazar and Maharaj Bazar – areas in the centre of the new part of town. In the heart of the old city, however, you still won't find any other type of cumin except the fragrant variety that grows in the valley.

Slowly and inexorably, however, things are beginning to change. Even in the old city, families now use spice mixes like Bawa Masala Company's (BMC) meat masala and garam masala. A few years ago, BMC would not have been sold in Srinagar at all – so minuscule would have been the demand. Kashmiri families are still traditionalists who believe that their way is the best, particularly in the most vital matter of food. Garam masala, containing as it does a plethora of aromatic spices, is never used in its ground form in Kashmir; instead, what goes into a dish a second after it is taken off the fire is the fragrant Kashmiri zeera. Crushed between finger and thumb, it releases its full aroma, whereupon it is sprinkled – uncooked and unbroiled – over any finished dish that contains lamb, which is to say, virtually every preparation in the valley, at least in Muslim families.

I have heard praises being sung of green split moong dal with a tempering of kala zeera sizzled in ghee. If it is true, it is certainly a novel use for shah zeera, quite different from anything that Kashmiris do with it. However, in Himachal Pradesh, kala zeera is used quite widely, a corollary of it being grown there. Housewife Rashmi Sood from Kangra sautés and uses it in those dishes that contain curd. For everything else, she sticks to regular, or safed, zeera. The only exception is kadhi. Though its base is curd, she uses regular cumin.

My friends, Yatish and Minu Sud of Shimla, show me the stash of Kinnauri cumin they have. Used only by the pinch, it goes into any dish where it does not have to be cooked. They claim that the higher the altitude, the better the quality of cumin: exactly like in Kashmir.

Away from the rolling mountains of Kashmir and Himachal Pradesh, in the arid plains of Rajasthan, I met Major Umaid Singh Rathore, who looks nothing like what one would imagine a cumin farmer to look like when he wears his army uniform, but is exactly that. With a full-time job that frequently takes him away from the Jodhpur region, where his ancestral fields are, Rathore has no option but to give his 25-acre plot out on a yearly contract. The only problem is that cumin, being the delicate crop that it is, cannot be the only thing cultivated; there have to be others as well. This is because while the spice is maturing, any rain or even cloudiness will turn the crop dark. And consequently, it will fetch a significantly reduced price. That is why farmers around Jodhpur hedge their bets by growing four different crops together, so as not to lose out if February and March are cloudy or rainy.

The same concern is echoed by Jyoti Jasol, who comes from the village of Jasol in Rajasthan's Barmer district. Though she now lives in the lush green oasis that is Udaipur, Jyoti's parents cultivate cumin in the homestead. It's not an easy crop to grow, they grumble. First of all, around Diwali, the price of the spice shoots up because of the demand-supply equation. It's the time of the year when agriculturists sow cumin and a quintal is required for every hectare. It is only a couple of months later that the seed forms in the diminutive fruit of this plant. Once this happens, the farmer's real headache starts. Jyoti explains that this is the time when watering has to be really careful and controlled, if at all. Watering leads to the seeds becoming heavy. Once the cumin plant becomes top-heavy, there is danger that it will bend to the ground. If that happens, it spells bad news, because the seed turns blackish and is nearly worthless on the market. The stalks containing the seeds don't even have to topple to the ground – rainfall at this crucial juncture will also blacken the seeds.

Curiously enough, cumin, like many other seed spices, grows best in soil that is not very rich. The poorer the nutrients in the soil, the richer the flavour of the spice. Once it is sown, it requires minimal watering. In fact, because it grows best on sandy soil, any amount of watering will do: The roots capture as much moisture as the plant needs; the rest filters quickly through the sub-soil. So it is no surprise that western Rajasthan, which is largely a desert, is where the most intensely flavoured cumin grows. This part of

Rajasthan also produces the largest size of cumin and because size really does matter – in so far as this particular spice is concerned anyway – it is the Rajasthani cumin that is exported to western Europe where premium quality is always sought.

Obviously, Jyoti Jasol has never bought a single packet of cumin in her entire life: Her mother comes to visit her in Udaipur with several kilos of the spice that last Jyoti a full year. It is the same with any member of the Rajput community: when they visit relatives, they gift them with, not apparel or handicrafts, but with the produce of their *thikana* or fiefdom. To Jyoti, it is not merely an organic spice (her family uses no chemical fertilizer), but a slice of a lifestyle, where women from the village of Jasol gather to thresh and sift the cumin, singing ballads all the while.

Threshing by hand is not an option in neighbouring Gujarat – the state that grows the lion's share of India's cumin – because the volume is far too large. Take for instance, Unjha, a crummy little town near bustling Mehsana, a two-hour drive from Ahmedabad on roads that would do any European country proud. Unlike towns like Jasol in Rajasthan, Unjha is not quaint and village-like. Instead, all you see are godowns, factories and the market yard. But the most characteristic feature of Unjha is, of course, the smell: The fragrance of cumin permeates the air. People who drive on the highway from Ahmedabad automatically know when they reach Unjha because of this fabulous fragrance. But don't sniff the contents of the jar of zeera in your kitchen to imagine the smell in Unjha: It's milder, well-rounded and sweet, rather than the sharp and astringent smell we've come to associate with zeera.

Hetal Dave, the managing director of Rasa Foods and Spices, allowed me to accompany him on a business trip to this town which is at the centre of the cumin universe. After five minutes in his supplier's factory, I began to feel mildly euphoric with the fragrance. It was certainly better than any essential oil I have ever encountered in a spa. The factory itself was a cavernous hangar-like building, one of several rows of similar buildings in that part of town. Several hundred bags of cumin, in various stages of processing stood in rows, and in one corner were the rather rudimentary machines.

When cumin is brought by the farmer to a factory, it doesn't resemble a spice as much as dried grasses and herbs. So many inch-long dried sticks and hay get packed into sacks along with the spice itself, that it becomes simply unrecognizable. I scooped up a tablespoon of the hay and sticks, popped them into a plastic pouch to examine at leisure and then promptly forgot all about them. Less than a month later, as I was leaving the Srinagar airport, with several spice samples, including the unprocessed cumin, in my handbag, an unsmiling female police officer demanded that I empty out my bag and show her the contents. She tried to prise away a free sample of body lotion that I'd been given at a shopping mall a while back, stared at my lucky rock crystal but positively hit the roof when she saw my precious unprocessed cumin. She demanded to know what it was, and when I told her, she laughed with a rather nasty twist to her mouth. She stomped off to her superiors and jeered, with a look in my direction, 'She's trying to tell us this is zeera!' It took a little white but eventually the whole thing was sorted out, somewhat amicably.

Coming back to the unprocessed zeera at Unjha, four processess turn it to the zeera we are familiar with. The first process sieves the sand and dust away; the second process takes away the loose sticks; the third separates the seeds by size and the fourth removes what is picturesquely called the *moocha* – the tiny whisker-like silken stalk on one side of the seed.

Hetal Dave's supplier is a processor, broker, godown owner, exporter and trader all rolled into one – not a very common combination in Unjha. Most people in the cumin trade fall into one category or the other. Minesh bhai is one of 1,500 traders in Unjha, one of 500 brokers and one of 15 exporters.

He explained to me that by the time a branded packet of cumin reaches our kitchen, it has already travelled a good deal. From the farmer, it comes to a factory to be processed. Since not all factories are run by brokers, it then travels to a broker who sells it in multiples of 12.5 metric tons, which is the bulk necessary to load a 20-foot container. A distributor then buys from a broker and supplies to cities and towns. Local suppliers, small-time brands, hotels and caterers, in all likelihood, purchase from a distributor while large brands like Ramdev in the west and MDH in the north buy directly from brokers like Minesh bhai.

So, what about contract farming? It is a concept that has gained currency in recent years, where a large buyer deals directly with the farmer and buys all of the farmer's produce. On the plus side, the farmer does not have to go looking for a buyer. On the other hand, the fixed rate usually favours the buyer, not the farmer. But Minesh bhai tells us that cumin farmers around Unjha are much better educated than the national average and are extremely aware of market conditions. They are unlikely to commit themselves to a non-competitive situation. A few farmers around Unjha drive their own cars, a dramatic departure of our city-bred image of an emaciated villager dressed in tattered dhoti-kurta!

Unjha has metamorphosed into the market yard for several other seed spices like fennel, sesame and fenugreek, notwithstanding the fact that farmers have to travel relatively far to reach it. The vast expanse of the market yard at Unjha spells prosperity, in a manner that beats the chilli market yard at Guntur in Andhra Pradesh and the turmeric one in Erode. Is it because zeera commands a higher price than these other spices? It is certainly the reason why farmers in Gujarat like to cultivate the spice more than the other spices that grow in the region like fennel and fenugreek.

As in the case of other spices, when farmers do not get the price they are hanging out for, they store their crop in godowns, for which they are charged a fee by the godown owner. Minesh bhai is a godown owner as well and has 5000 bags of cumin in his godowns, being held in reserve for a multitude of farmers, all of whom are waiting for the optimal time to sell.

Minesh bhai also tells me that McCormick's agent visits Unjha periodically. McCormick is a bona fide American brand that buys its spices from all over the world. Also, there are several other brands who are registered in western countries and sell there, but have tie-ups with companies in Gujarat. Thus, XXX Spices that sells in western Europe has cumin packaged in Ahmedabad, sometimes by YYY Spices. YYY Spices doesn't, however, suffer from an identity crisis – it undertakes the deal as a purely commercial one. Frequent as this sort of thing is, it is never spoken about publicly – perhaps because the relationship between buyer and seller in this tightly controlled world is usually considered as inviolate as the bond between a married couple and secrets are just as closely guarded as in a marriage.

India's love affair with cumin is well evidenced throughout the country, in well-nigh every dish from chaat to curries. Go to your neighbour's place for a hearty breakfast of potato curry with puri and the woody note in the curry will be a gift of zeera. Go out for a plate of chaat in the afternoon and among the medley of flavours, textures and spices, you'll catch a hint of cumin. You go shopping in the evening and stop at a street corner kebab stall and, lo and behold, there is a trace of cumin in that too. If you go to a more upmarket restaurant for kebabs, the regular cumin would probably be replaced by black zeera or shah zeera in the marinade. For dinner, because you don't fancy anything elaborate or heavy, you decide on a simple mixed vegetable pulao with a raita: impossible, once again, without cumin. As you turn in for the night, about the last thing on your mind is the relentless way that cumin has followed you around, yet, there has not been a single item on the day's menu that has not had cumin in it.

Travel to South-East Asia and it is the same story. Whether it is Penang curry in Thailand, ayam rendang in

Malaysia, Vietnamese chicken curry or Indonesian beef curry, they will all have cumin. However, because the spice is never roasted there as it is in India, and because it is combined with shallots, candlenuts, coconut milk and lemongrass, the cumin tends to be a base note rather than the star of the show, as it tends to be in Indian cuisine.

It is the same in the Middle East and Mexico. Both cuisines use cumin, but the accent is elsewhere. The only exception I can think of is the Middle-Eastern breakfast dish of ful – a hearty dish of stewed beans where you pick out your own accompaniments, all set out in little bowls. You can choose chopped cilantro, powdered roasted cumin, olive oil, chopped onions, chopped tomatoes, tahini and lemon juice. Put it down to prejudice, but for me, olive oil and cumin with ful is a marriage made in heaven.

In Mexico, where cumin grows, you will find it in the unlikeliest of preparations: from tortilla soup, mole sauce to chili. It may be halfway across the world, but the same operative is at work. If you think of mole as a curry with a mélange of various spices and herbs, it is not surprising that cumin is one of them. And chili, made with kidney beans – with or without the addition of beef – has to have the digestive action of cumin.

Back in India, there is no doubt that cumin is more prevalent in some parts of the country than others. Not only do members of the Vaish, Bania and Marwari communities in UP and Delhi use cumin in most of their cooking, they also take great pains to roast four days' supply and store it in an air-tight container on their kitchen shelf. (Roasting more than that would be counter-productive, because the essential oils of roasted cumin tend to evaporate after four days.) There is scarcely an item of food within the Vaish community, whether it is chaat, jal jeera or potato curry, that does not have cumin in it. But then, they do not use onions or garlic in cooking, so spices are all that can be used to add a robust dimension to the food. In combination with asafoetida (hing), cumin also helps to digest lentils, especially whole lentils with the skin on, and lentil dumplings like moong dal mangochis. There are, however, some rules for using cumin in this community. No dish that uses gram flour has cumin in it, with the result that kadhi made in a Vaish household will not be tempered with cumin, but with fenugreek and asafoetida instead. In addition, some vegetables: Spinach, kachalu, pumpkin and yam are not cooked with cumin. And milk-based gravy dishes like matar, makhana, khoya do not make use of cumin. Similarly, there are a few dishes in Punjabi cuisine in which cumin is not put: Fish, yam, mustard greens (sarson ka saag) and pumpkin are a few examples.

The signature pandhi curry, or pork curry of the Kodava cuisine of Coorg, is made by broiling a few tablespoons of cumin till it is almost black, and then combining it with black pepper and kachimpuli, the viscose souring agent of Coorg cuisine. It is then added to slow-cooked pork that has lost most of its moisture. Undoubtedly, the character of the dish comes from the cumin.

The only exception to this general fondness for the ubiquitous zeera is perhaps the Muslim community of UP where it makes its appearance in one or two dishes, if at all. I was rather taken aback when, on a visit to Varanasi, I asked a housewife how much cumin she used and she had to think and think. Finally, she came up with the answer, 'My mother sends me garam masala that she prepares herself. That has cumin in it.' The Lucknowi signature bandh gosht is made with cumin, but that is the only exception. For everything else, a mélange of aromatic spices and coriander powder are used.

Speaking of coriander, almost every cook in the country uses cumin and coriander together, so much so that the names of these two spices are often said in the same breath. Ask any Indian cook a recipe and they'll most likely start by saying, 'Sauté an onion, then throw in the zeera-dhania and then add the vegetables.' In Gujarat, all brands of spice that are sold in the state have a product called 'dhano-jeera'. In deference to the Gujarati population of London, spices stores like Dadoo's in Tooting and Patak's in Euston also sell dhano-jeera. Made up of 70 per cent dhania and 30 per cent zeera, it is also bought whole, in bulk, and ground by housewives in Gujarat when they purchase spices and ingredients together for the entire year.

It is slightly different down south. In Tamil Nadu, for any dish that uses coconut, cumin, whole black pepper and green chillies are used for sautéing. Coriander is used for an entirely separate set of dishes. In Goa, there's no talk of cumin and coriander in a single breath; instead, when you use cumin, chances are that you are also using whole black pepper in the same dish, so you'd speak of jirem-mirem in Konkani. Housewives who dish out whole spices to their maid to be ground on a stone speak of jirem-mirem with the same cadence their compatriots in the North use for zeera-dhania.

Cumin's fabled digestive properties also make it a part of an altogether different industry. Visit Manek Chowk in the old city of Ahmedabad, and through all the clamour of shining aluminium vessels on sale and piled in heaps right in the middle of the road, you'll see half a dozen carts. The carts belong to the purveyors of a uniquely Gujarati favourite collectively called mukhwas. Digestive pills (churans), candied betel nut (supari), spice seeds, processed dates – mukhwas is a treasure trove for the gastronome on a budget, because it includes fragrant ingredients at a fraction of the cost of, say, cardamom (elaichi). The chief purpose of mukhwas is to act as a mouth freshener, and indeed, you cannot leave a restaurant in most of Gujarat without being offered at least one type of mukhwas. In a sense, it is like the fennel seeds (saunf) and sugar candy (mishri) of a North Indian eatery. But while the two elements of saunf and mishri never vary, mukhwas in Gujarat varies from one restaurant to another, with quite ordinary eateries occasionally serving intriguing and uncommon mouth fresheners while much grander restaurants often stick to the plainest varieties. And cumin is the leitmotif that runs through most of these. On one of my visits to Ahmedabad, I chanced upon a semi-dried date filled with a churan that had zeera; zeera golis with a whole cumin seed in the centre; mixtures of various ingredients that invariably featured cumin, but the most intriguing was zeera 'dal'.

It is only in Gujarat that this industry exists, and make no mistake, it *is* an industry. Here's how it works: A cottage industry worker buys about a tonne of cumin, removes the insides, leaving an empty husk behind. The inside, which looks like a cumin seed except that it's flat, is moistened, mixed with salted water and dried. (A Gujarati friend who lives in New York and craved seeng dana, or salted peanuts, from home, one day figured out how to make peanuts the way they're sold on street corners back home. Buy peanuts with their skins on, arrange them in a micro-wave dish, add half a cup of water to which salt has been liberally added, and microwave the whole thing. In a while the water dries up, but the salt penetrates right inside the peanuts. It's the same principle for zeera dal.)

Try watching TV with a packet of zeera dal in your hand. Or munch a mouthful after a heavy meal. It's so addictive that I have to restrain myself from making a meal of the mukhwas itself. And meanwhile, what happens to the relatively worthless outer husk? Why, some unscrupulous tradesman buys it up, powders it and then sells it as zeera powder under some obscure brand name, making a killing.

SABUDANA KHICHDI

Jayesh Paranjape of The Western Routes takes tourists on food trails around his home city Pune as well on journeys around Maharashtra in search of the best local food. Whether it is the eye-wateringly spicy mutton preparations of Kolhapur or the alphonso mangoes of Ratnagiri, this young man knows his food exceedingly well. Below is his recipe for sabudana (pearl tapioca) khichdi.

INGREDIENTS

For the khichdi:

- 2 cups sabudana

- 2 large chillies, cut in medium sized pieces
- ¼ cup groundnuts, roasted, peeled and coarsely powdered
- 1 medium-size potato, boiled, peeled and thinly sliced
- 1 tsp cumin seeds
- Juice of 1 lemon
- 2 tsp sugar
- Salt, to taste
- 4 tbsp vegetable oil
- 2 tsp ghee

For garnish:

- Coriander leaves, finely chopped
- Fresh coconut, grated

METHOD

- Wash the sabudana and soak it in 3–4 cups of water in a large, shallow bowl. This is to allow the sabudana to easily absorb the water and double in size. Soak it for at least 7–8 hours, but preferably overnight.
- When ready, add salt, sugar, crushed ground-nuts and lemon juice to the soaked sabudana and mix well.
- In a kadhai (wok) heat the oil and add cumin seeds, chillies and potatoes and sauté for a few seconds.
- Turn the heat to medium, add the sabudana mixture and mix well.
- Turn the heat low and cover for 2 minutes. Once you take the lid off, make sure that you keep mixing the khichdi, as sabudana has a tendency to stick to the pan.
- Pour 2 tsp ghee from the sides of the pan and mix well.
- Garnish with grated coconut and finely chopped coriander leaves. Serve hot.

CHEF RAMON'S 'EAST-WEST' SAUCE

When Chef Ramon Salto Alvarez had taken over operations at The Leela, Gurugram, he and his team were doing a sit-down dinner whose theme was 'East meets West'. This sauce was such a marvelous fit (and tasted so great) that I snaffled the recipe before dinner was over! It was paired with some sort of roast chicken as far as I can remember, but I could be wrong!

INGREDIENTS

- 400 g black berries
- 200 g raspberries
- 100 g strawberries
- 300 g blue berries
- 130 g sugar
- Salt, to taste
- 1 tsp black salt
- 1 tpsp cumin powder, roasted
- 1 tbsp refined oil

METHOD

- Take a thick-bottomed saucepan and put on medium heat.
- Add all the berries to the saucepan along with salt, sugar and refined oil.
- Cook the berries on slow heat stirring after every minute. The berries will start losing moisture and become mushy. Once the berries become mushy, keep cooking till you achieve a chunky texture with very little moisture. Once the chunky and thick texture is achieved. Add the black salt and roasted cumin powder and give the chutney a nice stir.
- Check for seasoning, sweetness and sourness.
- Remove from heat, let cool and store in a container. Use as and when required.

Note: The fresh berries can be substituted with mixed frozen berries if berries are not in season.

PUMPKIN ERISSERY

Chef Arun Kumar is a film-maker and restaurant chef. He discovered his talent for cooking when he used to have to feed an entire unit on location, with little or no resources at his disposal. His caterings showcase the food of all four southern states, but there's little doubt that his heart beats for Kerala, his home state.

INGREDIENTS

- 250 g yellow pumpkin, peeled and sliced
- 1 tsp cumin
- 1 coconut, grated
- 2 green chillies
- Salt, to taste
- Curry leaves, to taste

METHOD

- Boil pumpkin till soft.
- Mix half of the coconut with cumin and green chillies to form a paste.
- Roast the other half of the coconut in a pan till brown. Keep aside.
- Sauté the coconut paste, add the pumpkin, and salt to taste.
- Mix well and cook for a few minutes. The pumpkin should become mushy.
- Add the browned coconut and curry leaves.
- Mix well, serve with steamed rice.

Turmeric

Some years ago, my family and I went on an extended vacation that lasted well over a month. During that time, every door in the house was bolted shut and every last window firmly locked. Our annual vacations usually last two weeks, so we reasoned that a couple of weeks more would not make much of a difference. Like every other year, we'd drive back to our flat, throw open the doors and windows, let in a bit of fresh air, and life would go on. Well, it so happened that in that particular year, Delhi had an unprecedented amount of rain. When we got back, we found that every single ingredient in the kitchen had become mildewed and had to be thrown away. The chillies were crawling with insects, the shah zeera had developed a blue overcoat and not even the cardboard cartons and plastic wrappers that contained my precious spice mixes had been spared. Only one spice was just the way we had left it: my good old haldi, that is, my turmeric. Moral of the story: When grandma tells you about the antiseptic properties of turmeric, she knows what she's talking about.

Turmeric is, arguably, the most elemental of Indian spices, along with cumin, perhaps. But unlike cumin, it is indigenous: born and brought up in India, as it were.

Chef Jacob Sahaya Kumar, the late Chennai-based restaurant consultant, researcher of Tamil Nadu's ancient cuisines and TV cookery-show host, was categorical that while many other spices came to India via other countries, turmeric is indigenous to India, and hence, it is the founding stone of Indian dishes. His theory was that though there are some dishes in which turmeric is not used, it is still the quintessential Indian spice: 'It is more allied to Indian food than any other cuisine and even its golden colour transcends cuisine and symbolizes auspiciousness.' Professor Pushpesh Pant, noted Indian academic, food critic and historian, goes a step further. He says that it is not merely the culinary use of turmeric, but also its medicinal and antiseptic uses that combined with its very colour, which is auspicious, that catapult it into devotional use. It is the only spice to have this distinction.

In my own opinion, the 'bite' of turmeric defines Indian food. It is a peculiar pungence, not shared with any other spice; not hot like black pepper or chillies, yet an unmistakably astringent bite.

Turmeric, or *Curcuma longa*, is native to South India, where hot, humid summers and plentiful rains together with loamy soil provide the ideal conditions for its growth. Turmeric is now grown in 22 states of the country: all over peninsular India, Bengal and some states of the north east. Other countries that grow turmeric include Pakistan, China, Taiwan, Peru and the diminutive French island of Reunion near Mauritius. It is used in a range of traditional cooking in Asia and North Africa. India, however, is the largest exporter and consumer of the spice, growing 80 per cent of the world's crop. (While the Western world has traditionally never used turmeric as a cooking ingredient, it is used as a colourant in condiments like prepared mustard.)

Turmeric is, essentially, a rhizome, whose shape resembles that of ginger. There is a fist-sized central part and numerous fiddly little projections, called fingers in the trade. The active ingredient in turmeric is curcumin, known for its healing antiseptic properties, as our mothers and grandmothers never fail to remind us. What varies is the percentage of it in the various crops that grow around the country: the crop of Allepey (Kerala) has the highest percentage of curcumin – 6.5 per cent, while Sangli in Maharashtra grows turmeric that contains 3.5 per cent, and the crop of Tamil Nadu can contain anywhere between 3 and 3.5 per cent, depending on the specific area. You tend to know how high the proportion is likely to be on account of the colour of the soil: Red soil yields brighter yellow turmeric, which in turn points to a higher percentage of curcumin. The higher the percentage of curcumin, the brighter the colour it imparts, and hence the better the quality of the turmeric the higher price it commands. The reasoning is that a stronger spice requires a smaller quantity to produce the same result. Other states that grow turmeric include Andhra Pradesh, Odisha, Assam, Karnataka and West Bengal. Meghalaya, which has always grown turmeric for its own consumption, can easily be a leader in this field with a modicum of government assistance.

Salem, in Tamil Nadu, has a naturally red soil, and the haldi grown there is exceptionally bright in colour. That may be a natural corollary, but nature has also bestowed Salem haldi with the quality of being larger and fatter than that grown elsewhere in the same district, and even the 'fingers' are more evenly shaped. The region is a force to reckon with: producing 10 lakh bags of 80 kilograms each which are kept in 170 godowns around the district. Seeding time for haldi is between May and July, while the harvesting period is February to March. After it is harvested, farmers tumble large quantities to rid them of the soil that clings to them and then wash them with cowdung. As both turmeric and cowdung are known to have antiseptic properties, it is something of a double whammy.

I had a chance to experience the country's turmeric belt – the area around Erode, Coimbatore and Salem – first-hand when I was taken by a friend to visit the turmeric plantation of S.P. Gnanasekhar, in Kilambadi village, 30 kilometres from Erode to learn more about this miracle spice. Gnanasekhar, who turned out to be the village headman of Kilambadi, was incredibly lucky to have all of his 60 acres more or less running right next to the river Cauvery. His fields are bound on one side by a tiny Vinayak temple, which in true Tamilian style had a panoply of brightly painted deities ornamenting the gopuram. On the other side is a gnarled old banyan tree with so many corners and crevices formed between its trunk and aerial roots that in the twilight hours it seemed vaguely menacing. Like all farmers around the country, Gnanasekhar too believes in not putting all his eggs in one basket, and grows rice and sugarcane in addition to haldi. 'As farmers, we are dependent not only on the weather gods but on market forces. If our haldi gets us a good price in the local Erode mandi, well and good. If the price nosedives, we just have to have a backup,' he tells me.

I ask Gnanasekhar whether he or his fellow villagers cook with the leaves of the haldi plant. After all, in Gujarat and Maharashtra, the rice-flour delicacy pankhi, is steamed between two haldi leaves and that is where it gets its subtle yet distinctive aroma from. Gnanasekhar looks thunderstruck. He stares at the leaves as if seeing them for the first time, then asks the friend, in a tone of horror, whether I eat haldi leaves. It is obvious that nobody here has ever thought about the usefulness of the leaves or the possibility that they can be put to use in cooking. In Goa, on the other hand, our family house has a kerchief-sized garden in which a large bit is used to plant haldi. Not for the spice itself, but for the leaves that are then used to make a classic Goan dessert called pathoyo. It is a dish that makes non-resident Goans weep with nostalgia when they remember the coarsely pounded rice flour and black jaggery paste that is smeared between two haldi leaves and steamed.

Our next stop is Erode and the Sakthi factory. Ask any Tamilian which brand of spices he uses and most probably the reply will be 'Sakthi'. I had managed to wangle an appointment to visit the Sakthi factory. When we get there, to my surprise I find that the premises are spotlessly clean though surprisingly low-tech for such a well-known brand. A notice, in Tamil, posted outside the gates informs farmers that the factory buys turmeric. The tone of the message seems to suggest that even small quantities of turmeric will not be sneered at. Sakthi started out life as a mom-and-pop business from a kitchen – the Duraisamys are believed to have started their empire by grinding and packaging locally grown turmeric – and though the brand has grown enviably, the very fact that small farmers are welcome to walk in and sell their crop indicates that they have – as yet, anyway – no intention of becoming impersonal as a multi-national company would. They do this regardless of the fact that it is a challenge to maintain a complicated billing system where amounts of 5 and 10 kilograms of haldi have to be paid for individually.

Despite the fact that we have an appointment, we are kept waiting endlessly while Shanthi Duraisamy, the owner, exchanges pleasantries with the parents of an about-to-be-married employee, who had come to invite the Duraisamys. Sakthi Masala is unusual in that the owner is a lady. A self-effacing one, let me add, because she goes out of her way to reiterate on company profiles that it is her husband who is actually the managing director. She takes us on a tour around the factory complex but by the time we come to the turmeric section, it is the lunchtime and staff members, in groups of twos and threes, are enjoying their lunch break. Many of those that we encounter are either blind or differently abled. It was later whispered to me that an offspring of the Duraisamys is differently abled, hence instituting a corporate policy. Mrs Duraisamy engages in animated conversations with the staff; she is clearly popular with the local workers. The owner of Sakthi Masala may not have much time to waste on food writers from Delhi, but her patience and sheer affection for the workers of her factory are boundless.

My next port of call is not too far away. Off a main road, along a narrow, potholed path stands a single-storey building with a tiled roof. It looks like a village shop, but is vital to the spice trade: It is a godown for turmeric. Inside the enormous dark room, it is surprisingly cool. There are thousands of jute bags full of turmeric, arranged in man-high piles with just enough space for walking between them. There are three small chalky lines on each bag and the smell is antiseptic rather than fusty.

The owner of the godown is none other than Kalyana Sundaram, the grandson of the great E.V. Ramasamy, respectfully known by the sobriquet Periyar, the legendary Dravidian social activist who founded the Self-Respect Movement of Tamil Nadu. He was also the founder of the Dravidar Kazhagam that later split into two, the other branch continuing to this day as the DMK.

Despite his illustrious ancestry, Sundaram is modestly dressed in a white shirt and lungi, like everyone else in the office, including the peon. He explains the entire process, from the need of a godown to the maintenance of one, in detail. The farmers need a godown because they need a clean, dry place in which to store the year's crop. The godown owner takes a fee from the farmers, but at the same time lends them money to buy seeds and pesticides. The fee includes money for fumigating the goods once every 70 days to avoid infestation by an insect that bores through the interior of the turmeric root, reducing the whole thing to powder. That is what the three chalky lines are – pesticide. Haldi traders buy from a market-controlled yard in Erode, and it is the farmers and the godown owners who attend the sales, though selling is the prerogative of the farmer: If he doesn't wish to sell at a particular price one day, he cannot be prevailed upon to.

After patiently answering all our questions, Sundaram excuses himself. He has to go home for breakfast. He steps out and starts his Kinetic Honda. There are no armed gunmen around him, no feverish aides hissing out to the public to make way for 'The Boss'. The thought of Farooq Abdullah's son or Bhajan Lal's grandson navigating the city on a Kinetic Honda is impossible to even contemplate, but my local guide puts it into perspective: 'He was, and still is, called Periyar because of his complete honesty. He was known for not favouring his coterie; nobody made a quick buck out of being related to him. In fact, I would have been horrified if Periyar's grandson drove a Mercedes Benz.'

Surprisingly, the familiar yellow spice is not the only kind of turmeric that grows in India. There's another type called mango turmeric that grows in the uplands of Idukki, near Thekaddy Wildlife Resort, in Kerala. It really does have a clearly mango-like aroma and is used, among other things, as a pickle. I promptly bought a bottle of pickle on my visit to the region, but found that the mango flavour came across as a trifle chemical. But whether that's because the manufacturers were tempted to give nature a nudge or whether mango turmeric really has an artificial aroma of mango will remain a mystery!

In India, it is a rare dish that makes no use of haldi. In fact, not using it in a dish is often considered blasphemous or at least idiosyncratic. My friend Sanjeev Goswami, owner of a slew of Indian restaurants all over China, tells me that he once hired a manager to look after the Shanghai restaurants (he has three in the city). The manager had been in Shanghai for just a week when Goswami left for Delhi. Three months later, the new appointee had settled in, but Goswami, sitting in Delhi, found that there had been no requisition for turmeric: Rather unusual, considering that all the dry ingredients for Goswami's chain of restaurants – spices, papads, ghee etc. – came from India. Curious, Goswami returned to Shanghai and asked the chef to cook him a dal and a vegetable. What came out from the kitchens had a curiously unappetizing colour. When Goswami expressed his shock and outrage, the sheepish chef admitted that the new manager, in his zeal to keep costs down, had urged the staff to make do without haldi once their stock was finished. Goswami lost no time in sacking the hapless manager, since 'there is no Indian cooking without haldi'.

This is not completely untrue; since this elemental spice goes into over 95 per cent of all dishes that any household in the country consumes. The use of haldi is also inextricably linked to its colour. In fact, out of all the spices, it is this one that is used more for its colour than for its somewhat astringent flavour.

The community that probably makes the most use of it are the Kashmiris. They even ladle it down the throats of new mothers in the form of soups that contain haldi, salt, garlic and little else, boiled with lamb, to (apparently) heal the mother internally and strengthen her bones. There is not a single dish into which haldi does not find its way in the valley, except two. One is haakh or spinach greens boiled with water to which salt and whole green chillies have been added. The other is tomato chutney, made by cooking tomatoes until all their water evaporates, and then adding oil, salt and green chillies to make a piquant, tongue-tingling thick sauce. For the rest, a dish without haldi is referred to in Kashmir as being 'unpleasantly white'. Indeed, a pinch of the spice is even sprinkled into hot oil when cauliflower is being fried so that the vegetable acquires a golden hue, notwithstanding the fact that it is soon going to be popped into tomato gravy. Similarly, yakhni, which is made with large quantities of yogurt, is made 'attractive' with the addition of a minute pinch of turmeric to save it from being completely white.

And perhaps because of Kashmir's love affair with turmeric, Kashmiris are very particular about how they cook this spice, given that they toss their spices into boiling water rather than sautéing them. If you put turmeric into water and let it boil without the lid on, or put it into cold water and then let it boil, you run the risk of what is known as 'lidder mushuk' or the odour of turmeric. As far as I know, no other community has ever faced this problem or is even aware of it, but that is probably because only Kashmiris boil turmeric powder – and all the other spices – rather than sautéing them. Why? To answer this question, I once went to the only Kashmiri wazas, or traditional hereditary caterers, who live outside the valley: Ahadsons, an extremely popular catering service based in Delhi since the 1980s, which is now run by the second generation. The dapper man-about-town, Shafiq Waza, is an MBA and his brothers Rafiq and Sharif cook wazwan food for the who's-who of Delhi. The three of them tell me that Kashmiris boil lamb with spices because they don't want their spices to burn, and they want them to penetrate the meat and vegetables completely. The steam, according to the Waza brothers, does the trick in a way that hot oil never can.

Another interesting use of turmeric is in vazhaipoo kola urundai from Chettinad, one of the very few dishes in the south where raw turmeric is ground to a paste with other ingredients. In the vast majority of cases, haldi is the first spice to go into the vessel, immediately after onion and/or tomato. However, in this dish, raw banana is boiled with haldi and kept aside. Oil is then used to fry the other spices with turmeric powder. It is the same in the cooking of the Nair community of Kerala: Two preparations that invariably use turmeric as a marinade are kaalan and avial. That is because the yam and plantain, used prominently in these dishes, tend to cause an itch in the throat unless smeared with turmeric and left for an hour or two. Cookbook author Hoihnu Hauzel from the Paite tribe of Manipur tells me that it is used in most fried dishes across Manipur. In its fresh state, it is also used in making a chutney, where it is combined with roasted tomatoes and dried fish and ground on a stone.

As a food writer, it is always tantalising to find exceptions to the rules. So while I know that almost everything cooked in India uses turmeric, I search of recipes that don't. Delhi-based Chef Arun Tyagi, who specializes in regional Indian cuisines, is cautious about committing himself to the unassailable position of turmeric in Indian food. Green vegetables, whole lentils including red kidney beans (raajma) and Bengal gram (chana), Kolhapuri meat, Bengali doi maach – none of these calls for haldi, he points out.

He is corroborated by Modhurima Sinha, Kolkata-based gourmet cook, who plies me with a list of dishes in the West Bengali (Ghoti) tradition that use no turmeric. First of all, there's the breakfast dish of aloo chechki with luchis. The potatoes are cut super small – it is the shape of the cut which is called chechki apparently – and do not have turmeric in them. Chochchori and shukto – both combinations of mixed vegetables – the former using vegetable peelings and stems that are usually discarded and the latter a standard mix of raw bananas, aubergines, potatoes and drumsticks in a slightly bitter gravy – do not have any turmeric in them. Lau chingri, the classic pairing of bottle gourd and prawns doesn't have the golden spice either. None of the handful of preparations of banana flower, called mocha, use turmeric, and masoor dal is not prepared with turmeric either.

In North-Indian food, exceptions are rare but not non-existent. Turmeric is not required in the crisp-fried okra dish called kurkure bhindi, in potatoes that have been soured with dried mango powder (aamchur aloo), in mutton/chicken dopiaza, cream chicken, or any other white gravy. You do not require it normally when you cook okra with mustard oil, you never require it for stuffed vegetables, which call for cumin, coriander, chilli and dried mango powder. No whole lentil requires turmeric in the tempering. Monish Gujral of the Moti Mahal Delux Tandoori Trail chain says that of the four most common spices, haldi is the least used. That, he is quick to explain, is because, none of the hottest selling items in his restaurants: butter chicken, dal makhni, tandoori items and shahi paneer, use turmeric.

Another community that makes minimal use of turmeric is the Muslim community of Delhi and UP. Restaurants like the iconic Karim's in Delhi use turmeric in just a couple of their preparations but for the most part, the familiar yellow colour is missing from their lamb dishes. Ask a member of the renowned Qureshi clan of Lucknow-based butchers-turned-chefs where they use turmeric, and the answer invariably comes after a long pause. There's a lamb curry called bandh gosht that uses onions, cumin, garam masala, grated dried coconut, khus-khus (poppy seeds) and yellow chilli in addition to turmeric. But it is an everyday dish, too home-style, to be put on restaurant menus.

'Haldi is not a spice,' say the chefs of the Qureshi clan scathingly. 'It is an Ayurvedic medicine. There's no flavour, no taste, no aroma. It cannot be called a spice.' One member of this remarkable clan adds, rather patronizingly, that paneer tikka is the only tandoori dish that makes use of turmeric, and that too, only because otherwise it would be white, and hence unappealing to Indian tastes. He probably does have a point.

Traditional Lucknowi cooks opine that turmeric is only used in their cuisine when a golden colour is required; nothing more. And it is crucial to determine the exact stage of the cooking process where it should be added. Too early and the colour of the finished dish will become an amorphous brown; too late and you risk serving raw turmeric! Nihari, the iconic winter dish of stewed lamb that is ideally left on a slow fire all night, is a case in point. The turmeric is added much later than the coriander seeds and chilli powder, so that the finished dish has a golden tinge. On the other hand, classics like the kormas, rogan josh and lagan ka boti do not require a 'sunehri' tinge and thus, do not use turmeric at all.

Chef Dirham ul Haque of The Oberoi Group explained that many of the lamb dishes of his community have khus-khus, curd, cashew paste and char magaz (melon seeds) paste in them, and it would go against the grain to stain them yellow with haldi. The two chief gravy preparations that do not have these ingredients are kaliya and nihari, hence the addition of turmeric in them.

It is interesting to speculate on the origins of the cuisine of the Muslims of Delhi and UP. Why don't they use this most quintessential of Indian spices? Could it be because their cuisine came from outside India? If it did, could it have really come from Iran? That is one theory about the conspicuous lack of turmeric in this cuisine, although there is no proof one way or the other.

In India, turmeric is much more than a spice: It has transcended the confines of the kitchen and become an integral part of our culture, our identity.

Across Tamil Nadu, India's turmeric land, the spice is used in ways that the rest of the country can't even dream of. Visit Madurai and you'll see ladies sauntering around the crowded markets that surround the Meenakshi temple with bright yellow faces. They look as if they are in the process of getting ready for a Kathakali dance performance, but all they are doing is getting the vast health benefits of turmeric on their faces. Why? I have yet to get a convincing explanation of this curious phenomenon. Theories do abound. One has it that Ayurveda prescribes a bath, oiling of hair and a turmeric face pack once a week. Another opines that using turmeric paste on the face protects you from the sun. But why use a face pack in the middle of the road in the middle of the day? This is one mystery I'll never figure out.

Other uses that turmeric is put to, in various communities of Tamil Nadu, are not as in your face, although just as interesting. In one community, brides and grooms wear white clothes that have been dipped in *manjal* (the Tamil word for turmeric) on the wedding day. Naturally, the clothes turn yellow. Nowadays, with ubiquitous wedding photos to be shared on social media, and the desire to look one's best on one's wedding day, the bridal couple usually resort to a compromise: they wear coloured clothes, but dip one end into turmeric water.

Dr R. Selvakumaran, the principal of Coimbatore's Sankara College of Science and Arts, tells me several uses of the spice that go far beyond merely consuming it in food. Manjal kulichi is an intrinsic concept in Tamil Nadu. It means bathing with turmeric water. Selvakumaran's grandmother never took allopathic medicine. When she had a cough or chest congestion, she'd hold a finger of dry turmeric over an open flame and use it as an inhaler.

Turmeric is an offering fit for the gods too. During Pongal, the state's most important festival, fresh haldi, along with the leaves are offered to the deity. Brides in the Kunkunad district of Tamil Nadu, where the giant's share of turmeric is grown, bring haldi and salt to their husband's house. Just bringing these two ingredients is considered enough. Even the taali pendant that every married woman wears around her neck is considered incomplete without a strand of turmeric-dyed thread in it. Indeed, when families cannot afford the price of gold for a taali, a piece of turmeric tied to a thread is considered a bona fide taali. When rural dwellers gift relatives on auspicious occasions, a blouse-piece, kumkum and haldi are considered appropriate gifts.

Modhurima Sinha tells me that haldi has exactly the same place in Bengali weddings. Turmeric is mixed with water to form a paste and a large blob is then sent to the groom's house for his thumb imprint, and then brought back to the bride's house where it is treated like a face pack by anyone in the family or neighbourhood. When Sinha went to attend a wedding in Dhaka, Bangladesh, she was taken aback to see her Muslim host's family doing exactly the same thing.

Turmeric is also used during worship to write 'Om' or make the Swastik sign. It is also used as a scrub for brides to be: their skin is polished with gram flour, turmeric and cream. Raw turmeric purifies the blood besides having antiseptic healing power, which is why it is sprinkled on wounds or when noses or ears are pierced. If you were prone to frequent colds as a child, your grandmother probably bustled around in the kitchen to prepare a nightcap of hot milk and turmeric. It is an age-old remedy for colds and coughs if you can bear to drink this less than pleasant concoction.

It would seem that Indian food is incomplete without this most elemental of spices, as much for the colour as for the medicinal value it imparts. And the global obsession with turmeric latte, also known as golden latte, tells us just how interwoven the colour and the taste profile of the spice is perceived to be across the globe.

PLA TOD KAMIN (TURMERIC FRIED FISH)

Ask Chef G. Sreenivasan of Hotel Radisson Blu Plaza for a recipe and he'll come up with a Thai dish, so often has he travelled to that country while setting up his award-winning restaurant, Neung Roi. Simple, fuss-free recipes that rely on irreproachably fresh ingredients is what makes his food stand out.

INGREDIENTS

- 4 whole red snappers of 300 g each
- 4 cloves garlic

- 1 tbsp sea salt
- 4 tbsp fresh turmeric
- 250 ml vegetable oil (for frying)

METHOD

- Rinse the snapper and pat dry. Slit across the body at an angle a few times.
- Pound the fresh turmeric, garlic and salt together.
- Rub the mixture into the snapper and marinate for half an hour.
- Heat oil in a wok. Scrape the marinade off the snapper and reserve it for frying later.
- When the oil is medium hot, gently add the snapper to the wok. Fry the first side for 5–6 minutes, then the other side for 4–5 minutes until the snapper is crisp and brown.
- Remove the snapper from the wok and set it on a serving plate.
- Add the marinade to the oil and fry for 2 minutes until the seasonings are crisp and brown.
- Drain the crispy seasonings and add on top of the fish. Serve hot.

ATUL SIKAND'S TURMERIC PICKLE

This turmeric pickle is oil free, and has a wonderful earthy, slightly bitter flavour. It is usually made in January when fresh turmeric is freely available and is eaten for its ability to ward off colds and coughs

INGREDIENTS

- 250 g fresh turmeric
- Juice of 4 lemons
- 1 tsp salt

METHOD

- Wash, peel and pat dry the turmeric, then grate it till you have about one cup.
- To this, add the lemon juice and a teaspoon of salt.
- Mix well and refrigerate. It will be ready in 2–3 days and will keep forever in the fridge! It is delicious, not to mention extremely nutritious.

RESHI FAMILY'S TEHARI

This is the most quintessential – and controversial – recipe in Kashmir! It is seldom or never made for just the family, but to distribute on the side of the road or near mosques and shrines in thanksgiving. And that is where its controversy stems from, as one school of thought considers it morally reprehensible to offer food as an appeasement. It is usually made for 50 to 100 servings. This scaled-down version will serve four.

INGREDIENTS

- 3 cups rice (golden sela or any thick grained variety)
- 1 tsp turmeric
- 1 tsp salt
- 1 shallot (if not available, use a medium-sized onion)
- 5 tbsp cold-pressed mustard oil
- 6 cups water

METHOD

- Wash the rice in three changes of water and soak till required.
- Take approximately six cups of water in a saucepan and bring to boil.
- Add turmeric and salt and stir briefly. Then close the lid until the water boils.
- Now add the drained rice and cook as usual.

- In a small kadhai, bring the oil to the smoking point and turn off the fire. Slit the shallot lengthways till you have thin juliennes (if using an onion, slice it finely).
- Heat the oil again till it's hot but not smoking and put the shallot/onion in and fry on low heat, stirring occasionally. You want golden, fried slices.
- When the rice is cooked through, drain the water and put the saucepan on a tawa on the lowest heat for 15 minutes for the extra moisture to evaporate. Turn off the heat.
- When the rice is barely warm, pour in the warm oil and shallot/onion, mixing well to ensure that every grain of rice is coated with oil. Check the salt, adding more if required. Serve warm.

Note: This dish is not served with any accompaniments, but eaten on its own.

MANGO TURMERIC ICE-CREAM

Chef Rishabh Anand, the pastry chef of The Leela Palace, New Delhi, always surprises me with his sugar-free desserts, but this one – using two bright yellow ingredients: turmeric and mango – was a complete revelation. I had never imagined turmeric would work so well as an ice-cream flavour.

INGREDIENTS

- 350 ml milk
- 750 g cream, preferably from Elle et Vire
- 2 tbsp turmeric powder, freshly ground
- 4 tbsp sugar
- 400 g fresh mango puree
- 1 tbsp ice-cream stabilizer

METHOD

- Infuse milk and cream with ground turmeric overnight.

- Warm the mango puree along with sugar and add to the infused mix along with stabilizer.
- Churn the mix in an ice-cream machine and chill in the deep freezer.

CHEF RANVEER BRAR'S CANDIED TURMERIC CRÈME BRULEE

I have known young Brar for far, far longer than his days as a celebrity chef on the Masterchef India programme. He has a good hand for cooking as well as an invaluable sense of combinations of ingredients.

INGREDIENTS

- 2 cups heavy whipped cream
- 1 cup whole milk
- 10 egg yolks
- 1 cup sugar
- ¼ cup fresh turmeric slices, candied (recipe below)
- Blackberries, fresh mint leaves and extra candied turmeric, for garnish
- 8 tsp raw sugar, for topping
- ¼ vanilla pod
- ¼-inch piece of raw turmeric

METHOD

- Combine the cream and milk in a medium saucepan. Add vanilla and the turmeric.
- Bring to a boil, take off heat and cover. Let stand for 15 minutes.
- Preheat the oven to 165°C.
- Remove the vanilla and turmeric from the cream and milk.
- Whisk the egg yolks and sugar in a bowl. Gradually whisk in the warm cream.

- Divide the custard into 8 single serving ramekins. Layer the candied turmeric in each.
- Place the ramekins in a large roasting pan. Pour enough hot water into the pan to come halfway up the sides of the ramekins, being careful not to splash any water into the custard cups. Carefully transfer the cups to the oven, and bake until just set in the center. Should take about 45 minutes. Remove from the oven and take out of the water bath to cool. Chill.
- Caramelize the top with a blow torch after sprinkling raw sugar.

CANDIED TURMERIC

- 500 g fresh turmeric, peeled
- 800 g sugar, plus additional sugar for coating the fresh turmeric slices, if desired
- 800 ml water
- A pinch of salt

METHOD

- Slice the fresh turmeric as thinly as possible using a sharp knife or a peeler.
- Put the fresh turmeric slices in a non-reactive pot, add enough water to cover and bring to a boil. Reduce heat and let it simmer for 10 minutes. Drain.
- Mix the sugar and water in the pot along with a pinch of salt and the fresh turmeric slices, and cook until the temperature reaches 107°C.
- Remove from heat and let stand overnight. Sprinkle some sugar on top and dry in an oven or dryer.

CORIANDER

Ask virtually any North-Indian home-cook how they make a particular dish and they'll start with the words 'Fry onions and tomatoes, then add your usual masalas. You know – cumin, coriander, turmeric, chilli powder.' To specialist chefs, it might be blasphemy, this adding of an astringent (cumin) simultaneously with a flavour as mild as coriander, because they would seem to cancel each other out, but to the vast majority of home-cooks in the northern states of India, as well as Gujarat, these two spices – together with turmeric and chilli powder – are what goes into virtually every dish that emerges from their kitchen.

Coriandrum sativum, to give coriander its Latin name, has a unique place in the spice world in several respects. While most other spices are assertive and strongly flavoured; coriander, on the other hand, has a mild, herby flavour with an earthy appeal. It is nutty and floral, as well as earthy with a mild hint of citrus too. Freshly harvested coriander seeds have a hint of insect pheromone, which some people find unbearable and others hardly notice. There's another attribute that makes it so special: its versatility. Finely powdered coriander seeds have quite a distinct appeal, as do ones that are coarsely pounded or simply broken open. It is almost like using three different spices. Of course, if you are using the leaves, stem and roots of the plant, you have three more tricks up your sleeve. Each variation has a sizeable difference in the flavour, far more so than any other spice. And if you grow a few coriander plants in your garden or in a pot in your balcony, and you pluck them while the seeds are green and unripe, then you have access to yet another variation of this fascinating spice, one that resolutely hides under the radar, letting others take the limelight.

Coriander is also one of the oldest spices in existence. The oldest coriander seeds have been excavated at a pre-pottery era Neolithic site in Israel that dates back to 7000 BCE, and the use of coriander seeds in Greece has been chronicled since the Greek comedies of the 3rd and 4th centuries BCE, specifically, *The Knights* by Aristophanes.

The general belief is that coriander is native to Morocco. It is one of the spices to be mentioned in ancient literature like the Ebers papyrus, dating to 1550 BCE and the Knossos tablets dating to 1375–1200 BCE, written in the Mycenian language. The Book of Exodus (16:31) compares heavenly manna to coriander seed – both being supposedly white. It is also believed to have been used in Egyptian burials as early as 1000 BCE: A few coriander seeds (15 to be precise) were found in the tomb of the boy-king Tutankhamen (1341–1333 BCE), leading to the theory that it was either traded along ancient routes or was cultivated in Egypt in that era. Coriander also makes its appearance in Sanskrit literature, namely Panini's Sanskrit Grammar, dated to the 4th century BCE, where it is called *kustumburu*, which is coriander's Aramaic name, used in Persia, among other countries. But nobody is entirely sure how it made its way into the country. Apart from vaguely worded theories about the introduction of the spice into India during Alexander's invasion (326 BCE), there is little in the way of recorded history. Today, it is not only found in every spice market in India, but also across the world, its use extending from all parts of Asia

Minor (present day Turkey) to the Mediterranean, North Africa, sub-Saharan Africa, Peru and Europe.

For a spice that is ubiquitous, especially in the Indian kitchen, coriander evokes strong, and often polarizing reactions, much like asafoetida. My friend Sangeeta Khanna, a microbiologist, says that the top-notes of petrichor remind her strongly of coriander. She does have a point: the muskiness and earthiness of one is echoed in the other. But many Westerners detest the fresh fragrance of coriander, comparing it to soap or even bugs. (In fact, the name coriander is thought to have come from the Greek word *koris*, which means bugs.)

Scientists have been intrigued enough by this phenomenon to conduct studies. Apparently, it is the aldehyde in cilantro that provokes the violent reaction. There are insects that produce the same aldehyde, which is why some say that cilantro smells like insects or chemical-like soap. The people who dislike the fragrance of cilantro have one of the two olfactory receptor genes that are missing in the rest of the population. There is a way to lessen the unpleasant smell, however, and that is by pounding the leaves, chopping them or cooking with them, rather than separating the leaves from the stem and then adding them at the end of the cooking process as a garnish.

There's one more attribute that coriander seeds, possessing little harshness, have: the power to tone down other spices. Coriander alone in the spice world has that attribute – every other spice not only has its own flavour profile, but is used solely on account of what it can add to a dish. It is a well-known axiom in the kitchen that if a dish has been over-spiced with too many cloves or cumin, the only way to counteract that is by adding a generous dollop of coriander powder.

Coriander seeds also have a far more varied flavour profile than any other spice. They are warm, nutty, almost buttery, even floral and slightly citrusy when left untoasted. When lightly toasted, the aroma turns nuttier and the citrus and floral tones recede. When the seeds are powdered, they lose some of their pungency and this is often used to bulk up a curry or tone down other sharp flavours. Coriander has the chameleon-like ability to change flavour not only with the amount of roasting but also with the amount of crushing. And this is just the seeds, let alone the leaves! One of the many surprises of this spice is that every part of the plant, from root to seed, is edible. Like the fenugreek plant that does double duty as an herb and a spice, *Coriandrum sativum* consists the familiar serrated-leaf fragrant herb that we get by the fistful from the vegetable seller, as well as the seed. In one of nature's mysteries, the aroma of one does not resemble that of the other.

You can either choose to grow coriander for its seeds as a spice or as a herb for its leaves only. You cannot do both, because the seeds form at the end of the stem that holds the leaves. In one case, you have to refrain from plucking the leaves in order to let the seeds form at the end of a season; while in the other case, you can keep picking the fragrant leaves for use, but in the knowledge that seeds will not form.

Jyoti Jasol's well-appointed home in a quiet, boulder-strewn hillside of Udaipur has a magnificent view: the City

Palace, seen from a distance of about 3 kilometres as the crow flies. This bungalow is surrounded by sprawling lawns, on the periphery of which is a vegetable garden. One of the herbs they grow is cilantro. They grow it for the leaves rather than the seeds, so work on the impossibly large vegetable patch never stops. Where coriander is grown for the seeds, the only other labour that is required – besides watering – is during harvest. Where the leaves are being used, it is a year-round effort. You pluck somewhat selectively, which means that at least twice a week your field has to be gone through. Growing cilantro only for the fragrant leaves is easy enough even in a shallow pot inside a modest flat that has the benefit of direct sunlight. It is not painstaking to snip off a couple of stems to add to a cooked dish; in comparison, what happens on a farm is that labour is required all through the year which is a most painstaking task.

As I walk in Jyoti's garden, I am mystified that I could not get a whiff of fresh cilantro. I had assumed it would be an integral part of the field. But then, it's just one of nature's little oddities. Jyoti tells me that it is only when you pluck the stems of cilantro that the fragrance is released and goes on to surround you all day long. It is the same with the seeds. When they are ready to be harvested, they change colour, the smell becomes fragrant and the carpel becomes tough.

Coriander is present everywhere you look in Rajasthan. Pal Haveli in Jodhpur's old town, for instance, is another of my favourite haunts. Its terrace is one of the best places in the city to watch the play of sunlight on the beautiful Mehrangarh Fort. Plus, there's another advantage of staking out a table at the only heritage hotel in Jodhpur's walled city – the excellence of its food. Thakur Bhawani Singh and Mahesh Karan Singh, the father-son duo, who own Pal Haveli, are as passionate about food as they are about their farm near their ancestral village Pal, where they grow coriander seeds besides wheat, jowar and moong dal.

Occasionally, the plan to plant coriander has to be abandoned for want of rain the previous year, which in turn, decides the amount of water for irrigation. The soil in the ancestral village, though, is ideally suited for the growing of this spice, because coriander requires loamy soil that forms clods of earth, the better to trap moisture: sandy soil through which water filters in seconds will just not do. At the best of times, the family farm, which lies between Jodhpur and Udaipur never gets the quantum of irrigation that is the norm in, say, Madhya Pradesh (MP), another state that grows a considerable amount of coriander. Far from considering it a disadvantage, Thakur Bhawani Singh tells me – as he makes preparations for the signature lal maas that his hotel is famous for – how this is a huge advantage, because abundant sunlight and minimal water intensify the flavour in the seed. The coriander seeds that he works with are far, far more intense than anything you can get in the supermarkets of Delhi and Mumbai. It is the same, he tells me, with cumin. These two spices, grown in the deserts of western Rajasthan are much stronger in taste than their counterparts grown in lush soil, well-watered with rain. I was mystified, because he had just finished telling me how coriander plants need soil that forms clods that retain moisture, in order to compensate for the lack of rainfall. But, apparently there is a vast difference between the bare minimum water and plenty of it, and the former appears to work far better than the latter.

Sure enough, the coriander seeds transformed the lal maas that was served to me at the terrace restaurant just as the Mehrangarh Fort began to glow golden in the evening light. I made a mental note to take some locally grown coriander seeds away with me, but the quaint little market, crowded with cows and motor-bikes around the landmark clock tower, didn't seem to have any locally grown coriander seeds. Perhaps the spice dealers weren't quite clear on what exactly it was that I wanted, or perhaps I was looking in the wrong place entirely, but I came back from my trip to Rajasthan empty-handed.

It was in Madhya Pradesh, namely Bhopal, where I had another curious encounter with coriander. I was the guest of the royal family of the erstwhile state and they were explaining to me the salient points of their cuisine on one lazy Sunday afternoon. An entire range of cousins and aunts were seated under the mild winter sun in the garden of their bungalow at Shamla Hills, the family stronghold. I was told that the single best-known Bhopali dish is the chicken rezala. It differs from the better-known Bengali version of the dish because the gravy here is green in colour. It is because of two factors: the famously hard water of Bhopal's lakes and rivers, guaranteed to give you indigestion; and the home remedy for it: cilantro. I had not previously known that cilantro was a digestive, but the entire family assured me that the reason why cilantro was so prominent in their cuisine was because it was an effective antidote to the hard water of the lake, from where the city's water supply originated.

Indeed, the preparation that I sampled – along with a dozen others – that afternoon not only had a green gravy but the colour had permeated the meat of the chicken too. What struck me was the amount of chopped coriander leaves that was used, both as a garnish and as a cooking ingredient, in that elegant meal. The rezala did not have any coriander powder, however: just a dash of aromatic spices and a few cups of chopped coriander along with a few spoonfuls of yogurt. In Bhopal, my hosts told me, you can distinguish a great cook from a good one by the final colour of the rezala, which has to be cooked together with the chicken for a considerable time, till the coriander attains the consistency of butter. Under those circumstances, too-dark coriander would be the order of the day, but in the hands of a capable cook, it does not have to be anything darker than a pleasant shade of green. Even in the family's hotel, Jehan Numa Palace, coriander is the single herb that goes into every last dish.

I was intrigued enough by this phenomenon to make my way to the innumerable farms outside the city limits, where coriander is one of the major crops grown. Hedging one's bets is the primary aim of the farmers in this belt, as a protection against years when the monsoon fails, and so coriander, fenugreek, and vegetables like bottle gourd and garlic all co-existed on the patch of land that I visited. The crop of cilantro was lush and verdant and the perfume wafted on the breeze as a group of women plucked branches with deft movements. In the entire Bhopal belt, the crop is not grown for the seeds but the leaves, which are harvested twice a week. The trick, as I learnt, is to keep the growth of the plants steady: too little cropping and the plant begins to flower. Once that happens, the leaves lose their flavour because all the strength of the plant goes to the newly developing seeds: it is nature's way of making sure a plant propagates itself. However, it is Bina and Ramgunj, two towns in MP near the border with neighbouring Rajasthan, that have the country's largest coriander auction centres, because the area north and west of Indore is where coriander is grown as a spice. MP itself grows 15 per cent of the country's entire coriander crop, while Rajasthan accounts for a whopping 58 per cent and Kota has become the largest auction centre in India.

The uninspiring road that runs through Yahiyaganj, not far from Lucknow's Molviganj, that passes for the city's wholesale spice market has a couple of tired, lonely dealers that trade in poppy and coriander seeds. Both spices sit in vast sacks, but instead of there being only one sort of each, there are at least six. I peer at the sacks of coriander seeds closely. One is off-white, another is brown, yet another pale green, a fourth is unevenly sized and coloured, a fifth looks like none of the others. After some wheedling, the dealer tells me where each sample has come from. They are all from around Lucknow except for one, which is from MP, but such is the difference in soil and water that each looks different. You'll find this in Indori coriander as well, the most prized among all Indian coriander, where brown, beige, lemon and green seeds are all mixed together, and that is how you can tell it apart from the crop of any other state in the country.

Every other time I have encountered coriander seeds in sacks at wholesale markets around the country, I have observed the difference in size and colour. In the crowded bazaars of Ajmer, where I met a dealer who sits with exactly two sacks of coriander seeds – nothing more, nothing less – the colour differs substantially from one sack to another. At the other end of the country, in the row of shops in Coimbatore's wholesale market, the colours of the coriander seeds are like an artist's palette. Some are beige, others are darker brown and still others are of a hue between green and yellow. The only other object in the spice market with such an attractive colour variation is jaggery, whose hues vary from golden to toffee: it is what makes the story of spices such a fascinating one, at least to me.

I find another variation of the coriander seed in Srinagar's old city, which always reminds me irresistibly of Central Asia, when I visit the oddly named Gaad Kocha market. 'Gaad' means fish, but for some mysterious reason that I've never quite understood, the market, a mere lane near the fourth bridge that straddles the river Jhelum, has metamorphosed into a spice and wedding-dress centre. I'm not even sure what the two products could possibly have in common: certainly the sight of metres of golden tinsel adorned dupattas has little to do with mountains of carmine chillies and crimson cockscomb flowers that every self-respecting waza adds to his rogan josh. As I walk through the lane, it suddenly strikes me that I have only seen one single sack of coriander seeds in just one shop. Far smaller and rounder in size than the coriander grown in the plains, the colour is dark brown as opposed to the myriad hues of greenish to pale straw to yellow that I've seen elsewhere in the country. In appearance, it is very much like the Romanian coriander that is sold in London. It is a feature of the spice when grown in cold climates. Perhaps the scarcity of coriander in Srinagar's old market can be explained by the fact that is only grown in tiny amounts in Kashmir, in the area around Chadoora. Cilantro is used more often by wazas. In my own family home in Srinagar, all that my mother-in-law uses coriander seeds for is the spice mix called ver (which she makes better than anyone else we know), where coriander seeds are just one ingredient among several others.

Pahadi coriander that grows in Himachal Pradesh is multi-coloured, but far smaller than other varieties. On a visit to the Gunj in Shimla, I saw that not one of the shopkeepers could be bothered to store the precious sacks safely in the dry interiors of their store. Row after row of dingy store had gunny sacks right out in the mist and drizzle that gives Shimla its irresistible charm. The sight of the slightly damp seeds open to the elements made me change my mind about buying any.

For every nonchalant shopkeeper on a mist-filled hillside in a corner of the country, there is an impassioned dealer. One of the most impressive of these is Vipin Gulati of Wazir Spices who doesn't just deal in spices, but also cooks, eats, sleeps and dreams of them. There is scarcely a hotel or a large restaurant in North India that does not source at least some of their spice mixes from Wazir.

Though his bread and butter comes from the wholesale market, his heart is in the spice blending business. Indeed, spices appear to speak to him. He claims that in his kitchen at home, he has three jars containing coriander: One with the seed coarsely pounded, a second with a fine powder and one that is the whole seed. According to him, it is the texture that is most important with this spice.

I've spoken to dozens of spice dealers, chefs, recipe writers and hobby cooks in the course of researching this book, but none know spices with the intimacy that Gulati can boast of. I mention an incident to him: Once while I was sitting in the reception area of a well-known spice dealer, a machine roared into life somewhere on the premises and the air-conditioned reception was suddenly filled with the glorious fragrance of coriander being ground. All coriander smells good, but this particular batch seemed so particularly fragrant that the incident was etched in my mind. Gulati at once asks me the month in which this incident happened. April, I replied. Gulati smiled with satisfaction and explained: April is when the crop is freshly harvested and if the seeds are ground around that time, they are more aromatic than they'll be the rest of the year. Had his name been Sherlock Holmes, he could not have been more prescient.

Gulati also claims that no non-resident Indian could live forever on cumin and coriander from other parts of the world. For that indefinable flavour of home, you would have to use only Indian spices.

I realized the truth in Gulati's sage words on my trip to Los Angeles soon afterwards. The first thing I bought, unsurprisingly, was a bottle of coriander seeds, not from an Indian store, but from a supermarket where every American went to shop for groceries. Most Indians who live in the United States make the extra effort to go to an Indian store because they know from experience that owing to the high demand, you are unlikely to get stale coriander seeds. But I wanted to taste the difference between coriander seeds grown in India and those grown in another country.

My 24 gram bottle by McCormick cost me over $4, for which amount I could have got several kilos here. Well, it was un-Indian, all right. It didn't smell like anything we have here. Although the instructions on the bottle recommended toasting it with cumin and fennel and using it as a rub on meats, I didn't take their advice, but crushed it coarsely in a limestone mortar and pestle a few seconds before sautéing it as part of a tempering.

The McCormick coriander had a lemony, almost grassy, flavour, quite unlike what we are used to in India

That, I later learnt, was because of the predominance of two terpenes – linalool and pinene. The varying proportions of these two natural oils in the spice determine whether it will have a woody, earthy aroma or a light, lemony one. Terpenes – a constituent of the essential oils of mainly medicinal plants, also occur in camphor oil and turpentine, and if you are ultra-sensitive to aromas, you may be able to make an extremely far-fetched, tenuous connection, but a connection all the same. Similarly, when you hear coriander seeds spoken of as lemony, it is because of the presence of linalool, an extract also found in lemon peel.

Kind friends often ring me up from the furthest corners of the globe, asking me if I want them to bring me any spices. I always say yes, and so I was able to procure coriander seeds from South China and from Iran. At first, I was excited. I had great plans for my samples. I would take them to a laboratory and have them tested for relative amounts of constituents. After frantic calls to several laboratories in Delhi and Hyderabad, one thing became clear: If there is any test for determining relative percentages of components of a spice, it does not exist in India. Every laboratory replied to my queries with the comment that they could detect any kind of impurity in a spice. But natural components? Heck, no.

The coriander seeds that I picked up from the superb Naqsh-e-Jahan square in Isfahan on my trip to Iran, was the greenest of all the samples. It was also the one with the most inclusions – grit, mud, sticks, insects – you name it and I found it in that half-kilo. When I tried to roast it, it remained the same colour, even though I roasted it on gentle heat for well over 20 minutes, stirring constantly. Another friend got me Turkish coriander, so tiny that it looked like it had been made for a doll's house. The colour of this one was dark brown. On the other hand, the glass jar of Moroccan coriander that I pounced on in Harrods' vast food halls on a trip to London were the diametric opposite of the Turkish variant: the colour of the seeds was the lightest, even lighter than the Chinese sample, and the size was huge. Far more common in London was Romanian coriander, packaged in simple see-through pouches by TRS, a UK-based importer. Romanian coriander, too, was dark brown, and though the seeds were small, they did not have the miniature appearance of their Turkish cousins.

Back home in India, most parts of the country use coriander in conjunction with cumin. In fact, every housewife in North India speaks of zeera-dhania as if it were a single spice. Gujaratis take this even further. They buy ready-made packets of the two spices together, called dhano-jiro. It is a bonafide spice blend, even if it is treated like a single spice. Gujarat giant Ramdev, the spice brand that has a huge presence not only in Gujarat but in Rajasthan as well, makes a dhano-jiro that is a 70:30 blend of the two – a fifty:fifty blend does not quite cut the mustard, apparently. (In fact, such is its popularity thatin London's Drummond Street, the shop that proudly refers to itself as the 'original Patak' sells TRS packaged dhano-jiro, as does Dadoo's in Tooting, a large venerable Indian-owned grocery store that clearly caters to Gujarati customers.)

Jagdish Patel of the iconic Mumbai spice store, Mangal Masala, tells me that the Parsi community too has a jira-dhano blend, though it is as different from the Gujarati version as it is possible to be. For one, the typical Parsi diet is meat and egg-based while the Gujarati diet is primarily vegetarian. So, there are a number of other aromatic spices that go into the Parsi version, making the name jira-dhano a bit of a misnomer.

Unlike the Parsi mix however, most meat-eating communities in India use a preponderance of just coriander seeds, since they are believed to have a cooling effect, the better to take away the 'heat' of meat. In the Muslim cuisine of Hyderabad too, coriander is much more widely used than cumin. In fact, I was told that using cumin 'blackens the gravy' and so, it is sparingly used and that too only in dishes where sourness is required. On the other hand, Lucknow's Muslim quarter uses coriander with discretion. In fact, their signature home-style bandh gosht contains powdered cumin in conjunction with other spices, but no coriander powder. The reasoning is that cumin is far stronger than coriander, and in combination, the former will inevitably overpower the latter.

Though coriander is used in most parts of the country – the Nadar community of Tamil Nadu uses this spice with uncommon flair. In fact, the basis of their cuisine is dark-roasted coriander powder, which is actually made from dark-roasted coriander seeds, saunf, cumin and rice powder. When the need for coriander powder arises, they use this mixture, which differs slightly from house to house. Like all such spice blends, this one too is a closely guarded secret, and is available in all spice, pickle and papad shops that are run by this community.

Each community also has its own set of dos and don'ts. In Gujarat, coriander is never used in a dish which has curd, because of the belief that it will turn an unsightly black. Examples are kadhi, potatoes, black gram and gourd with curd. Few other communities share this belief. In Himachal, a dish of black gram with curd that is called madra makes use of coriander powder but with caution. 'All you have to do is to take a bit of extra care,' Kangra-based housewife Rashmi Sood assures me. 'It's only a terribly inexperienced or careless cook that would cause the gravy to turn dark.' According to her, one way to ensure that the coriander does not burn is to keep it whole rather than powder it.

Even so, when you are sautéing spices to add to a dish, coriander usually goes in right after the onions, because it is generally acknowledged to be the spice that requires the longest sautéing time. Many experienced cooks are of the firm belief that you know the onions are sautéed when the coriander powder stops smelling raw. If you observe this cardinal rule, you will never suffer from partially cooked coriander powder.

Outside India, it is Portuguese food that uses the most coriander seeds in Europe. Soups, stews, even grills: It would seem that no dish is complete without a teaspoon of coriander seeds. So, it is entirely appropriate that Nando's, the worldwide chain of Portuguese/Mozambique fast food, uses a smidgeon of coriander powder in its hot-selling peri-peri chicken. But that's hardly surprising. Around the world, every time a cook wants to tone down the chilli component of a dish or round off the sharp flavours of cloves, he or she reaches out for powdered coriander seeds. And considering its mildness, it is almost impossible to make a mistake by using too much coriander. Some Moroccan and Algerian dishes even call for coriander seeds by the cupful as opposed to the teaspoonful!

Coriander root, stem as well as the leaves, form an integral part of many Thai curries. It is probably one of the reasons why Thai food, particularly their curries, tastes so different from coastal Indian food in spite of the fact that the spices used are almost identical. Cumin, coriander, turmeric, chillies – exactly what you'd find in India. But then, there's lemongrass, galangal, lime leaf and coriander root (with all the mud carefully washed off, of course). Add a bit of coconut milk and lo and behold, you've landed up with a different cuisine altogether, even though you have started out with the same spices.

But in all my travels, nowhere have I come across a worse

use of coriander than in Rome. Browsing through a gourmet store not far from the Trevi Fountain, I came across the funkiest object in Italy: sugar coated coriander. I bought it out of a sense of adventure, but as soon as I stepped out on to the street and popped some into my mouth, I wished I hadn't. To begin with, the coriander seed was whole – no attempt had been made to pound the seed, even coarsely, which would perhaps have released some of their essential oils. Secondly, they were long past their sell-by date, judging by their woody texture and singular lack of aroma. And thirdly, whoever told the usually discerning Italians that sugar and coriander was a felicitous combination? It isn't. Take my word for it.

On the other hand, one of the most delightful applications of coriander seed has to be the quintessentially Gujarati mouth-freshener cum digestive made out of the internal germ of coriander seeds. As flat as a disc, round and pale brown in colour, it is extracted, moistened with salty water and dried. The bustling street market around Ahmedabad's Manek Chowk sells a variety of mouth-fresheners amidst gleaming tin vessels and cut-price garments. Each mobile cart has a varied range of products, but every one of them stocks dhania dal, as it is called.

Though it is somewhat of an obsession in Gujarat, I've seen it sold in stores around the country as well, though admittedly not often. Judging by its low price and the casual way it is sold in piles along with churan and other lip-smacking digestives on the side of the road in towns all over Gujarat, it cannot be a high-technology venture. However, a surprising number of my friends, who are happy to munch on it after meals, could not make the connection between it and the spice. It is probably because of the texture – smooth and crunchy and mildly salty, these probably won't remind you of the spice you always associate with your spice rack at home.

But despite its many uses, and its prominent place in Indian kitchens, coriander, I feel, is not given its due, and often dismissed as a 'non-spice'. But no other spice is as versatile, in both seed and leaf form, than this humble little plant: As a base, as a garnish, as an aromatic, coriander rounds up the flavours in a dish in a way few other spices can. And for that, I think, it deserves a place in the 'big four' of Indian spices.

CHEF ARUN KUMAR'S LAMB CURRY

Mild and soothing, the coriander and the coconut milk work together to counterpoint the chillies.

INGREDIENTS

- 500 g mutton cubes
- 4–6 whole red chillies
- 2 tbsps coriander seeds
- 20 small onions (or shallots)
- ½ tsp fenugreek seeds
- 1½ cup coconut milk (fresh/packaged)
- Salt, to taste

METHOD

- Roast the red chillies and coriander seeds.
- Cool and then grind to a fine powder.
- Heat a tablespoon of oil. Crackle the fenugreek seeds.

- Add the onions and stir-fry till translucent. Add mutton cubes and fry till brown.
- Mix the ground powder. Fry for a few minutes. Add coconut milk, mix well.
- Add salt to taste.
- Simmer while covered till meat is cooked. Serve with rice or appams.

SIMPLE SOUP WITH CORIANDER POWDER

While researching for this book, I had to deal with dozens of packets of spices. Ingredients without their own strong flavour tended to be the best showcase of the quality of a particular spice. My two most oft-used ingredients, therefore, were potatoes and rice, but there's a limit to how much potatoes I could ladle down the gullets of my long-suffering family. So I hit upon this soup. As with many of the dishes that emerge from my kitchen, there's no fixed recipe. Use your imagination to add or subtract.

INGREDIENTS

- 200 g root vegetables. Choose from pumpkin, potato, carrot, beetroot etc.
- 4 tbsp good quality olive oil
- 1 small onion, finely sliced
- 4 cloves garlic, minced
- 1 tsp coriander powder
- 2 vegetable stock cubes
- Salt and pepper, to taste
- 4 cups water

METHOD

- In a large saucepan, heat the olive oil and sauté the garlic and onions.

- When the onions are translucent (but not brown) add the coriander and immediately after, the coarsely chopped vegetables.
- Sauté for less than a minute. Add the stock cubes and 4 cups hot water.
- Pressure cook till the vegetables are cooked.
- Add seasoning to taste.

Note: I usually serve the soup in mugs or bowls with a blob of whipped cream floating on top, with a pinch of coriander powder on the cream.

THE
AROMATICS

A Short History of the Aromatics

I vastly prefer the name 'aromatic spices' to describe the spices in this section, although the Spices Board of India's favoured term is the rather inscrutable 'tree spices', which conveys little of their magic or mystique. Plus, the term doesn't quite cover the provenance of either pepper, which is a climber, or cardamom, which is a shrub.

The aromatic spices – known for their use as preservatives, their medicinal value and the sheer flavour they impart to food – drove the spice trade for centuries. The western world competed fiercely for control of the routes that brought in these oriental spices, since they were worth their weight in gold. In fact, centuries before the age of Louis Vuitton handbags and private jets, it was the aromatics that were the definitive luxury item. Roman emperor Nero is said to have burnt a year's supply of cinnamon for the entire city at the funeral of his wife in 65 CE to atone for his role in her death. Considering the exorbitant price of cinnamon at the time, plus the sheer effort of transporting it from one end of the globe to another, it was the equivalent of covering a corpse with diamonds and emeralds.

It was the aromatics for which first Spain and Portugal, and then the Netherlands and UK, launched expeditions that discovered new continents. Christopher Columbus, Francis Drake, Vasco da Gama and Ferdinand Magellan are household names because of these aromatics.

Prior to Christopher Columbus' epic journey in 1492, spices reached western Europe through what would be known in bureaucratese as 'the unorganized sector', mainly through the hands of adventurers and black-marketeers. The trade was dominated by Arab traders who would arrive at the coast of Kerala or the islands of the Indonesian archipelago, load aromatic spices into their dhows and proceed to Egypt via an overland journey on camel back. From Egypt, they would load their cargo in boats and travel to Venice via the Mediterranean. None of this was formal; certainly there were no government-to-government links. On the contrary, the Arabs went to great lengths to conceal the actual location of where the spices grew and what they looked like. They concocted fanciful stories about fire-spewing dragons guarding impenetrable jungles where spices grew and of giant birds that built nests with cinnamon sticks. This was all done to impress on their interlocutors just how dangerous it was to actually try to get to the source themselves. When traders from the Arab world visited the Malabar coast in Kerala to acquire pepper and cardamom, they famously married local girls. Their descendants, the Moplahs, (a corruption of the word *ma pillai*, or 'son in law'), have a cuisine that is radically different from anywhere else in the state. Their biryanis too are nowhere close to what is served in the rest of the country. They are the only people in Kerala to use significant quantities of aromatic spices in their food.

The Arabs kept a tight leash on the trade so that by the time the spices arrived in Europe, their costs would have increased a thousand times or more. And so, it came about that for 400 years, from 1400–1800 CE, European expeditions from Spain, Portugal, UK and Netherlands set off to find the sources of these spices. Most famously, in 1492, Christopher Columbus sailed westwards from Spain, towards what he imagined was the East Indies but ended up in South America instead of India and the spice islands of the Indonesian archipelago.

Since the dawn of civilization, the centre of the world of aromatic spices was concentrated in two regions, of which one was as secure as a bank vault. The Banda Islands of the eastern Indonesian archipelago may not be the most prominent destination in the world today, but a large chunk of history was fated to be written around them. The five islands were the only source of nutmeg (and consequently mace) till less than 200 years ago. In the same neighbourhood, but a short way away, are three more islands that are considered as belonging to another geographical and geological group. These are the Maluku Islands of Ternate, Tidore and Makian, where cloves originally grew. The second location was the Malabar coast of Kerala, the source of green cardamom and pepper. Nearby was Sri Lanka, still the only location of true cinnamon.

Whatever else the Banda Islands are, you could not accuse them of being either large or prominently situated. Indeed, the island of Run is a mere 3 kilometres long and 1 kilometre wide. Yet, they were captured first by the Portuguese in 1511, then by the Dutch in 1599 and finally by the British in 1601 for the valuable nutmeg and mace that grew there abundantly and nowhere else. Today, the Islands are primarily a tourist destination for deep-sea diving. The sight of nutmeg drying on small pieces of cloth and matting in the courtyards of private homes is merely incidental.

On the other side of the Ceram Sea are the Maluku Islands where cloves grew. If the Almighty had wanted to hide His treasures from the rest of mankind, He did a mighty fine job of it. Even today, local flights to the area are erratic to say the least, and the local steamers are too primitive and too irregular to make travel easy, even with the benefit of accurate maps and navigational aids. It defies the imagination to consider what fleets of sailing ships were up against in the Middle Ages without knowing where the spice islands were, how to get there, what to look out for and even whether the world was indeed round, as some suspected, or flat, as maps of that time suggested. The miracle is, in spite of those odds, get there they did, in 1513, in the process changing the world forever.

It was in 1492 that Spain sent out a crack force to sail the seven seas and discover the sources of these spices. Christopher Columbus set out in the direction of the 'Indies' with only a vague sense of where he was going, but not much else in the way of direction and certainly no knowledge of what these coveted spices looked like in their natural state. In one of the best hoaxes of history, he landed in the Caribbean, saw allspice growing and mistook it for pepper. He then tried to convince his patrons back home that it was the real thing. Columbus neither realized that he had missed Indonesia and the spice islands by half the planet, nor that pepper and allspice were two entirely different spices!

The golden age of exploration was driven largely by consortiums hungry for spices. And when they succeeded in their objectives, they took pains to ensure that their riches did not travel: When the Dutch ruled Indonesia for 200 years from 1621, every last nutmeg was scalded in lime to ensure that it was sterile! In fact, so riveting are the stories that several books on spices deal exclusively with the provenance of aromatic spices, their discovery by Westerners and the vicissitudes of fortune of the spices and those that dealt in them.

A few facts however, do stand out. In the fight-to-the-finish rivalry between the two Protestant naval powers of the day – the Dutch and the British – for the key to the treasure chest of nutmeg and mace, the Dutch dominated most of the Banda Islands and managed to chase the British to the last one, Run, which was 10 miles away from its nearest neighbour Neira, and surrounded by reefs that made navigation to it fraught with technical difficulties. On the plus side, it grew abundant nutmeg and mace: its produce could fill an entire fleet of ships! The Dutch, however, were not content to banish their rivals to the smallest, furthest and most inaccessible island. They wanted monopoly over the nutmeg trade and so they signed a treaty giving the British another island, in another part of the world as compensation for Run. The name of this island? Manhattan. Scarcely believable in the 21st century. Even less believable is the fact the British accepted Manhattan with a long face: After all, what spice could grow on an island off the Hudson river! It is another matter entirely that today, you could claim to have never heard of Tidore or Run and not elicit gasps of astonishment but try telling your colleagues you've not heard of Manhattan!

The British did, eventually, have the last laugh, because they took saplings of nutmeg trees with them and planted them in their colonies in the tropics, thus causing the eventual decline of the Banda Islands.

Today, the flag of Grenada sports a nutmeg on it as a national emblem, which speaks of the successful planting of the spice from South East-Asia in the West Indies. Vietnam, in a twist of fate, has overtaken India as the largest exporter of pepper and Zanzibar and Madagascar, now export cloves to Indonesia! And if India holds any records, it is in the volume of chillies that we export, though that itself is a legacy from South America.

It's safe to say that the aromatics changed the course of history several times over. It is because of them that travel, trade and exploration became a way of life. Even as spices became the jewel in the crown, as it were, of these expeditions, subsidiary foodstuffs travelled to other parts of the world, thus altering the culinary landscape of the world forever. Today, corn or maize is never thought of as a Mexican ingredient, nor potatoes and tomatoes as from the Andes. Papayas, mangoes, bananas, apples, beans, aubergines: the list of foods that grow copiously in countries halfway across the planet from their original locations is endless, and it is the greatest testament to the vibrant spice trade that existed hundreds of years ago.

Cinnamon

I had my 'aha!' moment vis-à-vis cinnamon in quite an unusual place: The dried seafood market in Hong Kong, where every possible creature that lives under the sea, from seahorses and scallops to shrimps and octopi, was displayed proudly at the entrance of every shop on Des Voeux Road Central. I enjoyed photographing them to be sure, but the smell was quite another matter, even for someone who has walked around Mumbai's coastal villages when Bombay duck is being dried. More to catch a few minutes' break from the assault on my olfactory nerves than to actually explore Hong Kong's traditional medicine shops, I ducked into an air-conditioned shop and pretended to look around intelligently, but the jars full of gnarled branches and what appeared to be chopped wood meant little to me. I caught sight of a long piece of curving bark. 'Pretty,' I said to my guide, Fred Cheung. He turned to the shop-keeper and asked him conversationally in Cantonese what it was. Back came the reply, that was duly translated to me: cinnamon. I was thunderstruck. I had seen foot-long strips of cinnamon in Kumily, in Kerala, but I had never seen such a thick bark. Given that it had curved into an 's' shape, it was difficult to measure. What was even more intriguing was what cinnamon was doing at the very southern tip of China.

It was then that a bolt of realization forcefully hit me. Cinnamon is called dalchini in Hindi. 'Chinese wood' if you translate it literally. And what the shop-keeper had taken down from the shelf to let me see it at close quarters was as close as I was ever going to get to 'Chinese wood'. I just had to have it. To my surprise, the giant bark of the *Cinnamomum cassia* did not cost more than a couple of thousand rupees, and if I wrapped it in a clear plastic bag, I could carry it safely on my lap all the way home. Today, it is mounted in a glass-fronted box and hangs on a wall in my living room. Whoever has visited my house immediately demands to know what it is and to date, not a single person has been able to guess correctly.

Cinnamon is probably the favourite spice of many people all over the world: Its sweet note with an undercurrent of spiciness and its warm, aromatic fragrance has made it an instant favourite in kitchens and coffee bars, with chewing gum manufacturers, mouth-freshener brands and patisseries. And, in recent years, cinnamon has crossed the boundaries of the kitchen into the most unlikely of places: spas, hand-made soap stores, perfumeries, boutique candle stores, etc. I have received Christmas gifts of potpourri from Austria where its trademark curled bark was the star of the show, and I have had spa treatments on the Tioman Island, off the coast of Malaysia, where the scrub had so much cinnamon that the fragrance exhilarated me even while the languorous strokes of the masseuse were designed to send me into slumber.

Curiously, even though the spice is ubiquitous, the use of cinnamon is very different in the two hemispheres. In the West, you will almost always find it in bakery products, puddings, cakes and spiced sweet beverages like hot chocolate and cappuccinos. In the East, it forms a part of a set of spices that is added to meaty curries but seldom, if ever, to sweets.

One possible reason for this marked difference in usage of cinnamon is because the spice has a twin brother (or sister, if you prefer). Depending on whom you ask, and where you are from, cinnamon gets mistaken for its twin more often than you'd think. Confused? Let me explain. We are talking about two spices that are so similar that most people have no idea that they are different from each other. One is the thick outer bark of the evergreen tree *Cinnamomum cassia*. It is what most of us in India get when we ask the spice seller for dalchini. The flavour is sweet but there is an undertone of heat to it that goes superbly well with rich (or 'hot') ingredients, whether sweet or savoury. Thus, spice blends that include this type of cinnamon are usually used to cook red meats like lamb or beef. But here's the thing: it's not cinnamon at all, it's cassia bark.

At one point in history, most of the world's cassia came from China, although today cassia bark is also grown in Indonesia and Vietnam, and in a modest amount in Kerala. In fact, that's why we refer to it as as *dal-Chini* or bark of China! (We often don't realize how origins play a vital role in the naming of a food: The Arab world's reference to tamarind as *tamar-al-Hind* or 'dates from India', for instance, has now slipped into common usage without many of us being none the wiser.) True cinnamon is grown only on the island of Sri Lanka. Like cassia, true cinnamon also comes from a tree of the same genus, but a different species: *Cinnamomum verum*. It is one of the few aromatic spices that has never been successfully transplanted elsewhere, in spite of painstaking efforts over the centuries. You can identify true cinnamon by its look: Strips of bark that curl inwards, rather like ringlets. The colour of the bark is paler and the texture thinner than cassia bark. And the taste varies slightly as well: the presence of tannins in its bark makes cassia more pungent than cinnamon.

Though true cinnamon grows nowhere else in the world but Sri Lanka, cassia grows in China, Kerala, Indonesia and Vietnam and each variety is different, depending on the provenance. Vietnamese cassia is slightly less coarse in texture, a bit thinner and has less heat than its Indian counterpart. As a very general rule, cassia is used in eastern cuisines for curries and savouries while cinnamon makes it to the western world which uses it in sweets, baking and in coffee.

Don't bother to argue about which tastes better: cassia or cinnamon – it's a subjective matter. The former has a deeper, richer, spicier flavour and the latter is lighter and sweeter. Which one do I prefer? That's easy: Cassia for cooking meats and cinnamon for breads, puddings and desserts. And to flavour my morning coffee as well! There is one puzzle about cinnamon that I don't think anybody will be able to crack. How is it that despite Sri Lanka being so close to India, we have been procuring cassia from China? Perhaps in the distant past, it was traded overland. Or perhaps, given our usage of cinnamon in savoury dishes, the lighter, sweeter cinnamon from Sri Lanka was not as suitable a fit as the cassia bark from China. Or, maybe that too is not the case. Because, the US also uses cassia from China, but their usage is predominantly for cakes, pies and coffee. It is probably just another one of the enigmas of the spice world.

When it comes to cinnamon, there's a lot of skill involved in picking the spice from the plants, unlike most other spices, where what really counts is long hours, rather than technique. In the case of cinnamon, post-harvest processing is a highly skilled process, done by experts.

I had the chance of watching this process happen at a plantation in Sri Lanka, in the Negombo-Matara belt. The area is quiet and sparsely populated, surrounded by hilly terrain, but the hills are nowhere as high as they are in, say, Nuwara Eliya.

The plantation was owned by Shanta Rupasiri, whose son Manoj was in the tourism trade and known to a friend. Before we arrived, I had, in my naiveté, imagined that I would be entering a sacred grove, dark with the shade of towering trees and fragrant with the scent of my favourite spice. Alas! Unlike other tree spices like, say, clove, cinnamon entirely lacks girth and majesty. The trees and I were about equal height and as hard as I sniffed, there was no aroma of rich, warm, woody, sweet cinnamon.

Each bush – which is what they are called in the trade – is planted two feet apart, and yields around four or five shoots. The shoots are cut when they attain a certain growth, usually at around 18 months. Though the bush itself might be 100 years old, none of the shoots will be more than a year-and-a-half old. It is the 'trunk', for want of a more accurate descriptor, which is the main source of the spice, together with the longer branches. The bush is harvested twice a year, both times during the monsoon, which is when the bark is at its most soft and supple and can easily be formed into the quills that are the standard shape for sale in the international marketplace

The Rupasiris had chosen to harvest a few kilograms of cinnamon bark although it was not the correct season. Their simple, basic little outhouse with red oxide floors and bright, colourful flowers growing haphazardly around in a modest garden, strongly reminded me of my own grandmother's house in Goa. Even the rustic, rather basic furniture was similar.

Here, the cinnamon 'craftsman' – the person who harvests the barks and creates the cinnamon quills – was in attendance with what appeared to be his full family, seated on the floor of the living room. There were half a dozen family members of all ages busy with various tasks and several small children chattering excitedly. The craftsman-in-chief worked with an assortment of scrapers and sickles that their forefathers have used for centuries, including a dangerously sharp knife. A couple of sweeps of his arm down the length of a cinnamon branch, and the bark was peeled off. Long decades of practice made this seem effortless, though Shanta Rupasiri, the owner, told me that the same task would take him six times the effort. In fact, so integral are these craftsmen to the cinnamon plantations that when Sri Lanka has seasonal fairs, the peelers also attend, and even receive a share of the proceeds. This is one way of ensuring that their art continues to conform to a high standard.

Once the bark was peeled off, it looked very much like a parchment. Great care was taken to shoo the children away, lest they accidentally cause the whole bark to tear or crack. The international wholesale market traditionally requires that all cinnamon quills be 42 inches in length, so the craftsmen were taking special care to ensure that each bark was kept whole.

I was told that one day later a block of brass would be used to smoothen the bark carefully, without breaking or cracking it. Then, master peelers use a small sickle-like knife to cut the bark into 42-inch pieces. An inch less and the whole thing is worthless in the international market! Next, the barks are layered, so that when they curl as they dry over the next couple of days, they resemble very long cigars. When I asked Shanta Rupasiri for 12 quills, he reached up to a make-shift hammock near the ceiling that served as a drying chamber cum storage space, and handed me my quills for an absurdly small sum of money.

Back at Shanta Rupasiri's large, airy home, I asked what was done with the rest of the cinnamon branches after the bark had been stripped off. Instead of answering, Shanta took me to an outhouse kitchen with a wood-fire. All the sticks being used were branches and twigs of the cinnamon bush after the precious bark had been removed. And there was a distinct fragrance of cinnamon in the kitchen, which would, no doubt, find its way into the clay pot in which coconut, chillies and turmeric were being lovingly blended with the vegetables of the day.

Unsurprisingly, cinnamon is extensively used in Sri Lankan cooking, from vegetables to meats to desserts. The only instance where it is not used is in curries that call for vinegar. For the rest of the cooking, it is ubiquitous. Take, for instance, the lamprais, a meal in one, neatly prepared in a banana leaf, folded and heated when it is ready to serve. It is a speciality of the Burghers, the light-eyed, fair-skinned community of mixed Dutch and Sri Lankan descent, and is widely regarded to have been brought over from Malaysia by Dutch conquerors. Lamprais consists of cinnamon-flavoured rice, a fried egg, a cutlet, a chicken, pork or beef curry and a fried plantain or two meatballs. The Malaysian/Indonesian lemper, a bite-sized morsel of shredded chicken rolled in sticky rice and steamed, is thought to be the forerunner of lamprais.

The other dish brought over by the Dutch via Malaysia is gula melaka, a sago pudding where the steamed sago is plain to the point of tastelessness and two sauces, made respectively of coconut milk and melted palm jaggery, add the flavour. Although gula melaka is made in quite a few countries, the Sri Lankan version dutifully uses cinnamon in the pearl sago as a small but significant calling card, announcing to the world that Sri Lankan dishes have mastered the art of using their native spice, so beloved across the world, in their cuisine.

While true cinnamon is mostly used in the West to flavour sweets and breads, in countries like India, Mexico, the Middle East and South East-Asia, cassia is absolutely vital in biryani, kormas, rendang curries, pilafs and mole.

In India, in particular, although cassia is used mostly in conjunction with meats, there are a few examples of it being combined with vegetarian tea-time snacks. Gujarati bhakarwadi, for instance, features a sheet of dough made from wheat-flour layered with a spicy mixture strongly flavoured with cinnamon and cloves, rolled over, cut into slices and deep-fried in ghee. It is available in virtually every snack shop in Gujarat and it is a bit disconcerting to encounter the flavours at first. But then, all that ghee has to be made digestible, and what could be a more expeditious – and tasty – way of doing that, than to add ground cassia and cloves into the mix. Bhakarwadi has found its way to neighbouring Maharashtra as well, especially in Pune where it is available at every corner shop selling savouries.

However, bhakarwadi is the rare exception of a tea-time snack to use aromatic spices. For the most part, cinnamon is used in tandem with cloves and green and/or black cardamom and pepper in kebabs or main-course preparations that involve meats such as lamb, chicken and beef. In addition, cinnamon is ground into spice mixes such as garam masala, potli masala, even chana masala, wherever a hit of aroma is required. In Indian cuisine, it would be difficult to find cinnamon on its own, without the support of its companions, just as it would be challenging to find only cumin or only coriander in the vast panoply of Indian preparations.

From curries of lamb and beef to buns, breads and pudding, cinnamon seems to appeal to all kinds of palates, but that is only a fraction of what the spice can be used for. My grandmother's favourite remedy for a cold was a warm cup of water with honey, lemon and cinnamon. She even recommended oiling hair every week with a touch of powdered cinnamon and honey added to the oil. But that's not all. Because of its anti-fungal properties, it is used everywhere from room fresheners to spa treatments. Because it promotes the production of collagen, it is used in rejuvenating creams, and in lip-balms for its warm, rich fragrance. Diabetologists often advise patients to consume cinnamon powder first thing in the morning, along with their medicine, since it has properties that lower triglycerides and cholesterol.

However, there is, as the saying goes, too much of a good thing. Cassia – not cinnamon – contains the chemical compound coumarin, which is a blood thinner and can damage the liver. True cinnamon from Sri Lanka has a lot less coumarin, so it poses no health risks. The only problem is that in many countries, there is very little awareness regarding the difference between the two. In India, there is only one brand that packages true cinnamon; and even the US has postulated that there is too little difference between the two to make the distinction on labelling, with the result that it is perfectly legal to sell cassia as cinnamon!

From confectioneries to curry houses and from spas to Chinese medicine shops, the bark with the warm, toasty flavour manages to be relevant to butchers, bakers and candle-stick makers all over the world, despite being called misleading names by many of its closest associates.

JENNY LINFORD'S CINNAMON BUTTER

(MAKES 50 g)

Jenny Linford is a London-based food writer and chronicler of London's fascinating food scene. She is the author of several books, including *Food Lovers' London*, a cosmopolitan food shopping guide to the capital, *The London Cookbook*, a mix of recipes, food history and stories, *The Creamery Kitchen*, a celebration of dairy delights and *The Tomato Basket*. Her cinnamon butter, spread on hot toast, is a simple yet enjoyable British tea-time treat.

INGREDIENTS

- 50 g unsalted butter, softened
- 2 tbsp sugar
- 1 tsp cinnamon, ground

METHOD

- Using a fork, mix together the softened butter, sugar and cinnamon until well-mixed. Cover and chill until required.

CHEF MURTAZA SAIFEE'S DALCHINI MURGH TIKKA

Chef Murtaza hails from the Bohra community and the rest of his family consists either priests or scholars. Eschewing both professions, he became a chef and the food of his ancestors is never far from his consciousness.

INGREDIENTS

- 400 g chicken thigh, boneless
- 1 tsp chana powder, roasted
- 2 tbsp mustard oil
- 2 tbsp garlic
- 1 tbsp ginger
- 1 tsp red chilli powder (preferably deghi mirch)
- 1½ tsp cinnamon powder
- Salt, to taste
- 3½ tbsp hung curd
- 1 tsp tomato ketchup

METHOD

- Make a paste of the ginger and garlic.
- Clean chicken thighs and cut each into two.
- Now marinate the chicken with half of the mustard oil, cinnamon powder, ginger and garlic paste and red chilli powder and keep aside.
- Heat a little of the mustard oil in a pan to smoking point, cool down the oil and start roasting the chana powder.
- Once it starts becoming fragrant, remove from the pan and leave to cool.
- In a separate container take hung curd, add the remaining ginger and garlic paste, mustard oil, cinnamon powder and ketchup and make a homogenous mixture.
- Now mix the chana powder with the marinaded chicken pieces and coat them with the hung curd mixture.
- Grill the chicken pieces on a charcoal grill or in an oven.
- Serve with a light sprinkling of lemon juice, melted butter and chopped, fresh coriander leaves.

SAFFRON

The year was 1985. Harpreet Singh Chhabra, managing director of the 175-year-old company Baby Brand Saffron, was on his fifteenth visit to the Kashmir valley; this time for his honeymoon. He had been going there virtually every summer, for as long back as he could remember. After all, the Amritsar-based business that his grandfather had set up was based on saffron: the family has been important dealers in the spice for nearly two centuries. Choosing a destination for the honeymoon was, therefore, a no-brainer.

As Harpreet and his bride, like most other honeymooners in Kashmir, lounged in a shikara on the Dal lake, a small boat came up next to theirs. A salesman drew out a somewhat battered tin with a flourish. Inside was a pile of what could pass off as saffron.

Even today, these salesmen are a common sight, and they continue to sell what they pass off as 'genuine' saffron without any kind of assurance or guarantee: there's no brand name, no brick-and-mortar shop – nothing to which a customer can go back to complain if necessary. This particular salesman was confident that he had got hold of a pair of naïve fools and, as they showed a modicum of interest, he raised his sales pitch by a notch or two, always keeping his boat abreast of Chhabra's shikara. Harpreet played the part of a gullible tourist to the hilt. He looked at the saffron, pretended to examine it carefully, sniffed it for aroma and, when the salesman suggested that he place a strand on his tongue and let the aroma fill his senses, he did just that, even rolling his eyes as if in ecstasy though Harpreet knew with a single glance that the battered little tin contained little more than shreds of coloured paper. For his part, the purveyor of fake saffron believed that he had convinced a pair of tourists to buy his artificially coloured filaments as the real thing, never knowing that the 'credulous tourist' was a third-generation saffron dealer himself who saw through the ruse and played along only because it amused him to do so.

The salesman never did find out that it was *he* who was the credulous chump, and that the 'tourist' would, by 2000, buy around 50 per cent of the entire saffron crop of Kashmir – the genuine crop that is – every year.

Thirty odd years later, saffron is just as precious and there are just as many conmen around now as there were in 1985. The world's costliest spice attracts sharks, confidence tricksters and scam artists as a magnet does iron filings. It is not just in Kashmir either, let me hasten to add. I once visited a tiny handicrafts shop in Toledo, not far from La Mancha, Spain, where saffron was being sold in quirky glass bottles by an old lady in a funky headscarf. I bought a bottle, and after I came back to Delhi, took it to bona fide saffron dealers for certification. They all told me that I had been duped. It seems that what I had bought was three-year-old Iranian saffron that had lost most of its strength. So much for skilful marketing.

While Spain grows too little of the crop to make it commercially viable, Iran grows the largest quantity. While the Iranian saffron is known for its colour, having a high degree of crocin, Kashmiri saffron is prized for its aroma and flavour, being endowed with picro-crocin and safranal.

(Saffron has three active compounds – crocin, picro crocin and safranal – each responsible for colour, flavour and aroma respectively.) Greece, Morocco and Abruzzo in Italy are other locations where saffron is grown. Switzerland, New Zealand and France also grow minuscule amounts of the spice.

There are very few places in the world that have the right climatic and soil conditions, combined with cheap labour, that allows for saffron to grow, making it the 'caviar' of the spice kingdom, as it is sometimes called. Saffron is the name given to the spice obtained from the three maroon stigmas of the plant *Crocus sativus*. *Crocus sativus* has been around for an estimated 3,000 years, despite the fact that it requires human intervention to plant the corms (a short underground plant stem or bulb), since it is a sterile plant, incapable of reproduction on its own. What this means is that, at every stage of its history, every saffron plant has had people who have cared for it, planted it, transported it to various locations and used it. You can't say the same for many other spices, most of which do not need human intervention for their propagation.

A short distance from the city of Srinagar, is the town of Pampore, the only place in Kashmir – indeed India – where saffron grows. Drive through the cluttered little marketplace where the tin roofs of the shops glint in the sun, and you'll come to miles and miles of rolling plateau, an abrupt topographical departure from the broad river valley of Srinagar. For most of the year, there's nothing very special about these dry brown fields, which have been raked into several tens of thousands of neat mounds. It's only in the month of November, when the fields are carpeted with pale mauve blooms of saffron that Pampore's fame becomes apparent.

It is the very structure of families in Pampore – indeed, in the whole of Kashmir – that makes the cultivation of saffron saleable. Here, joint families have always been the norm, with families of 15 members not uncommon. It is the family members that are pressed into service during the month or so of harvesting and processing the crop. Without this large number of family members involved, paid labour would have to be procured, pushing up the price of an already expensive commodity. In the Western world, with nuclear families being the norm, hired help at European Union rates means that saffron grown in Europe is significantly more expensive than its Asian counterpart.

Besides the rolling plateaus of Pampore in the Kashmir valley, the spice is also grown at Kishtwar in the Jammu region, though Kishtwari saffron has dwindled to a fraction of its former yield.

The saffron crop of Iran is centred around the holy city of Mashhad, in the region of Torbat-e Heydarieh, in the Razavi Khorasan Province. Just as Pampore is an hour's drive from Srinagar, Iran's saffron-growing region too fans out in a circle, an hour's drive from Mashhad. The Torbat-e Heydarieh region is eerily similar to Kashmir – vast, open countryside – though somewhat flatter than the rolling plateaus of Pampore. However, the biggest difference is that here, saffron is but one crop among many. In Mashhad, saffron grows alongside cotton, sugar beet and barley. There are other differences too. During harvest season, growers in Iran sometimes simply pluck the flowers and take them to the saffron market where the pale mauve blossoms lie, out of the line of the direct sun, waiting to be collected by the armload. They are then taken to a dealer's house where they are sorted, dried and metamorphosed from a poetically lovely flower plucked from its plant to the costliest spice in the world. In Kashmir, because of the way society is structured, a grower never need to worry about not having enough hands to do the work, as he is sure to have a large family to separate the styles from the flowers and stamens. So piles of flowers for sale in a saffron market is simply not a part of the Kashmiri landscape.

Go to a saffron dealer in the holy city of Mashhad – where the traders tend to be – and you'll see rooms lined with shelves like a bank vault, packed from end to end with enormous plastic bags of saffron. As with saffron dealers all over the world, there's a carefully coded method to the placement of the bags. What bag to show to which customer is an unspoken art.

Not unusually, the world of saffron trading, buying and selling in Iran is primarily confined to men. But the private house-turned-office that I was privileged to visit in Mashhad had a courtyard separating the office from the packaging unit and males were rigorously kept out of the latter. That was where the ladies sat, busy pasting logos, aligning price tags, weighing saffron by the teaspoonful and placing it in attractive pouches. Mostly in their twenties; they sat with veils and chador scrupulously in place, filling and weighing with precision, till the sound of the Azan at the mosque next door made them keep their work aside for prayer.

In the bazaar around the tomb of Imam Reza, arguably the nerve centre of Mashhad, saffron was just one of the items on sale, but considering Iran is the biggest producer, there was a lot of it and in all shapes and sizes. Sugar candy on sticks, like lollipops, but coloured with saffron, to stir your tea with, saffron tea, saffron extract, saffron powder, saffron strands – the range was much more visible than anywhere in Kashmir.

It was also in Iran that I first heard of saffron biologists and a saffron research centre. That many countries have research centres for rice and wheat is expected; but for there to be a worldwide community of saffron biologists was, to me, surprising. Yet there are, expectedly from those countries where saffron is grown, but also others that have experimental farms that produce insignificant quantities. Hence, the symposiums are attended by saffron biologists from Spain, Italy, Greece, Iran, Afghanistan, Brazil, Argentina, UK, China and Japan. Some are interested in growing it commercially in their countries; others are in search of its remedial effects. They meet once every few years, and their somewhat long-drawn out deliberations are published in scientific manuals.

According to Vinayak Razdan, scholar of Kashmiri history and culture, there is a legend about how saffron entered the Kashmir valley. Like many other legends, this one too has its basis in verifiable fact. Vagbhata, the famous Ayurvedic physician who lived in the 6th century CE, had a patient with an eye complaint. No remedy that Vagbhata tried had any effect on the patient. Finally, suspecting that the patient was in reality a serpent deity (every fresh water spring in Kashmir had a specific serpent deity), Vagbhata asked him outright. When the patient identified himself as a Nag or demi-god associated with a spring, Vagbhata knew that the remedy had to include binding his eyes so that the fumes from his breath would not hamper the treatment. It worked, and the Nag presented Vagbhata with saffron corms in gratitude. Indeed, to this day, the fresh water spring of Takshak Nag at Zevan in Kashmir is visited by pilgrims and its water is considered sacred, not to mention that geographically, it is indeed very close to the area where saffron grows.

Other, similar legends associated with the Buddhist and Muslim faiths also exist, both of which were established in the Kashmir valley at different periods. Significantly, these legends too include the handing over of saffron corms by a religious figure in gratitude.

Saffron is widely thought to have been first grown in Croycus (now Korghoz) near Syria, from where the Arabs are said to have taken it to Spain in 961 CE. Literary references too provide clues about the origins of saffron in the Kashmir valley. When Kashmiri historian Kalhana wrote his *Rajataringini* or *Chronicle of Kings* in the 11th century CE, one of the crops he mentioned is saffron. And after Kashmir became a part of the Mughal empire in 1586 CE, Emperor Jahangir remarked on how the blooming saffron fields in Pampore caused him to feel drowsy, as referenced in the *Tuzuk-i-Jahangiri*. Legends and literary references aside, growing saffron is quite prosaic; in fact, it requires tedious, back-breaking work. Saffron flowers grow from corms and bloom for just one month in the year, always in autumn. The flowers have exceedingly short stems so, to delighted onlookers, it looks like the world's largest carpet – and quite possibly the prettiest too. However, to owners of saffron fields it means hours and hours of back-breaking work because machines just cannot take the place of human labour, much like tea estates. Each pale mauve blossom contains three yellow stamens and three maroon stigmas attached to a white style. Each corm yields anything from one to five blossoms that open at dawn. When a blossom is ready, it has to be plucked before sunrise, else the sun would weaken the colouring power of the trumpet-shaped stigmas. This means about six to eight hours of bending over double, every day, for at least two weeks in the year.

That's not the end, though: There's more labour ahead to make sure that the *Crocus sativus* transforms from a flower to a spice. The style has to be separated from the stigmas, and the quite worthless stamens have to be discarded. Next, the stigmas have to be dried in a process called 'fixing', and the more expeditiously this process takes place, the better the flavour and colour of saffron can be 'fixed'. In Spain, the fixing process is done over gentle heat, but in Kashmir – as indeed the rest of the saffron-growing world – the saffron is dried in the shade.

It is at this stage that rapid degeneration can take place, and experts have noted that Kashmiri saffron growers should put into place a system, not necessarily high tech, whereby a day's picking of saffron stigmas can be dried in one hour instead of the three days that it currently takes. But then, experts have been pursing their lips at many of the goings-on in Pampore. There is no irrigation system in place, no de-weeding, no pest control and no digging up of the corms every three years, as is the international norm. In short, nothing seems to be ploughed back into the system that is laying the golden eggs, as Harpreet Chhabra, puts it.

In fact, we don't even know how many golden eggs the goose lays. This is because all the landholdings in Pampore are in the hands of private families. In the absence of anything remotely resembling a wholesale market, purchase of fertilizers, a taxation system or a village co-operative, all one can do is guesswork. For example, it is known that it takes 150,000 flowers to make 1 kilogram of saffron, and that Pampore's production of saffron is anywhere between 15,000 and 20,000 kilograms. Given that one acre produces around one-and-a-half to two kilograms (whereas, optimally it should produce 5 kilograms), this means that there are probably 15,000 acres of land under cultivation, being looked after by around 20,000 families.

What we do know, beyond doubt, is that Kashmiri saffron has the thickest, longest stigmas and that the flavour is far stronger than its Iranian counterpart. It would be tempting to call it the 'best saffron in the world' but such claims invariably produce a host of angry rebuttals. One such is that Spanish saffron deserves to be called the world's best. Conventional wisdom has it that in Spain, the finest quality of saffron grows on the plateaus of La Mancha, with Rio and Sierra pitching in with lower grades of the spice.

However, Harpreet Chhabra tells me something completely different. He is the only Indian saffron supplier who attends international saffron conferences regularly. According to Chhabra, in all his trips to the plateau of La Mancha, Spain, he has never personally seen saffron cultivation, so it is probably grown in minuscule quantities today. The reason, he says, is one of simple arithmetic. The labour-intensive nature of the work – bending double for eight hours a day, two weeks a year, then separating the stamens from the stigma – can only be viable if you're in the third world. Pay daily wage workers European salaries, and you've automatically priced yourself out of the market.

Chhabra swears that Spanish saffron is all but over, and that traders in Spain resort to the simple expedient of buying saffron from elsewhere, packaging it as Spanish and exporting it – at a premium, naturally. This, perhaps, explains my unfortunate encounter with Iranian saffron in Spain.

It is this opaqueness in the saffron world that irks Chhabra. Iranian saffron – not the best quality, whether on the basis of colour, flavour or aroma, the three variables of saffron – is sold variously as a product of Kashmir and Spain. This gives rise to many discrepancies in quality as well, and can be completely befuddling for the lay consumer.

At one of my many meetings with Harpreet Chabbra, he put me to the test. In a small brief-case, he carried a variety of saffron and he had a game for me: I was to guess which were real saffron and which were fake. As he opened the suitcase and took out the samples, I observed them closely. There was a mushroom-shaped bunch of saffron with the stamens glued together: that was genuine Iranian. Another sample had long, elegant, thick stigmas, beautifully coloured: those were paper, dyed crimson to resemble saffron, and then passed through a shredding machine. Yet another sample was thin, wispy and unevenly coloured: those were the worthless, dyed stamens. Moral of the story: Only buy saffron that comes in packaging that has a brand name, address, email address and website. Such an enterprise can be presumed to have too much at stake to fob you off with shredded, dyed paper.

But sometimes it's not just the clueless customer who gets the short end of the stick. There are several other ways for a dealer to end up with a dud. One is to procure the saffron from a careless saffron grower. This is not difficult, given that most growers in India have little technological expertise. The kind of temperature variations that the newly plucked and graded crop is subjected to in a villager's home in Pampore is enough to render an entire consignment worthless. After being harvested, saffron needs to be dried so that no more than 12 per cent of its moisture remains. It needs to be stored carefully so that moisture and temperature variations do not ruin its flavour. In actual fact, however, the stigmas are stored in tins in Pampore, popped into a wooden cupboard, and all winter long are subjected to temperature variances: cold and damp followed by extreme warmth when coal – or wood-fired heaters are lit. While many growers are not sufficiently aware of the optimum amount of moisture in saffron strands, there are those who take care to keep more than the regulation 12 per cent of moisture to increase the weight of the product, But that, as a canny saffron biologist pointed out at an international conference, is akin to selling water at the price of saffron.

One of the other slips that can take place twixt cup and lip is the finishing of saffron. 'Raw' saffron contains many inclusions: dust, bacteria, styles and the odd stamen that has slipped in accidentally. 'Preparing' saffron by separating the stamens from the stigmas, then drying the latter, is done by growers, and a critical amount of pressure needs to be exerted while pulling bunches of saffron, seemingly carelessly. The right pressure will result in dust and pollen rubbing off and the style breaking off at the exact point that it joins the stigmas. The *wrong* pressure can result in all sorts of hideous consequences: Too light a pressure would keep the styles attached to the stigmas and would leave dust and insects clinging to the finished product, which would then have a very short shelf-life. Too much pressure, and the three chemicals active in saffron – crocin, picro-crocin and safranal – are in danger of being stripped away, besides the danger of the all-important stigmas breaking from above the style.

The other way for saffron to deteriorate in quality is the packaging itself. All of the saffron that is available in general merchants' stores and supermarkets is packaged in polypropylene containers, not the best of materials, given that saffron easily absorbs moisture and other flavours. Little wonder then that the common complaint is, 'The best saffron is probably exported out of the country, and we are saddled with third-grade stuff'. What people mean is that the saffron is adulterated, but here's the thing: adulteration is just as likely to afflict the export market. More to the point is that buying saffron, sadly, is an adventure fraught with risk, and you should only enter the arena with extreme caution.

That is why, a method for checking saffron has evolved. The buyers take a generous pinch of saffron in one hand, pour a few strands into the other palm and examine it carefully. Then, they throw the strands back into the receptacle and sprinkle a few more strands, the better to examine them. This usually tells them how carefully the crop has been processed, how even the length of each saffron stamen is and how uniform is the colour.

Saffron is used in various ways in cuisine all over the world. Iranians have their rice, we Indians have our biryani, Italians have their risotto and the Spanish have their paella: they are all flavoured with saffron. Saffron has a special affinity with milk: Both are seen as rich and nourishing, and one is seen as a value addition to the other. Plus, milk is the perfect medium for conveying flavours, no matter how subtle. In India, when saffron has to be used as a cooking ingredient, it is frequently soaked in warm milk, or rose-water in the case of sweet-makers, so that it releases its colour and flavour In Iran where saffron is used in many dishes, as you would expect from a country that produces ten times as much as India does, saffron is rarely soaked in warm milk, or even water for that matter. It is often ground to a paste in a marble mortar and pestle. Grinding is the thrifty way of ensuring that even the smallest possible amount is added to the food and in Iran this expensive ingredient is used more or less regularly. The more you grind it, the more the flavour develops, possibly because of the warmth that the friction of two stones produces. The only time I've seen it done here is by sweet makers, who are principally from Bengal.

In Marseille, France, the classic bouillabaisse, or seafood stew, uses saffron. (Curiously enough, saffron is never used with fish in India.) Bouillabaisse originated as a fisherman's quick stew, where at least six types of rock fish was to be thrown into a pot at the docks, boiled and reduced (bouillabaisse is derived from two words that mean precisely this) because no paying customer would buy these varieties. The saffron connection came about because it used to be grown in central France. In fact, at one point in history, Boynes in the Gatinais region was known to be the saffron capital of the world. Today, in western Europe, the gastronomy quotient of this fisherman's dish has gone through the roof and poor fishermen can no longer afford to eat it because of the scarcity of the spiny rockfish and other species that are the traditional components of a bouillabaisse.

In neighbouring Spain, paella is rice cooked with either seafood or with chicken wings and rabbit meat. Whatever the other ingredients may be, paella is always flavoured with saffron. In Italy, risotto atta Milanese always has saffron in the recipe. There does not seem to be much usage of saffron in sweets in the Western hemisphere; the Italian Christmas cake panettone makes use of saffron, and there may be a couple of others, but that's about it.

In India, saffron is used in both sweet as well as in savoury dishes and its usage is more prominent in the northern and the western parts. Besides biryani, of course, it is frequently used in kebabs and kormas, particularly those whose base is cashew-nut paste and, to a lesser degree, curd. That's because these curries are generally milder and you shouldn't use saffron as one element among a dozen others. A curry with cloves, cinnamon and cardamom, fried onions or red chillies is an unsuitable vehicle for this delicate spice. As for sweets, it is used often in rice and milk-based puddings and in sweets made with reduced milk.

Kashmir, however, breaks all rules of saffron usage that most other regions of the country so assiduously follow. It is used by every household to make kahva, the subtle tea made with 'green' tea leaves, brewed with saffron, cardamom, sugar and rose petals into a pale-coloured liquid that is a work of art as well as a marvellous digestive. And no wazwan, or banquet, is complete without lashings of saffron-infused water being poured atop ristas and rogan josh. Contrary to popular wisdom, all wazwan dishes of which it is an integral part, are rich with other spices as well, and have strongly flavoured bases, of which fried onions are only one example. And, in a radical departure from the worldwide norm, the milk or curd based dishes in Kashmiri cuisine never have saffron added to them.

Saffron is used in the greatest quantities by the Vaish and Marwari communities. In fact, it is one of the enigmas of the spice world that an upper-middle-class household in Kashmir would never use as much saffron as its counterpart in Gujarat or Rajasthan, which is surprising, because Kashmir is the only place in the country that grows saffron. In these communities, saffron is added to rich gravy dishes where charoli (chironji), char magaz paste and cashew paste are used. In the Vaish community, where new mothers and guests are considered next to God, dishes are devised to pay obeisance to this nexus, as the gods themselves are said to be saffron-hued. New mothers are fed chapattis flavoured with saffron for the first 40 days after childbirth; and a sherbet of saffron and pounded almonds is served to guests. So sacred is the spice that it is often stored in a container made from pure silver.

The Vaish community is not alone in its reverence of saffron. This spice is often taken to be a symbol of purity, equally because of its high cost and its auspicious colour. It is the colour associated with Lord Brahspati, who is the manifestation of the planet Jupiter. Brahspati, or Guruji, as he is also known, is associated with Thursday ('Brahspatwar' or 'Guru-war' in Hindi), and is vital in the pantheon of gods: every other deity prays to him for wisdom.

Saffron is also used in worship: Almost all priests throughout the country make the Navgraha or grid of nine squares (representing the nine planets), for every puja, whether it's for a new house or office space or for the success of a Bollywood film, and invite the gods by offering them saffron paste. It was saffron that lent boondi laddoo, the most common form of prasad all over the country, its signature colour. In Tirupati, till today, laddoos have a small quantity of real saffron added to them. The idol of Venkateshwar, an incarnation of Vishnu, in Tirupati, is bathed at 3.50 a.m. every morning by a host of priests with an amalgam of sandalwood powder, honey, tulsi, curd, ghee and saffron. The resultant liquid is distributed among the faithful as a holy offering called charnamrit.

Saffron is also used to ritually bathe the 58-foot idol of Bahubali outside Bengaluru. The ritual bath is performed once every 12 years by erecting a scaffolding atop which priests stand to pour thousands of pots of milk, curd, ghee, saffron, coconut milk, poppy seeds, almonds, gold coins and other substances. With each application, the immense statue changes colour. Swetambar Jains, who also worship idols, ritually purify them on festive occasions with a mixture of oils and unguents, of which saffron is one.

On bhaiyya dooj and raksha bandhan, festivals that celebrate the brother-sister relationship, in many parts of the country, sisters are required to mark their brothers' foreheads with an anointment that contains saffron soaked in water with a couple of grains of uncooked rice. Among the Muslim community in Kashmir, even today, the taweez or religious amulet is sometimes written in saffron mixed with water instead of ink.

In fact, so potent is the mystique of this coveted spice that no less than 25 to 35 per cent of saffron is used outside the kitchen in India, with uses as diverse as skincare, religious festivals and even reproduction – many even believe that male virility is helped along by regular doses of saffron! And it is not only in the home-grown school of Indian medicine that saffron is endowed with magical properties: According to Chinese medicine, drinking alcohol to which a few strands of saffron have been added will prevent a hangover. Incidentally, large-scale users of saffron include chewing tobacco (pan masala) companies and a brewery in Rajasthan that seeks to re-create a traditional liquor called kesar (saffron's Hindi name) kasturi, that used to be imbibed by kings.

The cosmetic industry is also a large user of saffron because it is believed to promote fairness. That's the reason why many expectant mothers are fed milk into which a few strands of saffron have been soaked. Whether it actually helps a couple to have a fair baby is a hotly debated issue but what has been fairly well-established by Ayurveda is that saffron is good for the texture of the skin. It is also considered to be a brain stimulant, a cure for asthma and an aphrodisiac. In fact, the colour of saffron (incidentally, one of the colours in the Indian flag) is so auspicious, that any self-respecting mithai seller catering a wedding will definitely top a few of his sweets with strands of saffron.

RISOTTO WITH KERALA PRAWNS, TOMATO AND SAFFRON

Ritu Dalmia burst on to the Delhi scene a couple of decades ago, much before anyone could appreciate her way with food, particularly Italian food. However, Delhi has since come to appreciate what she does, in her restaurants and trattoria, as well as in her numerous recipe books. Here, she accords saffron the place in the sun that it deserves.

'I like risotto. For me it is like khichdi, something which comforts me when I have a cold, or something I can stir mindlessly when I need to relax. However, this risotto will simply beguile you. Fresh and aromatic, whenever you cook this you will always get a pat on the back. Saffron adds delicacy and luxury to this otherwise humble rice dish often eaten in the Veneto region,' says Ritu Dalmia.

INGREDIENTS

- 300 g medium prawns, deveined and cut into small pieces
- 100 g unsalted butter, divided as specified
- 1 small onion, finely chopped
- 2 cloves garlic, minced
- 200 g high-quality imported Arborio rice
- 100 ml dry white wine
- 200 g cherry tomatoes, halved
- Pinch of saffron strands, soaked in warm water
- Handful of parsley leaves, chopped
- 500 ml fish or prawn stock (if you are too lazy to make

stock, just use chicken stock made with a cube)
- Salt and pepper, to taste

METHOD

- In a heavy-bottomed saucepan, heat one third of the butter over medium-high heat. When the foaming subsides, add the prawns and cook till light pink (about 2–3 minutes). Remove the prawns from the pan and set aside.
- In the same pan, add another third of the butter and sauté the onion until translucent. Add the garlic and cook for a few minutes more. Add the rice and stir until well-coated with the butter. Sauté lightly for a few moments, until the rice starts to turn translucent, then add the wine and stir constantly until evaporated.
- Begin adding the stock by the ladleful (about ½ cup), stirring constantly. After about 10 minutes or so, add the tomatoes. Continue the process of adding the stock and stirring for another 10 minutes until the rice is creamy and al dente. Always make sure there's enough liquid to cook the rice; it should bubble gently like old-fashioned oatmeal. If it dries out or becomes clumpy, add more stock or water.
- Add the saffron. Stir in the prawns and parsley. Season to taste with salt and pepper.
- Now add the remaning knob of butter, remove from the fire and cover it. Let it rest for 2 minutes or so.
- Give it a good stir and serve it right away.

PESCE IN ACQUA PAZZA (FISH IN CRAZY WATERS)

'I ate this flavourful plate for the first time in a tiny restaurant called Cumpa Cosimo in Ravello in Italy, and fell in love with the simplicity of this whole dish. I was informed by the very chatty owner that every true Neapolitan fisherman ate this for lunch, and no trip to Naples is complete without eating this at least once. I have a feeling that these poor fishermen did not add saffron to the recipe, but this is how I like to prepare it in my restaurant,' says Ritu Dalmia.

INGREDIENTS

- ½ kg firm fleshed white fish fillet like red snapper, sea bass or sole
- 2½ tbsp olive oil
- 1 tsp chilli flakes
- 1 medium-sized onion, sliced
- 3 cloves garlics, mashed
- 100 g cherry tomatoes, halved
- 1 tbsp capers
- Couple of bay leaves
- A pinch of saffron, soaked in warm water
- 3½ tbsp dry white wine
- ¼ cup water
- 1 tbsp lemon juice
- Lemon slices, for garnish
- Salt and pepper, to taste

METHOD

- Preheat the oven to 200°C. Wash the fish thoroughly, sprinkle with salt and pepper, and place in a large baking dish. Set aside. In a large frying pan, heat the olive oil over low heat. Add the chilli flakes, onion, bay leaves and garlic, and sauté until translucent (about 5 minutes). Add the cherry tomatoes, raise the heat to high and keep stirring. Add the white wine, capers and saffron. Cook for another 5 minutes, until super fragrant.
- Take off heat and add the ¼ cup water and lemon juice.
- Let cool for about 5 minutes and pour over fish, add the lemon slices to the top. Bake in the oven for 15 minutes. Serve immediately.

Note: You can prepare the same recipe with prawns instead of fish. Fillet is easier to eat, but if you want the 'wow factor', use a whole fish instead of a fillet. However, in that case the baking time needs to be increased to about 25 minutes.

CHEF MURTAZA SAIFEE'S ANAR AUR ZAFRAN KA PANEER TIKKA

In this recipe, that became his signature dish in Vietnam where he ran a hotel for two years, Chef Murtaza highlights the richness of saffron and the sweet-sour appeal of pomegranate, that are central to the core of Bohra cuisine.

INGREDIENTS

- 300 g paneer
- 2 tsp fresh cream
- 1½ tbsp hung curd
- 100 g fresh pomegranate seeds
- 1 tsp deghi mirch powder
- 1 tsp dry ginger powder
- A pinch of saffron, soaked in warm water
- Salt, to taste
- 2 tsp mustard oil
- 1 tbsp ginger and garlic paste
- Processed cheese
- 1 tsp butter

METHOD

- Cut the paneer into 1.5-inch square cubes. Sprinkle some salt and a little saffron water and mix well.
- Now grate the cheese in a flat pan and cream it till it becomes a smooth mixture.
- Add the ginger and garlic paste and mix well.
- Now add the hung curd, fresh cream, remaining saffron

water, mustard oil and salt and make a homogenous mixture.

- Separately, make a paste of the fresh pomegranate seeds.
- Heat a little oil in a pan and add the deghi mirch powder.
- Now add the pomegranate paste and cook on a slow heat.
- Add the dry ginger powder and keep on cooking till the mixture becomes thick, like a relish. Add salt. Now make a small slit in the paneer cubes and stuff this pomegranate relish in the paneer. Coat the paneer with the mix and cook it on a grill or in an oven.

NUTMEG AND MACE

Chef Srinath Sambandan, formerly of The Park, Visakhapatnam, and now an independent restaurant consultant, was spoiling me rotten. He had brought me to the city's Poorna Market, where fresh vegetables vie for space with fruits, fish, and spices. It was in Poorna Market that I caught a glimpse of mace at a spice stall, but this was no ordinary mace – it had been processed to resemble long strands of saffron. However, unlike saffron, this heap of mace was light, and you could literally see each strand. Mace is far from being the most popular spice in the country, so I was a trifle surprised at seeing it so lovingly and painstakingly processed. Chef Sambandan then told me that the combination of mace and star anise is vital to chicken curries and pulaos in coastal Andhra. The aroma of mace defines the dishes that make use of it. I didn't know it at the time, but that is probably the most intensive use of mace by any community worldwide. Usually, it is used much more sparingly.

Nutmeg and mace are usually spoken of in the same breath, and quite legitimately too. After all, they come from the same tree. Mace is the red mesh that encloses the hard, nut-like ovoid seed that in turn encases the nutmeg. Native to five tiny islands called the Banda Islands in the Indonesian archipelago, 600 miles away from its nearest landmass, Australia, the story of these two spices is a tragi-comedy in which the Arabs, the Portuguese, the Spanish, the English and the Dutch all play their respective parts, and who are all finally outsmarted by French horticulturist and missionary Pierre Poivre – whose surname, somewhat ironically, means pepper, and who is sometimes identified as 'Peter Piper' of the well-known tongue twister, 'Peter Piper picked a peck of pickled peppers'.

As I've mentioned in the introduction to this section on aromatics, the history of these two spices is tied to the early expeditions of Portugal and Spain, and later the English and the Dutch, who all wanted to discover the source of these rare aromatics. At the time, the Banda Islands was the only part of the planet where nutmeg and mace grew. It should come as no surprise then that, the islands soon became a hotbed for international struggle, where first the Spanish and the Portuguese, and then the English and the Dutch slugged it out for trading rights. The Dutch won in the year 1599, and guarded their privilege so jealously that every last nutmeg that grew on 'their' islands was sterilized with lime before being exported, so that they would be incapable of reproducing. Consequently, they did maintain their monopoly over the nutmeg trade. (The Dutch, however, had not reckoned with the birds that flew over the islands, eating the fruit and dispersing the seeds, and not always on Dutch territory!)

The history of the Banda Islands is not a pleasant one. The Dutch massacred a large percentage of the native population, ruthlessly shook off Britain from occupying territory, and even traded the island of Manhattan for Run, the nutmeg-rich British stronghold in the Banda Islands, in order to consolidate their monopoly on the nutmeg trade. But before the Dutch retook control of the Banda Islands according to the Treaty of Breda that was signed in 1667, the British transported many nutmeg trees to other British colonies like Grenada, Sri Lanka and the West Indies.

The vicissitudes of history also played a part in dispersing nutmeg to other lands. In 1755, Pierre Poivre, an adventurer, sailed to the Banda Islands with the express intention of purloining a few nutmeg plants. It was a daring idea to be sure, because if he was caught, the punishment was certain death: Not only for him but for all those who helped him. However, Pierre Poivre actually managed to lay his hands on a couple of nutmeg plants and smuggled them to Mauritius, which was then a French colony.

In one of the twists of fate that makes the history of spice such a fascinating subject, the Banda Islands are shrouded in obscurity, while the image of a nutmeg makes its appearance on the flag of the island of Grenada, one of the largest exporters of nutmeg and mace today!

It is one of my greatest wishes to visit the Banda Islands, but in the meantime, I have devoured accounts by travel bloggers who have been luckier than I. Traces of the Dutch presence still, apparently, live on, in ruined hilltop forts, planters' bungalows built in the signature Dutch style, with verandahs running on all four sides, and once-grand gateways, now falling to pieces slowly yet inexorably. The sea around the islands is myriad shades of blue, with coral reefs that draw in deep-sea diving enthusiasts. Each of the Banda Islands has a perfectly conical shaped volcano in the centre that towers over the 30-foot tall nutmeg trees that grow in its shade. From all accounts, any patch of flat land, including courtyards of unassuming private houses, is likely to have a series of mats on which shiny nutmeg seeds have been spread to slowly dry out in the sun. The rain that falls every single month of the year in the region serves two purposes: It keeps the spice gardens watered and serves as a dampener for all but the most determined visitors.

It is no surprise then that, after such evocative accounts of the Banda Islands, it was a great disappointment to see the nutmeg trees in the uplands of both Kerala, the only state in India where they grow, as well as Sri Lanka. To my dismay, there was no waft of fragrance: Early travellers, whether from Portugal, Spain or Netherlands, have all claimed to have been able to smell the plantations of Banda Islands from the sea even at a distance of 10 kilometres, much before their ships docked. Even the sheer height and girth of the nutmeg trees in Banda Islands isn't even remotely echoed in South Asia, where a tree of a puny four-meter height is considered perfectly acceptable. Also, the dense plantations of hundreds of nutmeg trees are conspicuous by their absence in our neck of the woods.

What I did see on a plantation in central Kerala, not far from the elephant reserve of Thekkady, was a yellowish fruit whose pulp has to be discarded, inside which is the bright red mace. If you are imaginative enough, it will look like a many-fingered fist tightly enclosing the seed, inside which is the nutmeg. Even if imagination fails you, it still looks like a tightly furled protective covering for a dark brown shiny shell that encases the nutmeg seed. The best quality of mace is as bright a red and as fully formed as possible. When the fruit has just been split open, the mace is as shiny red as a sports car and turns dull with exposure to air. Broken bits of orange or dark yellow mace are near the bottom of the quality barrel. In the spice trade, the lowest grade is known as BWP: broken, wormy, punky. This grade can be used to distil oil, but certainly not to sell to unwary customers.

Crack a nutmeg in half vertically and you'll see a pattern of light and dark striations, rather like worms, that are characteristic of betel nuts too. The dark streaks are the oil-bearing veins. Nutmeg that is past its sell-by date (and most spices, being agricultural products, are best used within one year of plucking) will not have striations because most of the oil has evaporated. The fruit that encases the two spices – nutmeg and mace – resembles a peach, and though it does not have a whit of sugar, it is used to make what is called 'nutmeg jam' in countries as far apart as the Banda Islands, Grenada and even Kerala. Not for any extraordinary gastronomic value, I must add, but rather like a subsidiary industry to make a bit of money on the side. The jam does have a faint echo of mace in it but unlike the immediate appeal of, say, strawberry jam, nutmeg-fruit jam, if it can be called that, is much more subtle and can only be appreciated by someone who is familiar with the context of the two spices and the fruit that binds them together in a tight embrace.

Out of all the aromatics, nutmeg is the one that has to be treated with the most care. Add too much pepper or too much cinnamon in a dish, and all that will happen is that the flavour of that spice will predominate, perhaps a tad unpleasantly. Use too much nutmeg, however, and the dish will become inedible, even hallucinogenic, depending on the volatile oil content. Take Kaveri G. Ahuja, for example, a passionate foodie from Coorg, who went on a driving holiday in Kerala and, tempted by the peach-like fruit that encloses both nutmeg and mace, took a large bite. It didn't taste good at all, but she kept chewing on the pulpy fruit, hoping to get a whiff of either nutmeg or mace. Soon, she began to feel drowsy, and dropped off into a deep slumber that lasted several hours. That's not unusual, because the volatile oil in both nutmeg and mace contains myristicin and elemicin, hallucinogenic and narcotic substances.

But it certainly has its uses. In Chef Sheikh Arif Ahmed's extended family, every woman who goes into labour is given a betel leaf smeared with ghee and two generous pieces of nutmeg. The leaf is for digestion, the ghee helps it slide down the digestive tract quickly and the nutmeg heats up the body, so that the baby usually pops out in record time. Or so they believe. Arif, hailing from a prominent catering family in Hyderabad, says he has noticed that those family members who refuse this fiendishly tasteless concoction usually have to undergo caesarean sections!

This is not the first time I've heard the connection being made between nutmeg and body heat. In Zanzibar, one of the countries that produces nutmeg and mace, a whole nutmeg is often grated over porridge and consumed as an aphrodisiac or for its hallucinogenic properties. Closer home, Aligarh Muslim University did a series of studies to establish the aphrodisiac qualities of nutmeg – using rats in a series of controlled settings – which they then proved beyond doubt. Besides being an aphrodisiac, nutmeg is also hallucinogenic. The great food scientist K.T. Achaya, in his *A Historical Dictionary of Indian Food*, notes that the Chinese monk and traveller, Xuanzang was provided with 20 nutmegs daily during his stay at the Nalanda monastery in the 7th century. You can almost see Achaya pursing his lips!

Hyderabadi cuisine uses nutmeg and mace in a dessert called badamkand, made of almonds and flavoured with nutmeg, mace, green cardamom and saffron. In Lucknow, as a general rule, mace is used in combination with green cardamom, where the latter is used in double the quantity as compared to the former. Most of us would never use aromatic spices in a dal, but there is a Lucknowi arhar dal that contains nutmeg and mace along with green cardamom, curd and raisins. They are also used as a principal flavour in Salmani kebab, a minced lamb kebab with a hint of crushed sesame seeds. Any korma from Lucknow also has top-notes of nutmeg and fennel.

The doyen of all Lucknow chefs, Imtiaz Qureshi, says that it is tricky for a novice cook to get the perfect balance between nutmeg and mace, and the safest way to do so is in combination with cloves, cardamom and bay-leaves. His rule of thumb for using nutmeg and mace together is to use six times more nutmeg than mace. And coincidentally, nature bears him out perfectly: a whole nutmeg is exactly six times the weight of one 'blade' of mace. (Just why it is called a blade is a mystery I'll never solve. To me it looks more like a flower, but recipe books, especially those written in the 1960s and earlier, never fail to refer to mace in terms of blades!)

One of the most unusual uses of mace I've come across is the vegetarian 'settu' soup of the Chettinad community, which has become the somewhat unlikely star of many of the communities' weddings. It is on the repertoire of every caterer; in fact, 'settu' is the Tamil pronunciation of 'set' and refers to the whole set of dishes that a caterer does. Though it is a simple, clear tomato or cauliflower soup amidst a panoply of grand meat dishes, its light but distinctive spicing of fennel, turmeric, mace, clove, cinnamon, star anise and pepper has made it greatly sought after at weddings and other gatherings.

However, the most intensive use of this spice seems to be in the East and West Godavari districts of coastal Andhra Pradesh, a rich alluvial belt. There, every biryani and mutton or chicken korma, made by the enthusiastically meat-eating Naidu community, has a strong flavour of nutmeg, mace, cinnamon and cloves. Chef Sambandan calls it the signature flavour of the region. Travel to Telangana and the nutmeg and mace are replaced by cardamom; go further south to Rayalseema and seed spices with incendiary amounts of chillies dominate the flavours. So, coastal Andhra Pradesh ranks as the country's top user of nutmeg and mace for a reason that nobody has quite been able to explain.

Worldwide, the trade makes a difference between the nutmeg and mace that comes from the Banda Islands (called East Indian in the spice trade) and those that come from Grenada (called West Indian). The former tend to be exported to India and Europe and the latter to the United States. Though nutmegs are graded into specific sizes (8 grams per nutmeg, 6 grams, and so on) the largest sizes are normally sold jumbled up together and are collectively called ABCD in the international trade. The less attractive but still excellent quality bears the less than felicitous name of 'shrivels' and merely indicates the outer appearance: the oil content is the same as the ABCD grade. Lower than this is the BWP grade which is fit for oil distillation, but not used in food.

Nutmeg from the West Indies (principally from Grenada) is lighter in colour than its Indonesian counterpart and has a lower volatile oil content. It is usually exported to the United States in a single grade called SUNS or sound unassorted nutmegs.

There are also a couple of 'fake' nutmegs that have neither the aroma nor the oil content. One grows wild in South India and is called Bombay nutmeg in the trade; the other grows in Papua New Guinea. Neither contain the precious volatile oil and are used to bulk up the weight in large orders by unscrupulous dealers.

Given how vast the Indian market is for spices, the nutmeg and mace section seems unnaturally modest: Only about a dozen or so large traders between Mumbai and Delhi, whereas the far more pricey saffron has double that number of significant dealers. Most of our nutmeg and mace come from Indonesia, but it is known as Singaporean in the trade, and in Kerala and Colombo as well. Historically, whole nutmegs have been the norm in the Indian market, but as convenience foods and short cuts are gaining ground in domestic kitchens, powdered Kerala and Sri Lankan nutmeg is now preferred. They are easier to grind than the far harder Indonesian nutmeg.

Nutmeg and mace both have a warm, soft, sweet, faintly cloying smell that reminds me, personally, of a children's nursery. Internationally, both are used in milk-based puddings as well as in sauces that use milk. In this regard, the use of these two spices, whose flavour profiles are not unlike one another, resemble saffron, which is also used internationally in milk-based desserts and sauces. The only difference is that while nutmeg is also often grated on to cauliflower in the western world, saffron is almost never used to flavour vegetables. Other international uses for nutmeg and mace are in sausages and other processed meat products like luncheon meat, salami and meat pies, especially pork pies. In India and internationally, nutmeg and mace are also used in cakes and cookies, in golden latte (known to Indians as haldi doodh) and in eggnog. Specifically, in India and Pakistan, it is also a part of spice mixes that are used for biryani, kormas and even rogan josh.

Not surprisingly, both nutmeg and mace have identical components, albeit in different proportions: the myristicin, responsible for hallucinations in nutmeg, is present in minimal quantities in mace.

One of my more interesting brushes with nutmeg was in Istanbul, Turkey. I was happy to let my guide, Gulgun, do the ordering when we visited the restaurants. So when a rice pudding at a nameless eatery near the Grand Bazaar made its appearance on the table, I took little notice. Created from pounded rice cooked with milk and left to sit under a gentle heat till a pale golden crust formed on top, it seemed, at first glance, to be the same as the versions I had enjoyed a few times previously at other eat-and-run outlets in the area during the same trip. But as soon as I took a bite, the subtle flavour of nutmeg hit me and I was hooked. My short holiday in Istanbul became a race-to-the-finish search to eat as many bowls of rice pudding as I could to see if any other restaurant bettered the version I had already had. Sadly, none contained any nutmeg at all. One lesson I did learn, though, was that for nutmeg to shine through, the rest of the the ingredients in the dish have to be as simple as they possibly can.

Nutmeg is such an intrinsic part of my spice rack, that I got a shock when my parents-in-law visited me in Delhi for the first time. They wanted to know what the 'round marbles' were in my spice box. They loved the smell and the flavour, but would they use it themselves? No thanks. It was too foreign for them.

Nutmeg and mace are the wild cards of the spice world. They always grow together but have very different appearances yet very similar compounds. I always think of them like fraternal twins who have stayed in a tight embrace in the womb, are born together but who then live apart. Some use them in sausages, others in rice puddings and still others in spice blends to sprinkle over deeply savoury kormas with several layers of flavours. Some use only the nutmeg; others just the mace. And whatever they use, the twin spices blend right in and enrich their surroundings immeasurably.

ATUL SIKAND'S PANEER MAKHNI

Although there are several spices in this recipe, the dominant flavour is that of mace alone: All the others miraculously recede into the background. The main part of this dish is the gravy. The recipe is written following the steps of preparation and the ingredients are given separately for each step.

MAIN INGREDIENT

- 500 g paneer, cubed to desired size

Step 1

INGREDIENTS

- 800 g tomatoes
- 2 mace flowers
- 5 green cardamoms
- 1 cup water

METHOD

- Coarsely chop the tomatoes and place with water, mace and cardamom (barely broken open) in a large saucepan.
- Bring to a boil, then leave on low heat, covered, for about 15 minutes.
- When cool, carefully remove the tomatoes on to a plate with a slotted spoon.
- Peel and discard the shrivelled skins, removing as many as you can.
- Heat up the liquid used to boil the tomatoes. Bring to a boil with mace for another 10 minutes then discard the mace and cardamoms, retaining the water. Puree the tomatoes with the water.

Step 2

INGREDIENTS

- 1 tbsp ginger paste
- 1 tbsp garlic paste
- 1 medium sized onion, finely chopped
- 1-inch cinnamon stick
- ½ tsp carom seeds
- 100 g ghee/butter

METHOD

- Heat the ghee or butter, add the cinnamon and fry till it turns brown. Then add the carom seeds.
- Add the onions and fry till they are translucent. Then add in the tomato puree prepared in Step 1. Cook covered on a very low flame till the gravy reduces to half: This will take about 30 minutes. You should be left with a semi-thick gravy.

Step 3

INGREDIENTS

- ½ tsp cumin powder
- 1 tsp coriander powder
- 1 tsp Kashmiri chillies
- 1 tbsp sugar
- ¼ tsp garam masala
- 1 tsp fenugreek powder
- Salt, to taste
- Lemon juice, to taste
- Coriander leaves, for garnish
- Green chillies, slit, to taste

METHOD

- Add the above ingredients to the gravy prepared in step 2.
- Cook for 1–2 minutes to blend all flavours. Then take the cubed paneer and fry in the gravy for 2–3 minutes.
- When well coated, stir in the cream, adjust flavours; you can add a bit of lemon juice.
- Garnish with green coriander and slit green chillies.

Note: When you add the cream, stir constantly and on low heat as the cream shouldn't boil, just heat up slightly.

JENNY LINFORD'S BAKED RICE PUDDING

A few simple ingredients combine here to make a satisfying pudding, very much a comfort food. The little touch of grated nutmeg is essential to the dish, a tribute to the power of spices.

INGREDIENTS

- 600 ml full-fat milk
- A pinch of salt
- 1 tbsp sugar
- 3 tbsp short-grained rice
- Nutmeg, freshly grated

METHOD

- Preheat the oven to 150°C. Butter an ovenproof dish.
- Heat the milk to simmering point in a small pan. Remove from direct heat and stir in the salt, sugar and rice.
- Transfer the mixture to the buttered ovenproof dish and grate nutmeg over the top.
- Bake in the oven for 2–3 hours until the rice has softened and expanded and the milk has been largely absorbed.
- Serve warm from the oven.

CHEF RAVITEJ NATH'S NIZAMI JOUZI HALWA

Jouzi (the urdu word for nutmeg) halwa was one of the favourite desserts of the Nizam of Hyderabad. In fact, he liked it so much that the maker of this halwa was instructed to name his shop after the Nizam's son, Hamid. Till today, the halwa is available only at Hameedi Confectioners in Hyderabad. The use of nutmeg balances the richness and sweetness of this halwa.

Chef Nath hails from Hyderabad, where he has been sampling jouzi halwa since his early childhood. To him, nutmeg is synonymous with this rich yet superb dessert that is fit for a king.

This recipe will make approximately 3 kilograms. Serves 30.

INGREDIENTS

- 5 l full-cream milk
- 500 g ghee
- 1 kg sugar
- 1 kg grated khoya
- 500 g whole wheat
- 4 tbsp mamra almond flakes
- 4 tbsp Afghani pistachio slivers
- 1 tsp nutmeg, freshly grated
- 6 silver varq leaves

METHOD

- Sprout the whole wheat for 72 hours and then grind to a paste.
- In a heavy-bottomed kadhai, bring the paste and milk to a boil and let it simmer for 2–3 minutes.
- Reduce to a low heat and cook, stirring continuously, for around 25–30 minutes until it turns thick.
- When thick, add khoya, and stir well, scraping the bottom continuously to prevent it from burning.
- Add all the ghee and mix till incorporated.
- Next add the sugar and cook for another 15 minutes, until the halwa leaves the sides of the pan.
- Add the freshly grated nutmeg powder, stir in half the almonds and pistachios.
- Remove to a container and garnish with varq, pistachios and almonds. Serve hot or warm.

Pepper

One of the oldest occurrences of black pepper is in a rather unexpected place: Up the nostrils of the mummy of King Ramesses II of Egypt, who died in 1213 BCE. It does not tell us about the trade between the Malabar Coast of Kerala, where pepper (*Piper nigrum*) has grown since the beginning of time, and the rest of the world; nor how exactly it was discovered to be a spice that could be used to flavour food. It does, however, tell us a great deal about how advanced civilization was over 3,000 years ago and that trade was conducted between Egypt and India, possibly by sea as boat-building was already known to the ancient Egyptians. It also shows that the preservative quality of pepper was already known at that time!

Black pepper is the single most widely used spice in the world, making its presence felt in all parts of the globe. And I wouldn't be overstating if I said that pepper is, perhaps, the single spice that has changed world history. More than the any of the other aromatics, it was the search for black pepper that provoked the great explorers – Vasco da Gama, Magellan, Christopher Columbus and Drake – to set off on their voyages. All this was due to the preservative nature of the spice, more than any flavour profile that it had. Today, looking at the pepper mill commonly found on every table at a high-end restaurant, it is difficult to believe that these tiny round devils were the cause of wars and intrigue, and were once so expensive and luxurious a product that they were considered equivalent to cash!

Pepper has always grown on the west coast of India, and you can still find parts of the tropical rainforest in both Kerala and Karnataka that have the original strains of wild pepper clinging tenaciously to host trees. Thousands of years ago, that is what the forests of north and central Kerala must have looked like, with pepper vines clambering up the trunks of the nearest trees, waiting to be discovered by man. Today, when you look at the 'spice gardens' in Kerala and the coffee plantations in Coorg, with pepper clinging to corral trees, you cannot help but notice the symbiosis between man and nature.

Pepper has been intrinsic to Indian food for millennia, which is unsurprising, since along with turmeric, ginger and cardamom, pepper is a spice native to the country. However, the arrival of chillies on our shores a mere 500 years ago have made us forsake the lingering depth of pepper for the far hotter bite of chillies. The reason is that chillies can be grown around the country, whereas there is only a relatively small area of suitable land that is available in Kerala, Tamil Nadu and Karnataka where pepper flourishes.

On the secluded island of Kumarakom, in the backwaters of the Vembanand lake, in the Kottayam district of Kerala, is Philip Kutty's farm. The widowed mother-in-law daughter-in-law duo that run the homestay that their respective husbands started are renowned for their cooking. Their style of cuisine is Syrian Christian – just one among Kerala's confusing welter of Christian denominations, albeit the one best-known for their style of cooking. I had been staying with them for a few days, and one afternoon, over lunch, the mother-in-law was telling me about the spice blend that they used as a dip for idlis, chammanthi podi, as it is called in Kerala. They couldn't find the blend, so I went with them into their cavernous kitchen, with black basalt counters and polished red floors, to look for it. There were rows and rows of spices on their racks, so I started by taking them down, one by one, opening them, sniffing the contents and returning them to the racks. A few jars later, I thought I had found what I was looking for. The colour was dark and speckled, and the fragrance was poetic: It transported me to the spice gardens that are the highlight of all my trips to Kerala. 'Is this it?' I asked triumphantly. Mother and daughter looked at me with narrowed eyes. 'That's black pepper,' they said, incredulous that someone who called herself a food writer could not identify this most elemental of all spices, one reputed to be the most widely used spice in the entire world.

I could scarcely believe my eyes either. The spice in that plastic jar was absolutely nothing like the pepper that pretentious South Delhi restaurants crush on your plate of carpaccio with a pepper mill the size of a bludgeon. On my way back to Delhi, I stopped at Kochi and bought a modest amount of black pepper (the variety that I bought is called Malabar Garbled Extra Bold, one of the most premium peppers produced in the world) and I now know the true taste and fragrance of black pepper. But I don't think the Kuttys will ever let me within a mile of their island again.

There are several types of peppers, but the International trade, however, centres around black pepper (*Piper nigrum*), although white and green pepper are offshoots of the same plant, in different stages of ripeness and processing. A cluster of peppercorns on the vine turns red at first. When it turns green, it is plucked. If the peppercorns are then dropped into brine, the enzyme that turns the outside surface (called the pericarp) black is halted, and the peppercorns remain green. If they are allowed to dry, they turn black and the pericarp wrinkles, giving black pepper its characteristic crinkled look. If the pericarp is sloughed off, the inside is shown to be smooth and white – this is white pepper. Sloughing can be done by a dry or wet process, depending on the country of origin. While South-East Asia has developed a long-drawn out soaking process, India has a dry process for the sloughing off of the pericarp. Because the pericarp, that contains sugar and part of the volatile aroma compounds of pepper, is sloughed off, white pepper has a slightly different flavour than black pepper, and is primarily in demand because its use doesn't interfere with the appearance of a finished dish.

Though the coast of Malabar has historically been where the lion's share of the world's black pepper has come from, in a rather cruel twist of fate, today it is Vietnam that exports the largest amount of pepper, and India has been reduced to number four. Vietnam's skill in removing the pericarp of black pepper has made it the number one exporter of pepper in the world. However, the common consensus is that the pepper indigenous to the coast of Malabar has the best flavour. This is because these hills are lashed by monsoon winds at precisely the time of the development of the flower into the spice. The pollination of pepper is done by gentle rain in April–May. No rain at all or rains that are too heavy can be a disaster for the crop.

The pepper plant is a climber as opposed to a creeper. It is often planted around corral trees whose thorns allow the pepper vines to grow upwards with a good grip. Travel out of Kochi into almost any upland region of the state, and you'll catch sight of trees wrapped with vines of the pepper plant. Once upon a time, the sight was common only in the heavily forested regions around the coast of north Kerala and later in Thekkady and Wayanad, but with the constant climb of international pepper prices, even farmers whose land is not quite as high in altitude manage to coax pepper vines around host trees. Black pepper drying in the sun is one of the distinctive sights of Kerala's countryside. Even in Kochi, around the tiny lanes of the Jewish quarters, you can see able-bodied men raking tons of pepper set out to dry on coconut leaf mats. This is done to ensure that each berry dries to a moisture content of 12 per cent. More than that and there's a chance that mildew will set in.

It quite often does, especially in cases where farmers have intentionally kept the moisture content slightly higher than 12 per cent to make a quick buck: effectively, what they are doing is increasing the weight of the spice.Once this happens, some crooked practices are often set in motion for the spice's recovery. The most common of these consists of hurriedly drying the berries on high heat and then spraying them with oil – any oil – to give them a glossy appearance, effectively conning customers into buying pepper that is not of very good quality. I have bought many an attractive packet of glossy black peppercorns. However, whenever I've tried to grind them in the limestone mortar and pestle I use for my spices, they had no taste whatsoever, which has now made me wary about suspiciously shiny peppercorns. As a general rule, there is no substitute for tasting a tiny pinch of a spice before buying it. It goes without saying that a freshly harvested spice that has been stored carefully can make all the difference to a cooked dish, just as a spice that is long past its sell-by date would not add value to a preparation, even if added in great quantities. This is especially so for pepper, which can either prickle your palate with its pungency or have the appeal of sawdust.

The other state that is associated with pepper is Karnataka. The uplands of Coorg have many hundreds of privately-owned estates that are planted with pepper and coffee. Coffee needs a shade tree. The shade provided by tall trees that vary from rosewood to teak to silver-oak. It is on these that pepper vines are then trained, so that pepper, in a manner of speaking, becomes subsidiary to the all-important coffee, unlike in Kerala, where pepper is king, with the corral tree being completely incidental, though the soft wood of the corral tree is good for making matchsticks.

Many of these old estates in Coorg have now been turned into homestays, which provide a quiet and secluded stay away from the bustle of everyday life. I found out how secluded they really are on my three-day visit to Varuna Plantations, not far from Virajpet, the main town in the region. For the three days of my stay, I met nobody but my hosts, Sagar and Kavita Muthappa. I did not even speak to anybody but them, not even on my cellphone, because given the topography of the region, I would have had to trek for a kilometre or two to get a signal. There were no neighbours visible, no blare of a television set or voices of children playing, no tradesmen calling out their wares, no vegetable vendors, no postman, no courier delivery boy, no rumble of a local bus: nothing at all. As much as I love silence, it was ever so slightly unnerving. In the evenings, we would sit in the garden and talk desultorily till the silence would suddenly be broken by a dog barking in the distance. My hosts pointed out that as sound travels easily across the hills, the dog was likely to be at least five kilometres away.

The Muthappa's estate primarily grew coffee, with shade trees that included jack and silver oak. It was up these that the graceful pepper climbers were trained, with their artistic, heart-shaped leaves trembling in the breeze and curved drupes of glossy peppercorns clinging tightly to the central stem. The small but furiously efficient team of plantation workers on the estate appeared to know each individual coffee bush (and there were thousands!). They knew under which bush a patch of wild mushrooms might sprout in another week. In Coorg, varieties of wild mushroom and bamboo shoots grow near the coffee bushes during the rainy season, but you can only find them if you know where to look. During the torrential three-month monsoon, the estates are even more secluded than they are during the rest of the year. Hence, stocking the larder becomes a necessity, and the home-made wines and pickles that are sold in the shops all over the area point to the industriousness of these estate owners.

The largest plantations in Kerala and in Coorg have some similarities. In both states, there is a lifestyle that revolves around the estate and its crops. The planter may be at the top of the chain, but he and his family are dependent on the staff, who, in most cases have lived on the estate for generations. When you compare the growing conditions in south Karnataka and in Kerala, though the plantations in Kerala are marginally closer to the sea than Coorg plantations, both states have similar soil and climate conditions: red laterite, and approximately equal humidity. However, the piperine content in Kerala pepper – the alkaloid responsible for its pungency – is marginally higher: 6 per cent compared to the 5 per cent in the Coorg crop.

I once tasted a recreation of a meal from the 6th-century Tamil treatise *Pakadarpana*. The late Chef Jacob Sahaya Kumar Aruni, who used it as inspiration, made it clear that the text was a sort of home-science treatise and not a recipe book, but if you read into it, you could extrapolate which spices and ingredients to use for a particular preparation. Of course, the meal was just an approximation based on a manuscript written in Tamil, but the broad details had been meticulously adhered to. The only spices used, for example, were the ones that were known at that time, which meant it had been spiced entirely with long pepper as, at the time the treatise was written, black pepper was something of a novelty. (Long pepper, *Piper longum*, which looks like a tiny pine cone with seed-like projections, was common in India as well as Greece and Rome till black pepper ousted it from its position of prominence around 12th century CE. Today, it is used, if at all, in Ayurvedic medicine.) In our meal, it was used in conjunction with ginger, and the bite was pungent, because *Piper longum* has a hotter bite than *Piper nigrum*, but nothing like the blast of hotness from chillies that we now have come to expect in an Indian meal, since, of course, there were no chillies in 6th-century India. Even though in that particular meal, the use of pepper was controlled, it made me wonder whether the predilection Indians have for spicy food has something to do with the fact that pepper is indigenous to our country. And while in most other parts of the world, pepper is primarily used as a seasoning, rather than a spice, in India we use it in a wide range of dishes: from rasams and curries to panjiri to sweetened milk-based drinks like thandai. In North India, black pepper is one of the ingredients in garam masala, but it is by no means used in every version. Chef Manjit Gill of ITC Hotels jokes that the most visible signs of the use of pepper up north is in matthis, the deep-fried, flaky flour savouries that are a feature in both Punjab and UP. For a matthi to be 'authentic', it has to have a whole peppercorn pressed into its centre.

Of course, there are other quintessentially Punjabi dishes that black pepper goes into. All types of wadis – dried, pounded and spiced urad dal dumplings, usually cooked with one or two vegetables – have to have black pepper in addition to cumin, coriander powder and chilli powder. In fact, the city of Amritsar uses far more black pepper in its cooking than many neighbouring states. Chana masala, tawa-fried meat, even raita, all use ground pepper for its hot bite and colour, since pale fish, mutton, chicken and lentils are not looked upon with much favour in Amritsar.

Most restaurants in North India also have a special dish called chicken kali mirch that is something of a trick up their sleeve. The heat of black pepper goes well with the mild blandness of chicken and the best conveyor of the heat is the creaminess of a dairy product. So a curd-based gravy with just a few spices is mixed with a strong dose of crushed pepper powder before being taken off the fire. It all works well against the canvas of two mildly flavoured ingredients, yogurt and chicken, amidst which is a hit of black pepper.

The state with the highest usage of black pepper is, predictably, Kerala. There, it goes into every last stir-fry of vegetables, shrimp and red meat. Even curries are not exempt from a few peppercorns added to spices while they are frying. It is what sets Kerala's cuisine apart from its neighbours, though as a general rule, all rasam/saaru, by definition, have a powerful punch of freshly pounded peppercorns.

Ayurveda also plays a part in accounting for much of the usage of black pepper. According to Ayurvedic tradition, pepper helps temper *pitta* – which governs heat and metabolic functions of the body.

When peppercorns are moistened with a little water and ground on a grinding stone, they are said to lose their heating properties and become cooling to the system (which is why thandai, drunk in summer, always contains ground pepper along with rose petals, almonds, poppy seeds and fennel). There is also a prevalent belief that when uncooked mutton is marinaded with a very strong dose of ground black pepper for a few hours and then washed off with boiling hot water, it rids the meat of its cholesterol-causing properties. Many patients who have been warned not to consume red meat by their cardiologist, resort to this practice when overcome by cravings.

It is believed that there are more than 63 varieties of pepper, not all of them edible or even closely related to what we know as pepper. Like with so many other spices, in the case of pepper too, etymology leads to confusion. Take Sichuan pepper, for instance, which is not really a pepper at all but the fruit of a bush called the prickly ash. And thereby hangs a tale. The English named the bush thus for the thorns that the branches undoubtedly have, but the word 'ash' probably comes from the leaves of the tree that *resemble* those of the ash (*Fraxinus excelsior*), without being related to it in the least.

Sichuan pepper comes from plants in the genus Zanthoxylum, which includes so many species, from so many various continents, that it is a botanist's nightmare to separate all of them. It is neither a chilli pepper nor a black pepper. And besides the common Sichuan pepper, there are many other variants: a Japanese version whose leaves are crushed to make sansho pepper, a Korean version, one version from Nepal, another from Uttaranchal and one from the west coast of India, which includes Goa, north Karnataka and parts of Maharashtra. Here, in the western part of the country it is known variously as triphal, teflem, jumman kai and teppal. Like all its cousins across the globe, *Zanthoxylum rhetsa* (the Indian coastal variant) grows from a thorny tree.

One can spot the teppals in any market in Goa, sold in bunches tied with twine and, depending on which month you visit the market, they will be either dark green and not quite open, or brownish-black and open, with the central shiny seed removed. (The seed has to be discarded in all species of Zanthoxylum, for it has a bitter taste and a gritty texture.) All the essential oils are carried in the pericarp or leathery outer skin. It does bear a cursory resemblance to Sichuan pepper, but the skin of teppal is far from being papery and brittle. Bite into one, and in a few minutes, you will feel your mouth becoming strangely numb: the reason why it is referred to as 'mouth-numbing pepper'. However, to achieve the strange but not unpleasant mouth-numbing sensation, one has to follow a few rules: You do not grind teppal; when the your dish is almost done, you add three or four berries whole, but without the seed, and let it cook; by allowing the cooked dish to stand for fifteen minutes, the character of the teppal infuses through the preparation.

Its astringency cuts out the fattiness of certain fish like mackerel. Potatoes, beans and lady's finger – all the vegetables that, according to Ayurveda, have a heavy effect on the digestion – benefit by being cooked with tirphal, and the iconic Goan shark curry, ambotik, always contains triphal.

People from the Konkan region settled all over the world discover, to their horror, that they are unable to replicate the tastes of home without it. That's when a quick search on Google yields the similarity between Sichuan pepper and teppal, and a fortuitous compromise is reached.

It might be appropriate to mention here another instance of a pepper that is not pepper at all. What is commonly touted as 'pink pepper' in that assorted mix of peppers you see in the posh glass pepper grinders at your local café is, more often than not, the fruit of a South American tree called *Schinus terebinthifolius*, and not pepper at all. Be careful not to use them in large quantities though; its sap can cause severe itching in sensitive individuals. Consuming a number of them at one sitting may also cause nausea.

There *is* a way to ripen black pepper on the vine so that its colour is forced to turn crimson – the 'true' pink pepper, if you will – but it is a job for specialists and the cost is high because of the wastage that results. To my knowledge, this process is only undertaken by one single pepper plantation in the entire state of Kerala.

One of the culinary puzzles in the world of spices is that while pepper is endemic to India, there is no use of it in its green form. In Thailand, on the other hand, stir-fries make copious use of drupes of green pepper, glossy and tongue-tingling. In traditional Indian cuisine, the concept of garnish is virtually non-existent, which probably explains why green peppers are rarely found in our cuisine.

And while pepper is used in all parts of the world – it accounts for 20 per cent of all spices traded internationally – it is by no means used equally. In the West, it's treated primarily as table seasoning while in India, we consider it a spice. Even within the country, some cuisines rarely make much use of black pepper. Take our traditional Kashmiri family for instance. We take the prize for the most frugal use of black pepper: About six peppercorns a week, for 10 people. In our extended family, our only use of black pepper is for lamb koftas which appear on the menu once a week. It is pounded in our mortar and pestle along with black cardamom, shallots and fennel over which the minced meat is added and whole lot is hammered till the mince becomes silky and the spices are amalgamated into its very fibre. And why don't we use black pepper for other preparations involving lamb? Because it is tradition – the one thing you don't question or argue with!

ATUL SIKAND'S BLACK PEPPER LAMB

Atul Sikand literally lives for food. On his farm are cows and vegetables. On his Facebook group are over 20,000 souls who post recipes with rapid-fire speed, and Sikand tests each and every one of them before uploading them to *Sikandalous Cuisine*. This recipe is his own creation.

INGREDIENTS

- 500 g mutton
- 2 tbsp thick curd
- 1 tsp (heaped) garlic paste
- 1½ tsp black pepper, coarsely crushed
- 1 tsp whole black peppercorns
- 2 tbsp coconut, grated
- Salt, to taste
- 15–20 curry leaves
- 3 tbsp ghee

METHOD

- Sauté the coconut till aromatic and lightly coloured and then make into a paste.
- Marinate mutton in curd with garlic paste, salt, crushed pepper and half of the curry leaves. Cling-wrap and leave in the fridge for 12–24 hours.
- Bring mutton back to room temperature. Place the mutton and juices in a pressure cooker and cook for 3 whistles. Allow to cool down.
- In a kadhai, heat ghee, splutter peppercorn and then add

the remaining curry leaves. Now scoop out the mutton without the stock and sauté the meat, slowly adding the stock from the pressure cooker.
- Cook covered for 5 minutes then add the coconut paste and cook another 5 minutes or so till done. Adjust salt.

BUTTER PEPPER GARLIC CHICKEN

This is my family recipe for when my two children wanted to eat something tasty and uncomplicated that would be ready at lightning speed: The quest of most mothers all over the world!

INGREDIENTS

- 8 chicken joints
- 3½ tbsp butter
- 4 tbsp garlic, finely minced
- 1 tsp salt
- 2 tsp black pepper, coarsely pounded
- 1 tsp lemon juice
- 2 tbsp fresh coriander leaves
- 4–5 black peppercorns, to garnish

METHOD

- Wash the chicken.
- Bring a pot of water to the boil and give the chicken a quick turn in the water till it changes colour. Discard the water. The chicken will now fry evenly.
- Heat butter on medium flame and add the garlic. Sauté till golden.
- Add chicken pieces, salt and pounded pepper and fry on high for 5 minutes till the chicken changes color.
- Lower heat and cook the chicken covered for 15–20 minutes or until tender.
- Remove the lid, increase heat and add lemon juice.

- Cook until completely dry. The trick is to cook the chicken till done without causing the garlic to darken too much.
- Pound the whole peppercorns coarsely and sprinkle over the chicken.

CHEF G. SREENIVASAN'S HONEYDEW AND WATERMELON GAZPACHO

INGREDIENTS

For the gazpacho:

- 600 g honeydew melon (cut into chunks)
- 600 g watermelon (cut into chunks)
- 125 g cucumber (peeled and seeded)
- 2 tbsp green onion
- 50 g mint leaves
- 3½ tbsp coriander leaves
- 3 tbsp honey
- 1 tsp black pepper
- 1 tbsp rock salt
- 2 tbsp lemon juice

For the garnish:

- 4 tbsp feta cheese
- 1½ tbsp pumpkin seeds, roasted
- 8–10 mint leaves

METHOD

- Puree all ingredients in a blender, keeping aside 100 grams of both melons for garnish.
- Place the melon chunks in the serving bowl, pour in the puree over it.
- Serve garnished with pumpkin seeds, crumbled feta cheese and mint leaves.

Cardamom

At a Lebanese restaurant in Delhi, two friends were undecided on which dessert to order. 'All your desserts reek of rosewater,' they complained to the chef from Beirut. This proved to be an insult to his Lebanese pride, so the chef shot back, 'Like all Indian mithai is flavoured with elaichi.'

The Lebanese chef did have a point. Perhaps we Indians don't realize how ubiquitous the use of cardamom is in our daily cuisine: From the countrywide favourite masala chai to pedas topped with a pinch of coarsely pounded black cardamom seeds, or the single spice note of green cardamom in most of Kerala's sweets.

This isn't surprising since green cardamom is endemic to Kerala's uplands, and there is a school of thought that says it grew wild at one time. That was almost certainly the case for at least a millennium and during that time Arab traders landed on the Malabar Coast to trade in spices and made a temporary home in north Kerala, often marrying local women and setting up home.

For the better part of the last century, the cultivation of cardamom as a crop has taken place in the central Kerala district, generally in the hands of the Syrian Christian community. Why this is so is the subject of much conjecture, and there are several theories about it. One theory that I was told by almost every plantation owner I met is that when the British were constructing the Mullaperiyar dam in the 1800s, they needed plentiful labour. There was only one problem: The area was virtually devoid of any human habitation. They invited people from the neighbouring district of Pathanamthitta, which had an overwhelmingly large Christian population, perhaps with the promise of being granted tracts of land to settle in. And thus began the reign of the Syrian Christians as the growers of spice. Today they account for approximately 80 per cent of all growers. Only growers, mind. There are remarkably few members of the community who trade in the spice.

Rival theories, however, scoff at the idea of growers coming in as late as the 1800s. They claim that as early as the 13th and 14th centuries, Syrian Christians were appointed as port revenue officers by local rulers and given land to settle down in the spice-growing regions. But in the absence of reliable written records, it is impossible to trace this history conclusively.

Green cardamom flourishes in Kerala because the rain-lashed hillsides have provided the ideal growing conditions for millennia. Black cardamom, however, grows nowhere near Kerala, but there are some commonalities in their growth patterns. Both require hillsides rather than flat land, both grow on similar-sized shrubs, and require the protection of shade trees. Though the shrub is approximately as tall as a man, the spices grow from rhizomes near the root, which means painstaking squatting for hours on end, up and down hillsides, during harvest time. There are more commonalities. Both are air-dried in wood-fired ovens in the plantations themselves using the wood of the shade-giving trees. A poet might point out that having shaded the spice throughout its life, the shade tree then gives up its life to make its protégé a marketable commodity.

When the green cardamom plants are mature enough to bear fruit, they send out foot-long shoots that remain on the ground. The cardamom pods grow on alternate sides of the shoot and mature once every six weeks, throughout the year. That makes it seven times a year. There are more interesting details about the plant. The flower gives a hint of the pattern in which the cardamom pods emerge – alternately, on either side of the shoot. Hold a tiny white flower close enough and you will notice the maroon design on the inside of each petal – a shoot-like line, with striations appearing alternately, exactly the way the pods do on the shoot. It is just one of nature's little tricks or enigmas and what makes the world of spice such an endlessly fascinating subject.

Similar to pepper, green cardamom grows in two contiguous states: Karnataka and Kerala. While Kerala has spice plantations where coffee and tea are also grown; upland Karnataka, mainly Coorg, has primarily coffee plantations and cardamom and pepper are cultivated alongside. Similar to the tea industry, which needs precise geographical and climatic conditions, as well as plentiful, cheap, highly-skilled labour, cardamom also needs labourers that have a high degree of expertise and efficiency. Fortunately for the Idukki district of Kerala – where cardamom and pepper grow, almost to the exclusion of any other crop, on rows of densely-forested hills – there is an endless supply of female workers from neighbouring Tamil Nadu, more precisely, from the Theni district, just seven kilometres away. At harvest time, busloads of women thread their way to the border post between the two states and clamber aboard plantation jeeps that will take them to work.

It is not comfortable working in a cardamom plantation. You have to assume a squatting position for eight hours a day, inching up or down a hillside on your haunches.

Plucking cardamom is tricky too. You have to wait for the pods to turn from pale pink to yellow, and then commence picking. The only catch, however, is that not all the pods on a single stem ripen at the same time, so you cannot jerk the delicate stem for fear of spoiling the unripe ones.

The good ladies of Theni are able to work with speed, each collecting an average of 15 kilograms of pods a day. It seems to be a hereditary skill, because many, if not most, are third-generation cardamom pluckers, each working for the same plantation as their mothers and grandmothers did.

Travel around the Idukki district of Kerala and you'll never be far from a cardamom plant. They're ubiquitous, so the sight of their long, spiky leaves rising to man-height soon becomes a familiar one. If you visit the many spice plantations in the area – this is spice country, so there is little else besides plantations, many of them on the main road, and some even offering home-stays – you can see cardamom plants at close quarters.

That is exactly what I have in mind when I head to Green Park Ayurvedic and Spice Plantation. Hidden away near the village of Attapallam, this plantation offers a show garden where visitors are taken around by informed and highly educated staff members. My own guide – Noushad P.S. – has a college degree in biochemistry and makes the two-hour-long walk through spice fields an engrossing experience. He and owner Benny Joseph Muttathukunnel are the embodiment of that old cliché: be passionate about what you do. So, while Noushad sets off to climb a corral tree to try and fetch me a sample of unripe pepper, Joseph crawls on all fours around the cardamom plants to find a shoot that was beginning to bear flowers. 'All the flowers will eventually grow into cardamoms,' he says triumphantly as he comes back bearing a lone blossom with the trademark striations.

Joseph reckons that the Thekkady area must have around a hundred show gardens of varying sizes. Some, like his, are virtually classrooms for both children and adults to be exposed to the mystique of spices while they are still agricultural plants. Others are thinly veiled excuses to buy, buy, buy. However, if you do happen to get the short end of the stick, I would say that it is better to have visited a show garden to get up close and personal with spices on the tree, as it were, than to have stayed away from for fear of incessant requests to purchase armloads of pepper, cardamom and honey.

Despite the spice trade being so lucrative, Joseph tells me that older plantation families are struggling to maintain their ever-dwindling plantations. When settlers first began to come into the area, virgin forest land could be had for little or nothing and large families made sense since everyone needed to pull their weight and build a plantation. But today, long-drawn out inheritance battles among multiple stakeholders across generations has whittled down large parcels of land over and over again. Plus, the allure of office jobs, particularly overseas, has tempted many sons and grandsons of plantation owners to move away from the family business. This isn't surprising to me. I personally know several people who possess valuable land in Kerala's uplands, but who would rather slave away in some corporate job in Dubai or Delhi, while the homestead is trustingly left in the hands of old caretakers and retainers.

Not far from Green Park, in Thekaddy, is Elephant Junction, which represents one of the more unusual facets of a spice plantation. This 86-acre land was bought from the government over 72 years ago by owner Raju K.G.'s grandfather from the government. Since elephant dung makes an excellent fertilizer for cardamom plants, five elephants tramp up and down the path where cardamom grows, sometimes taking tourists for rides, sometimes not. It is clear that Raju loves elephants and it is his evident love for them that has made Elephant Junction the attraction that it has become. You can feed elephants and even have a bath with them (though how clean you will be after the bath is arguable!) During our hour-long ramble up the cardamom section, Raju's voice is husky with emotion when he addresses the elephants. It is clear that they all reciprocate his sentiments, extending their trunks to sniff his palms and generally showing their affection for him.

The whole plantation is far too large to be covered on foot, so we decide to take Raju's jeep. The quiet, self-effacing Raju, with his folded up mundu, looks anything but a reckless driver, but once we climb in, we careen up and down hillsides, up steep, stony slopes at top speed to get to the upper reaches of the plantation where nutmeg, cloves and coffee are cultivated. We finally stop in front of an ancient structure that is now used as a storage barn. Inside, I am taken to the original chamber for cardamom drying. It looks, not unnaturally, like a large oven of the size you might see in a commercial bakery. The stout metal door would look more at place at a bank than in a spice plantation. Cardamoms that have been plucked need to be spread out on a net in a dry spot in the shade at 50°C for the first 12 hours. After that, into the oven they go, where, for the next 12 hours, they are subjected to 100°C heat, or until a crop of say, 200 kilograms is reduced to a mere 40 kilograms. It is why the price of green cardamom is so high.

If you want a good price on your cardamom crop, it has to make the grade. Cardamoms are graded according to size. However, it's not length that is counted but the width. The fattest cardamom pods measure 8 mm around and have the most seeds in them – between 26 to 28; the size after that has 22 to 24, and the smallest, puniest size, around 5 mm or less, contains anything between 18 to 20 seeds. Though there is no difference in taste between the best and the 'worst', the best quality commands a premium because you would have to use proportionately fewer pods than if you choose from the opposite end of the scale. The brighter green the skin and the fatter the outline, the costlier the spice. Cardamoms with open skins don't make the grade: they have been picked too late. Those with white skins have been artificially bleached to be in keeping with the vogue of a bygone era that now, fortunately, has passed.

Nature has endowed both the skin and the seeds of the green cardamom with slightly different flavour profiles. The skin is earthy and fresh with sweet tones while the seeds are distinctly lemony and have a menthol-like coolness about them. That accounts for why their most popular use is as a breath freshener all over India; cardamom seeds coated with silver leaf are as sophisticated an after-dinner mint as any. Cardamom is also used to soothe a sore throat, gum infections, lung infections and even as an anti-depressant. It is also used in tea mixes, most famously in masala chai across the country. And while hardly any Indian would be brave enough to drink coffee scented with cardamom, in the Arab world, few people would think of drinking coffee – called qawah – *without* it.

Although green cardamom is endemic to the Kerala highlands, it is now being cultivated in countries as far apart as Guatemala, Vietnam, Papua New Guinea, Tanzania, Sri Lanka and Thailand. Cardamom was introduced to Guatemala in the 1920s, and in less than a century, it has overtaken India as the world's major producer. A kind friend from London once presented me with a packet of Guatemalan cardamoms, telling me that she used no other kind in her biryani, which was the toast of the town. I was initially wary, but was soon impressed by the rich green colour of the shell and the punch of flavour that a single pod imparted to the rogan josh I cooked. Even accounting for the difference in quality of the spice one can buy in India versus London, there's a lesson to be learnt from Guatemalan cardamom. It reminded me of the tagline of the advertisement for a car rental company: *When you're number two, you try harder. Or else.* Guatemalan cardamom has a history that is much shorter than that of Kerala's crop, but the ease with which the quality has overtaken ours shows that provenance or antiquity alone cannot be a factor in growing spices.

On the other hand, Thai and Java cardamom can hardly be used as a substitute for green cardamom because of the vast difference in flavour. In fact, the first time I bit into Thai cardamom, I was not able to identify it as cardamom at all! The colour of the skin looked yellowish and the cross section of both varieties was round rather than triangular. Thai cardamom, I learnt, is used in the extreme south of the country, to make the paste for massaman curry.

While the uplands around Thekkady specialize in growing green cardamom in plantations that are carefully tended and shaded by cinnamon and nutmeg, or silver oak and jackfruit, with almost no endemic species of trees, black cardamom is perhaps the only spice in the country that is grown in otherwise natural forests. All the shade trees on black cardamom plantations are those that are endemic to Sikkim.

In fact, two more divergent approaches to spice growing could not have been imagined than the cultivation of green and black cardamom. While Kerala's plantations are mostly family owned, and tend to have a hands-on approach to spice cultivation, Sikkimese plantations are mostly owned by aristocrats who delegate the job of plucking and drying cardamom to, primarily Nepali, workers. Additionally, the Sikkimese almost never cook with black cardamom and are seemingly indifferent to its presence on the landscape. On the other hand, central Kerala's cuisine is scarcely identifiable without the presence of green cardamom and black pepper.

Nowhere was this point brought home to me more closely than on my first visit to Gangtok. It is the only place in India where black cardamom is grown, if you don't consider Darjeeling, which accounts for only a minuscule amount – less than one-tenth of Sikkim's crop. Yet, practically no one in Sikkim actually uses it in cooking: Not the Lepchas, not the Bhutias, not the Nepalis and not the Bengalis – the four communities that more or less make up the population. Neither is it available in the markets of Gangtok in any significant quantity.

K.T. Gyaltsen, a bureaucrat in the state government, and one of the indigenous Lepchas who constitute around 20 per cent of the total population, admits that he's never given the puzzle of black cardamom much thought. This is in spite of the fact that it is with cardamom money that most members of his extended family have been educated. Gyaltsen belongs to the aristocratic class of Sikkim, called kazi (they have nothing to do with Muslims who have studied jurisprudence, also called kazis), who have traditionally held large landholdings, and it is the produce of their land that has underwritten the public school and prestigious college education of families like Gyaltsen's.

And what, pray is the produce of these lands? The single most important commodity is, undoubtedly, black cardamom. Gyaltsen drives me to Tashi View Point, a must-see on the itinerary of most tourists. However, we are not going to have our picture taken while wearing furry hats and silk robes as the other tourists are; Gyaltsen merely wants to give me a sense of cardamom country. 'This,' he says with a sweep of his arm, 'is north of Gangtok. Can you see how densely forested the hills are? It is where cardamom grows.' We are standing on the most picturesque spot of real estate in the entire state, and a phalanx of tourists is eagerly immortalizing the scene wearing local garb. 'Now look towards the east. See how the landscape changes. All you can see are terraced rice fields. There's little cardamom there.'

Drive to Gangtok from the nearest airport at Bagdogra and you'll notice how fields give way to sal forests and then gradually to dense, mixed deciduous forests as you approach the border of Sikkim. Tiny as the state is – a mere 115 km in length and 65 km in width – Sikkim is divided into north, south, east and west, and it is only the southern half of the state where black cardamom grows.

In the few days of my stay in Gangtok, Gyaltsen's entire family tries to pitch in to help piece together the black-cardamom puzzle. This involves visiting a bunch of relatives, all unfailingly charming and gracious hosts, who keep impeccable tables. I enjoy steamed bamboo shoot with fresh yak cheese and flavourful, homely nettle soup, but there's not much in the way of enlightenment about black cardamom.

I do learn, however, that black cardamom is not planted as extensively as, say, green cardamom is in Kerala. It is just one of the many plants that form the undergrowth in the forest. Earlier the Lepchas gathered it from the forests to sell. Over time, they started cultivation to adapt to optimum elevation, water availability and frost conditions. The plant requires a shade tree to protect it from direct sunlight, and nature has provided the perfect solution: the Himalayan alder (*Alnus nepalensis*) which not only provides shade throughout the year, but also makes sure that valuable nitrogen does not get leached from the soil.

Because all of Sikkim is mountainous – the little state veers from subtropical to permanent snow – there is a virtual absence of flat land on which to practice agriculture.

Rice and other cereals are grown on terraced hillsides, but that – as well as rampant building activity in the capital Gangtok – predisposes the land towards crippling landslides. So it is agro-forestry that is a perfect solution for Sikkim. In a single solution, trees in the forests are left untouched, and some undergrowth is cleared, but only to make way for black cardamom plants. There, in the midst of kilometres of hillsides, I spot the now-familiar black cardamom plants, dwarfed by deciduous trees. Shoots bear a fist-sized receptacle in the shape of a pine cone. Each receptacle contains around half-a-dozen pods of black cardamom. During harvest time, which is once a year from October onwards, the whole receptacle is removed so that individual pods can be separated later. Each large plantation owner has a drying chamber on his land. To help fire these up, branches of Himalayan alder are burnt; in a few months' time they will have grown back.

Part of the smoky taste of black cardamom comes from the hours it spends in the drying chamber: Certainly, when I bit into a seed that was picked straight off the plant, it had a sharper, slightly acidic flavour to it. It didn't even have the gnarled, somewhat pre-historic appearance that black cardamom gets after a stint in the drying chamber where it acquires its trademark charred eucalyptus undertone, with an undeniable sweetness in the finish.

The most intriguing part of Sikkim's odd relationship with this spice is the connection between black cardamom and the Marwaris who trade in it. My Sikkimese friends tell me that

Marwaris from Kolkata migrated to Sikkim for the express purpose of buying and selling the spice. I am given directions to the shops-cum-godowns of a couple of Marwari traders near M.G. Road, as 'un-Indian' a road as I have ever come across: tiled pavements, no traffic, only benches, fountains and shops that have stood here for decades. On the far side of M.G. Road is a row of far smaller, less impressive shops that act as grocers-cum-wholesalers of black cardamom.

As I walk into virtually every one of the twenty-odd shops selling singularly unlovely blocks of washing soap and an assortment of dals, I enquire about black cardamom. Invariably, the shopkeeper calls out to the youngest boy in the shop who then climbs like a monkey on to sacks of rice and dal, perches his foot on a shelf of Maggi noodles or MDH Masalas, stretches himself with an almighty effort to the very top of the shop and, from just below the ceiling, brings down a dusty packet of black cardamom. The packets are never larger than 500 grams and they are never in mint condition, so I am not tempted to buy them.

Clearly black cardamom is seldom sought in Gangtok's shops, even by tourists. I find it extremely strange to see how easy it is to buy panch phoran, in deference to the number of Bengalis that live in or visit Gangtok on long weekends, but how difficult it is to come by the produce of the land. In Jammu's Raghunath Bazar, by comparison, every tourist worth his salt buys at least one kilo of raajma, which is the local produce. And in Kashmir, tourists go in search of saffron, its price notwithstanding. So why the hesitation in Gangtok? I wish I knew the answer.

Far away from Sikkim, in Punjab, however, you'll find a stash of black cardamom in every kitchen. It has a digestive quality, which is why it is used in garam masalas and many whole dals which are heavy on the stomach. According to tradition, in every Punjabi household when there is a new-born baby, a jug of water in which black cardamom has been boiled steadily is given to the mother to drink. The belief is that this helps to flush out the toxins from their body; and the baby is not prone to colic because of the digestive nature of black cardamom. Old-fashioned barfi and pedas, too, are invariably topped with a sprinkling of coarsely crushed black cardamom seeds.

Somewhat unsurprisingly, in Kerala, there is no use at all of black cardamom among the community that owns plantations of aromatic spices: the Syrian Christians. That is understandable because no black cardamom grows in Kerala. What little black cardamom is used in the state is mainly by the Muslims, in the form of garam masalas for mutton preparations and biryanis. Abida Rashid, a Kozhikode-based authority on Muslim cooking, tells me of an intriguing warm drink for the breaking of the daily fast during the month of Ramadan. It is made from roasted semolina and fried shallots and flavoured with black cardamom.

For me, black cardamom has never held any personal appeal. This is probably because, as a teenager, I overheard a conversation in Goa between the owner of the local Punjabi restaurant and a customer who was obviously from Delhi. The restaurateur was recounting that the first time a Goan customer walked in, he ordered a dal and then raised the roof about what he thought was a dead cockroach. It turned out that it was a black cardamom, but young and impressionable as I was, the connection between cockroaches and the spice was irrevocably made in my mind.

A chef of a well-known group of hotels reiterates the

appearance of black cardamom to cockroaches. Apparently, at the chain of hotels in which he works, there's a standing instruction that black cardamom is only to be added to food in its ground form. On several occasions, Western guests mistook whole black cardamom for cockroaches and complained so bitterly (and noisily) that the instruction is now immutable.

Over the years, I've never been tempted to change my mind about this spice. The pungent, incipient sweetness of black cardamom has (to my palate) always overpowered every other spice it shares a dish with. In my in-laws' kitchen, it goes into every single preparation, including those where only one aromatic spice is required. Though I am biased against it, I will say that it is not an inferior or coarser version of green cardamom, but an altogether different spice and has to be treated as such.

PAPUTTU

Kaveri Ponnapa has a most beautiful blog that celebrates the cuisine of her beloved Coorg as intertwined with the culture and lifestyle. She is the author of the only definitive book on the Kodavas, *The Vanishing Kodavas*, and writes about the food of her community for several publications.

INGREDIENTS

- 1 cup tari*
- 1 cup milk
- 1 cup water
- Seeds from 1 pod of green cardamom, very lightly crushed
- ¼ tsp salt

- 1 tbsp sugar
- ¼ cup or less coconut, freshly grated

METHOD

- Soak the tari in water and milk, with the grated coconut for an hour.
- Next, add the salt, sugar and cardamom, and squeeze the coconut in the liquid gently by hand, until it releases milk, and the mixture becomes creamy.
- Prepare a steamer, bringing the water to a boil. (You can also cook the puttu in a pressure cooker, without the weight, in case you don't have a steamer. Make sure you place the puttu on a stand above the boiling water.)
- Pour into a shallow enamel plate approx 8½ inch in diameter, 1½ inch in depth.
- Place the plate in the steamer, close the lid and cook on medium to high heat for about 15–20 minutes, until done.
- To turn out, allow the plate to cool a little, then place your palm on the base, and slam down firmly on to a cloth spread on the kitchen counter. Cut into 8 wedge-shaped slices. Puttus should be firm to the touch, soft but not mushy, and a delicate scent of cardamom should rise from them.

**Note: Tari is short-grain rice that is washed, dried and pounded. It's possible to make this at home by washing, drying and pulsing the rice in a food processor. Take care to sieve out any powder, and retain only the bigger pieces of rice. Rice rava is not an appropriate substitute. Paputtu is traditionally eaten with mutton curry.*

NADIYAH AKRAM'S PANI POL (COCONUT CREPES) WITH GREEN CARDAMOM

This recipe is simple, quick and filling.

INGREDIENTS

- 2 cups coconut, freshly scraped or desiccated
- 1 cup kithul jaggery, scraped/crushed
- 3 whole green cardamoms, lightly bruised
- Sugar, to taste (in case jaggery is not sweet enough)

METHOD

- Melt the jaggery in a pot over the stove on a low flame with the cardamom.
- Once the jaggery has dissolved, fish out all cardamom pieces and remnants.
- Add the scraped coconut to the warm jaggery syrup and stir rapidly over a low flame for a minute. Remove from heat and allow to cool.
- Make paper thin crepes using a batter of eggs, flour and milk and roll with pol pani filling.

GAWALMANDI KA KAHIRA

Chef Dirham ul Haque is the shining star in the firmament of The Oberoi Group. He specializes in Mughlai food and though many of his recipes are too complicated for the hobby cook, this rice-based dessert is guaranteed to yield perfect results.

INGREDIENTS

- 200 g basmati rice
- 2 l full-cream milk
- 250 g sugar
- 250 g danedar (granular) khoya
- 10 green cardamoms
- 3½ tbsp almond slivers

METHOD

- Soak rice in water for an hour.

- Gently roast the cardamom; make a fine powder of it.
- In a heavy-bottomed copper vessel, simmer the milk for 30 minutes on low heat with the cardamom powder, add sugar and grated khoya.
- Cook till the milk reduces to half its volume.
- Add rice and cook it for 30 minutes, stirring constantly.
- Set in earthenware moulds. Refrigerate; garnish with almond slivers.

CHEF RANVEER BRAR'S CASHEW NUT 'HOLLANDAISE' WITH BLACK CARDAMOM

INGREDIENTS

- 200 g unroasted cashew nuts (broken ones are a good option)
- ½ tsp black cardamom seeds, pounded
- Approximately one cup neutral-tasting oil, such as rice bran oil

METHOD

- Wash the cashew nuts in running water to remove any grit or inclusions/salt. Soak for at least 8 hours. Drain.
- Place the cashew nuts in a wet grinder and blitz till you are left with a paste. Slowly add in the oil, drop by drop, while the mixture is being blended at high speed.
- When it becomes stiff enough that it can be turned upside down safely, it is done.
- Sprinkle over with the black cardamom powder and fold in well.

Note: This can be used as a topping for canapes, as part of a filling for sandwiches, as a dip or even in a seafood dish that has to be gratinated.

RASHMI SOOD'S PEDAS

Jawalamukhi – the part of Himachal where my college friend Rashmi lives – has a mithai shop that makes mithai in the old-fashioned way. Hence, black cardamom is still used, albeit the price keeps shooting northwards! The mithai maker has kindly given Rashmi his recipe.

INGREDIENTS

- 500 g khoya
- ½ cup sugar
- 1 tsp milk
- 2 tbsp ghee
- ¼ cup water
- Seeds of 10 black cardamoms, a few reserved for garnish

METHOD

- Sauté the khoya in a pan on medium heat, stirring continuously for 10 minutes. If it begins to stick to the bottom of the pan, add a few drops of ghee at a time and keep stirring till the colour changes to golden brown.
- Take the pan off the heat and set aside to cool. In another pan, cook the sugar with the water on medium heat.
- Add half the cardamom seeds, coarsely broken in a mortar and pestle.
- Stir till the sugar dissolves and the mixture becomes syrupy.
- Take the pan off the heat and add the khoya mixture to the sugar syrup, mixing well.
- Now, divide the mixture into flattened balls of equal size and shape. Use your palms for this, after applying a bit of ghee.
- Press the remaining cardamom seeds into the pedas. You may coarsely pound them before-hand, so that you have some almost whole and others almost powdered.

Clove

If there was ever a beauty contest for spices, clove would be a strong contender. The tree itself grows to majestic proportions, attaining heights of ten metres easily, its shape an almost perfect cone. The flowers – that later become the spice – form pretty clusters at the very tip of every twig and, after they are picked and dried, the chocolate brown stem holds its 'head' in exactly the same manner as a four-claw ring holds a diamond. If that sounds poetic, there's more! The harvesting too has to be done with skill and precision, because each bunch of ten to fifteen buds ripens at a different time from its neighbour on the next branch and the picker has to know which bunch to pick and which to leave for the following week. What's more, the picker cannot be too rough with shaking the branches, because there is a superstition that clove trees only flower completely once every four years and for a good harvest in one year, the tree has to be treated with a certain amount of delicacy the previous year!

Cloves come from the Myrtaceae or the myrtle family. On the face of it, eucalyptus, allspice and guava have little in common with cloves, but they are all from the same family. The word clove itself comes from the Latin word *clavus*, which means nail. In fact, the word for cloves in several languages, including Tagalog, Russian and Hebrew is the word for nail, and it appears that most of the world has named this spice after its shape: possibly the only instance of such a happening.

One of the earliest occurrences of cloves has been recorded as far back as 1721 BCE at an archaeological site in modern-day Syria, in what appears to be a home kitchen. It is tantalizing to speculate on how they made their way to ancient Mesopotamia from a handful of obscure islands in the Indonesian archipelago. By the 4th century CE, there was an established trade route between the Maluku Islands (collectively known as Moluccas) – the five islands in the Indonesian archipelago where cloves have grown since the beginning of time – passing through the South China Sea, crossing the southern tip of India, and traversing Arabia and going into Syria by caravan. It truly beggars the imagination to visualize that in a world without maps and compasses – even the existence of iron had not been discovered – a cargo of cloves could make its unerring way from the tropical islands of the Moluccas to Syria in a journey that still confounds historians and researchers!

The story of cloves as we know them today started in the Maluka Islands that comprise islands such as Bacan, Ternate and Tidore, among others. These were the original 'spice islands' and, alongside Banda Islands which were famous for nutmeg and mace, were the crown jewels in the battle for the aromatics that raged between Spain and Portugal, the English and the Dutch. Before the 16th century, if you wanted either cloves, mace or nutmeg, you'd have to visit these diminutive volcanic islands. Plenty of people did. The Chinese sailing in junks, the Arabs in dhows, the Spanish on expeditions, the Dutch conquerors and the French adventurers – the Molucca received plenty of visitors.

Today, the Molucca have lost most of their shine. They are no longer the world's only producer of cloves. One of the reasons is that the islands are quite hard to get to and because of the rioting that took place there, between 1999 and 2002, boat service is not only rudimentary, it is liable to get cancelled without prior notice. As a result, not too many visitors come to their shores. Plus, English is not widely spoken, so unless you have a Bahasa-speaking escort, you have more or less lost the battle before you've even started.

Although Indonesia is still one of the largest producers of cloves, producing more than double of its closest competitor Madagascar, they are not self-sufficient, and have to import from other countries. This is a rather shocking reversal of fortune, since the Moluccas once used to provide the entire world with its quota of cloves. The single largest reason for this reversal is the high consumption of kretek, a clove-flavoured cigarette. Almost every Indonesian who smokes seems to favour clove-scented cigarettes, which crackle when you puff on them, probably because of the presence of essential oil in them, adding another dimension to a quiet smoke.

As long as the Dutch ruled the Maluku Islands, they fiercely controlled every single clove plant, but the enterprising French adventurer, Pierre Poivre, managed to overcome this in the 1750s. He purloined several thousand clove plants with the help of locals and shipped them to Mauritius. The cloves – as well as the other spice that he acquired in the dead of the night in the Moluccas: nutmegs – never did flourish in Mauritius. But when, after Poivre's death, they were once more shipped to the French-controlled island of Mozambique, they grew in profusion. It is the cloves from Mozambique that are now exported to Indonesia every year for use in their kretek cigarettes!

Today, by contrast, most of the world's cloves come from Zanzibar and Madagascar, while a modest amount comes from Idukki district in Kerala. There is one difference between the two. In Zanzibar, cloves are dried in the sun, whereas in Idukki, they are shade dried. The result is that the top bud remains an appealing chocolate colour in the case of India, whereas the Zanzibar bud becomes as dark as the rest of this nail-shaped spice. It is important to note that Zanzibar and Madagascar have very limited consumption of cloves, as compared to the Moluccas where the giant's share is consumed in the domestic cigarette industry.

Knowing that the Dutch occupation of Indonesia was precisely for its precious crop of cloves, I was enthused when a friend brought back a gift to me from Amsterdam: Dutch Edam cheese with whole cloves. When I tasted it, however, it had not a trace of subtlety. There was no reason indeed, for the cloves to have been there at all, let alone in such a vast quantity. Two hundred years – the amount of time the Netherlands ruled Indonesia – is obviously not long enough to learn about how to make the optimum use of spice.

Cloves only become a spice when they're taken off the tree; when they are on it, they are the flower buds. Traveller accounts tell us that sailors knew when they were nearing the Molucca Islands because the fragrance of spices used to waft out to them. Even today, a small grove of even half-a-dozen clove trees will produce the pleasant, astringent fragrance of the spice. It is difficult to find such a grove in India though. In India, spice plantations usually grow endemic species like pepper and cardamom, so that vanilla, cacao, cinnamon and cloves are relegated to a few trees, if they are grown at all.

Shinoj Kallamakal, whose spice plantation is on the main road in Kumily in Kerala, a few kilometers before Thekkady, tells me that his average yield per clove tree is two kilograms per annum. Those buds that are allowed to develop on the tree instead of being picked, become worthless, so it is crucial that every last bud is plucked, the height of the tree notwithstanding. Kumily is the nerve centre of the spice plantations in central Kerala. There are over a hundred show gardens in the area, some, as another plantation owner Benny Joseph Muttathukunnel tells me, are a part of traditional spice plantations while others are modest plots of land along the main road just to show tourists how spices are grown, something for which the local government gives attractive incentives. Benny's show garden, simply called Green Park, is in Attapallam, a dimunitive village near Kumily. It is here that I see a clove tree and taste a clove in the making. Not nearly as hot and spicy as dried cloves are: this one is at the stage where it would be called a bud, and there is a faint hint of the trademark astringency so familiar in some brands of toothpaste.

I heartily endorse the idea of show gardens, because school children, tourists and people who would otherwise never be able to see spices in their growing stage, are exposed to one of the most magical experiences of the food world. The bud that my guide opened out for me at Green Park was pale lemon in colour and resembled the shape of a clove. It was hard to believe that a soft and delicate flower would metamorphose into a dark brown spice so hard that it's impossible to break it into two with one's fingers. The flowers, I was told, keep changing colour, from lemon to green, then pink and finally to brown, when they are ready to be harvested.

I have often been at the receiving end of surprise dishes at restaurants, where chefs with boundless enthusiasm have dehydrated or transformed a particular ingredient in their molecular kitchens and asked me to guess what it is. Try eating Nutella as a pale pink powder on a plate and see if you can make the connection between the thick hazelnut spread and a barely sweet powder. I mention this because when you walk through a spice plantation and are fed a random bud, bark or seed and asked to guess what it is, you squeeze your eyes shut in concentration and try to place the ingredient, but sometimes, even an everyday spice proves to be so elusive in its unripe form that it is unrecognizable. No wonder we need more show gardens!

It is a widely held belief that cloves are best used whole. Other spices combine well – and taste good – when they are pounded to a powder, but somehow cloves acquire a sour edge once they're powdered. Of course, they have to be pounded to be used in garam masala, but few people would think of storing clove powder on its own, the way cinnamon powder is stored. And though cloves are assertive, astringent and leave behind a stinging sensation, if consumed in large doses, many classify it as a sweet spice. Thus, Chef Kaizad Patel whose Parsi catering firm keeps him busy around the year, tells me that his cuisine is characterized by cinnamon, cardamom and nutmeg, but not by the sweetness of cloves, which, however, are used in dhansak masala to make the signature rice, lentil and cutlet set. Like garam masala used in most of the country, Parsi garam masala too uses cloves, but that is where the usage ends.

It is similar in Maharashtra. Chef Mandar Madav, who hails from Sindudurg, says that because cloves are a sweet spice, they are used judiciously in very few cases, the most common one being katachi amti: the watery legume preparation made with the liquid drained off from the dal used to stuff puran poli with. Puran poli is a sweet dish, with a hint of jaggery and katachi amti is slightly spicy and sour, so counterpointing the two is a stroke of genius. The community from which Madav hails never fails to add powdered clove to each and every last dessert, so subliminally, the connection between sweetness and cloves is complete.

Rocky Mohan, cookbook author and food impresario, tells me that in Lucknow, the very first spice to go into the *lagan* (cooking pot) is a whole clove. First ghee is warmed up, then a clove and a few drops of water are added and the pot is covered immediately. The effect of this is to cleanse the ghee of any impurities, as they cling to the drops of water which becomes steam and hits the lid of the lagan, all by the action of the clove. Traditionally, ghee needed to be purified and this was the most expeditious way of doing so. Ayurveda does, however, bear Mohan out, because indeed, in spite of its piercing astringency, cloves are considered a sweet spice. Chef Sheikh Arif Ahmed, a native of Hyderabad, is the lone voice who says that cloves are very far from being a sweet spice, and calls them spicy and astringent. He says that the only time cloves are used in their powdered form is in garam masala, and that too, in small quantities to offset the spiciness they generate when ground to a powder. This is perhaps because of the presence of so much essential oil: a whopping 15 per cent, as against the 7 per cent in other fragrant spices like cardamom. Also, perhaps because of so much essential oil, the powder tends to clump together into a mass, which happens with no other spice powder.

The essential oil in cloves is eugenol. It is this that gives cloves their characteristic astringent bite and medicinal properties. Anyone who has ever suffered from a tooth ache has either been told to place a clove between clenched teeth or has been given a piece of cotton wool dabbed with clove oil. As a corollary, prominent brands of toothpaste advertise themselves as containing clove oil to keep tooth decay at bay. And though eugenol is also obtained from other spices like cinnamon, nutmeg, bay leaf and even basil, its presence in cloves is astonishingly high. The little 'head' of the clove contains the giant's share of essential oil, followed by the 'nail'. I'm told that even the leaves of the clove tree have a percentage of clove oil but the trees are not stripped of their foliage because of the belief I mentioned earlier: harsh treatment of the tree will deplete the following year's harvest.

The rather unfortunate fallout of obtaining clove oil is that unscrupulous dealers often sell the nail-shaped spice in the market after most of its oil has been extracted. They do this by boiling the spice and what the consumer is left with is something in a shape that resembles cloves, but with a marked depletion of its qualities.

Outside their natural habitat in the Moluccas, clove trees tend to not grow as high as 12 metres and hardly have the same dark-leafed majesty. But the essential oil component in the spice is always an astonishing 15 per cent as against the 6 per cent found in black pepper. This means that cloves have to be added much more judiciously than other spices if they are not to overpower the dish.

One of the best ways to use a clove is to perfume a dish with the smoke produced by lighting a single clove. Dhungar, or smoking, is used to greatest effect in Rajasthani cuisine and improves the most ordinary dish. Here's how to do it: Finish cooking a dish of, say, mince. As soon as you take it off the fire, place a lighted coal in a katori (steel bowl), position the clove on top of the coal, moisten with a drop or two of clarified butter, place the katori in the cooked dish, immediately cover the cooking vessel and leave for half an hour. The eugenol in the clove will be released by the lit coal and the vapours will spread in the tightly closed vessel. The astringency of the clove will transform into an attractive smokiness that will perfume the mince in an extraordinary way. You could, in theory, perform an identical routine with any other spice that has aroma, for example cinnamon or peppercorn. But it is only cloves that will give you that rich irresistible fragrance. Is it the property of eugenol or the high percentage of oil that creates this magic? It may take a food scientist to answer that one, but it certainly was a genius who first thought of it.

There are few kitchens in the world that do not have a small stash of cloves in them, whether to stud a leg of ham before baking it, to add to a mulled wine, to sprinkle atop a korma or even to give relief to a toothache. And innocuous as the tiny 'nail' looks, it has quite a long and intriguing history, having made its way to far-off Syria by land and causing major upheavals in Portugal, Britain and Netherlands when these countries sought to perpetuate their control on the clove islands. Today, cloves are one of those spices that represent how much of our history has been shaped by these tiny ingredients, and how far they've travelled in time and space to land on our plate.

EVA SUD'S STEWED PEARS

Eva Sud and I have known each other for nearly 50 years. As a pre-teen, she showed not the slightest inclination towards the culinary arts, but her life as an air-force wife taught her that delicious food need not be painstaking.

INGREDIENTS

- 1 kg pears (hard, any variety)
- 1 cup sugar
- 10 cloves
- 1 tsp lime juice

METHOD

- Peel, core and quarter the pears and put in micro-proof dish.
- Add the sugar, cloves and lemon juice.

- Microwave cook on high for 7–10 minutes till pears are soft but still hold their shape.
- Serve with custard or cream.

EVA SUD'S APRICOT FOOL

INGREDIENTS

- 250 g dried apricots
- 4 tbsp sugar
- 1 cup water
- 1 cup milk
- 2 tsp custard powder
- 1½ tbsp sugar
- 3 whole cloves, pounded in a mortar and pestle

METHOD

- Soak the dried apricots in hot water for 3 hours to soften them.
- Mix the sugar into the water and bring to a boil, adding the apricots. Simmer for approximately 30 minutes or until the apricots soften.
- For the custard, heat the milk in a pan and add the cloves. Leave on a very low fire for 5 minutes.
- Strain out the cloves and discard.
- Add the sugar and continue to simmer till the sugar dissolves.
- Now add the custard powder, whisking well. As soon as the mixture thickens, take off the fire and leave to cool over a large bowl of water.
- Arrange two or three apricots in a stemmed glass. Pour the custard over them. Repeat till the glass is three-fourths full. Chill.

RESHI FAMILY TOMATO SOUP

Like almost all my recipes, this one uses whatever vegetables you have to hand, rather than those listed here. If you are making it for a vegetarian friend, omit the chicken/beef stock cube and use a vegetable stock cube instead.

INGREDIENTS

- 500 g ripe tomatoes, chopped into chunks
- 50 g pumpkin, one stalk celery, half a carrot
- A splash of good olive oil (say 4 tbsp)
- ½ a large onion or 1 small onion, sliced
- 4 cloves garlic, finely chopped
- 1 stock cube (chicken or beef – your choice)
- 4 whole cloves
- Salt and pepper, to taste (preferably white pepper)

METHOD

- Sauté the tomatoes in the olive oil with pumpkin, carrot, garlic, onion and salt.
- When the tomatoes have more or less lost their moisture, add the stock cube, the chopped celery, whole cloves and approximately four cups water. I use a pressure cooker, but you could use a deep, wide-mouthed pan with a close-fitting lid.
- Cook for 10 minutes in a pressure cooker or 30 minutes in a saucepan.
- Check seasoning and consistency. I usually blend the solid bits in a food processor for a thick soup.
- You could also add a teaspoon of tomato ketchup and/or sugar to it before serving.

Note: Grandmas tell us that tomatoes are cooling to the system. The only way you can consume them in winter is with whole cloves!

Asafoetida

If you're ever in Delhi, take a walk through the crowded Khari Baoli in Gadodia Market, Chandni Chowk – once a gracious haveli with a courtyard that has now been co-opted by the spice trade. The narrow arched alleyway that forms the entrance is lined with chilli sellers, making it obligatory to carry a moistened handkerchief – even the porters whose business it is to transport sacks of chillies and other spices on their backs cough and sneeze at the entrance. Immediately afterwards, there are sellers of rock salt, eight different types of coriander seeds, whole turmeric, where every sack has a slightly different intensity of colour, cumin in shades ranging from grey to greenish and brown, and every other imaginable spice, with specializations in each taken to heights that you and I could not possibly imagine. But my favourite is the asafoetida, or hing, shop, at the corner where the market begins, because of the aroma that surrounds it.

Opinions are divided on asafoetida's signature smell. I used to have a neighbour from Andhra Pradesh – a strict vegetarian – who was in search of a wife. Because of the persistent belief that garlic is an aphrodisiac, many traditional vegetarian communities avoid its use and instead favour asafoetida. This neighbour of mine was no different – he couldn't bear the smell of garlic. Every time his parents arranged for him to see a young woman, he would have a standard list of questions. First among them was, 'Do you eat garlic?' The correct answer was no. Anyone answering 'yes' was not entertained further.

My erstwhile neighbour would be interested to know that at least as many people are put off by the smell of asafoetida. In fact, in many European languages, the name translates as 'Devil's dung' and it's mainly because of its powerful odour. (Can one call it a fragrance? The very same people who refer to it as 'devil's dung' also compare it to – hold your breath – black truffles!) Gernot Katzer, the author of the most definitive spice pages on the worldwide web, tells a hilarious story about asafoetida. When he was first told that Indians use it as a spice in cooking, he thought that his leg was being pulled. He could not believe that anybody would actually want to ingest something that smelled like that. Katzer, who comes across as an avid Indophile, now loves asafoetida, as he does every other Indian spice. While the Portuguese brought chillies to Indian shores, according to Katzer, we have Alexander's army to thank for bringing us asafoetida. In the 4th century BCE, when the army crossed the Hindu Kush mountains (then, as now, the spice grew in a swathe that includes Iran and Afghanistan) to enter India, they noticed a plant that resembled silphium, a once-rare spice that was used to tenderize tough meat. Mistaking asafoetida for silphium, they carried it with them into India.

Back at my favourite hing shop in Khari Baoli, two unusually dour brothers preside over a series of white enamel bowls. Each is filled with a small lump of asafoetida. Even the untutored eye can tell that there is an appreciable difference between each sample. On one of my several walks through the market, and to the shop, I ask them how many different types of hing they dealt in. 'Seventy-four,' comes the immediate answer. And, could they please tell me what the difference between each was? Again, the answer is immediate: 'No.'

Sanjay Bhatia of Chetan Das Lachhman Das in Tilak Bazar, also in Khari Baoli, is much more helpful. He educates me about the qualities and varieties of asafoetida. As an importer, he knows of just 10–15 varieties. Seventy-four, he thinks, is a gross exaggeration. 'With an inventory of 74 products, even we would not be able to tell one apart from the other. Besides, billing would be a nightmare.'

Asafoetida is derived from the ferula plant, part of the carrot family. The roots of the ferula plant are enormously thick: up to 6 inches at the crown. In March, when the plants are just about to flower, the upper part of the root is laid bare and the stem is incised. Milky latex starts to ooze from the incision, and when it stops, the latex is collected and another incision is made at another spot, and so on, till the plant gives up all its resin. This usually takes about three months. A healthy plant of four to five years of age can usually yield a kilo of resin with two incisions.

One type of asafoetida differs considerably from the next. The first difference is classified in terms of provenance. Kandhari asafoetida is considered the best, followed by Iranian, and then by the Afghani variety from Herat, near the Iranian border. However, Bhatia assures me that the trade in India makes no distinction between the provenances of the various crops. No matter where they are grown, they all come to the market at Kabul from where Bhatia's agents procure them. Bhatia himself can tell apart the crops of one region from another, but not many others can, not even his own customers. The Iran strain is far lighter in aroma and flavour and has slightly citrusy undertones. The crop of Afghanistan has a far more pungent smell. Almost the entire crop of both countries makes its way straight to India. The 5 per cent that is at the bottom of the barrel in terms of quality is exported to countries like Germany where it is used as a pesticide, for which quality is not critical. But they are not the only ones who've had this idea! In Maharashtra, there are housewives who grind a year's supply of spice every summer and preserve it by placing a small lump of asafoetida on top, daring insects to attack.

Pure asafoetida, that trickles out of the cut root of the plant, doesn't lose its potency for years together. At first, the resin is viscid and greyish white, but as it dries, it becomes progressively darker and hardens into a substance that resembles glass. Dealers stabilize it by adding starch and edible gum to it. This is usually wheat flour in North India and rice flour in South India. Spice companies based outside India have now taken to using rice flour to circumvent gluten intolerance. The more the flour, the cheaper the product. At one point, you can actually sell asafoetida as a powder, owing to the sheer volume of flour in it. Needless to say, it is not of the best quality.

There is about as much obfuscation about asafoetida as there is about saffron. The truth of the matter is that being a resin, this spice does not decompose and can be safely left with only a mild degradation of the odour occurring even after five years. All compounds of asafoetida harden over time and as it is extremely difficult to find pure asafoetida in the retail market, it can be safely said that hardly any of us know what the real thing looks or tastes like.

The best quality of asafoetida is tinged with pink and is yielding to the touch. I have found it almost impossible to keep it that way – no matter what I do, it hardens in my kitchen, and then I have to use a mortar and pestle to break it into pieces. A friend's mother always bought asafoetida in large quantities – about a fist-sized lump – and stored it either in her turmeric jar or in the coriander seed container. This, she claimed, had a dual effect. It preserved the asafoetida perfectly and flavoured the turmeric, so in time, you had to use progressively less quantities of asafoetida, because the turmeric kept becoming stronger!

Although India uses the greatest proportion of asafoetida, none is grown in the country. Which is why importers like Bhatia often have to negotiate sudden price rises. The day I met Bhatia, he was deftly juggling two landlines and two cell phones simultaneously, while lamenting that the price of the crop had just gone up yet again. 'That country [Afghanistan] has so much going for it. It has everything from world-class dry fruits, asafoetida, black cumin and medicinal drugs, but because of their tenuous politics, the country and its produce are going to rack and ruin.'

Bhatia is one of only 22 or 23 dealers and importers of asafoetida in the entire country – so small is the quantum of business for this spice. By comparison, dealers of other spices in the same league number in the thousands. Delhi-based wholesale dealers, whom I have spoken to, say that, once upon a time, a significant part of their business came from selling asafoetida to wandering merchants, in addition to spice merchants and owners of branded spices. Today, the market that importers like Bhatia cater to includes Unani and Ayurvedic medicine companies, manufacturers of hing ki golis, exporters, big brands and wholesale dealers in small towns. It is not unusual for him to have customers who buy volumes of around three tonnes per annum: A rather modest quantity when seen in the light of the rest of the spice trade.

As Bhatia is licensed to process asafoetida as well as to trade in it, part of his business includes mixing wheat flour with it in carefully graded proportions, so as to be able to sell to all sections of the market. The least expensive grade today costs ₹350 and the most expensive ₹12,500 a kilogram. Not unnaturally, he sells to the trade, rather than to individual buyers and he has observed, over the decades, that brands who want to re-sell asafoetida under their own label buy the product of Afghanistan while those who want asafoetida to use in a spice blend invariably ask for the product of Iran.

Some towns across North India have itinerant hing-sellers. All through the 1960s and 1970s, Shimla's Lakkar Bazar and Lower Bazar always saw a line of chattering Tibetan ladies chanting, '*Heeeeng le lo*', periodically in sing-song voices to attract passers-by. My earliest recollection of the crowded Lower Bazar, bustling with pack-horses and shoppers, was the musical sound of these hing sellers. However, the last time I visited Lower Bazar in 2010, they seemed to be few and far in between. I chanced upon just one Tibetan lady with the trademark diminutive weighing scales of hing sellers. She sold two qualities – poor and very poor. Her other wares were much more interesting: nail cutters, sewing needles and handkerchiefs, but since she was probably the last one left of the hing-sellers of my youth, I felt obliged to make a small purchase. I also chatted with her about the trade. Surprisingly, she had a perspicacious insight into it. Apparently, in her youth (I put her age at 75 years, so roughly in the 1930s), the hing trade in the area was in the hands of itinerant traders who would travel on horseback from Afghanistan through mountain passes to Nepal and Tibet, and the ladies of Lower Bazar would buy high quality stock from these merchants. Now, said the lady sadly, the conventional route of whole-sellers in the organized sector is the accepted mode of operation, relegating adventurous merchants to the pages of history.

In the countries where asafoetida is traditionally grown, the spice is used in small amounts. In Iran, I am told that a grain of asafoetida is rubbed onto a plate till the plate acquires the smell. Thereupon, kebabs are placed on the plate. It is the same principle by which the French rub a cut clove of garlic onto the walls of a salad bowl and then add lettuce and other leaves to the bowl: the perfume becomes infused. In Afghanistan, for instance, dried meat is often flavoured with asafoetida.

But the use of asafoetida in food is far more widespread in India than in the countries where it is grown, and that is because of vegetarianism. Exactly how this came about is a mystery that we will never solve. Perhaps it is because Ayurveda recommends using asafoetida for every preparation that has *vata*: therefore, kachoris and other fried morsels always have the trademark earthy pungence of asafoetida, as does the flavoured water of pani puris, and preparations of lentils, cabbage, green peas and beans. Also, strict vegetarians who don't eat onions or garlic –

traditionally considered aphrodisiacs – need a substance in their food that can be used as a digestive, and asafoetida plays that part to perfection. The smell of asafoetida has a marked resemblance to onions and garlic, courtesy of the amount of sulphur compounds present in all three. And, just as cooked onions and garlic lose their pungency, so does fried asafoetida, making it easy for the smell to pervade the cooked dish. The spice is used in almost every dish in the vegetarian cuisines of the Vaish community of Delhi and UP, Marwari and Gujarati cuisine, and in the Iyer and Iyyengar dishes of Tamil Nadu.

Although the use of asafoetida is primarily in vegetarian cuisines across the country, it makes a wild-card entry into the heavily non-vegetarian cuisine of Kashmiri Pandits. Unlike most Brahmin communities, Kashmiri Pandits are avowedly non-vegetarian, perhaps because of the cold climate of the valley. But they still eschew onions, garlic and tomatoes, flavouring their food instead with asafoetida. The flavour of asafoetida in their preparations is marked, whether it is in khichdi or in their signature potatoes or elongated meat-balls. As Suman, my Kashmiri Pandit friend who is a great cook, remarked, 'Hing is all we have for flavour.' While that is not strictly true: There is turmeric, fennel powder, ginger powder and the aromatics too, Suman's remark was indicative of the sheer weightage that is given to asafoetida.

Most members of the community who have lived in Kashmir recollect their mothers and grandmothers using a form of the spice – resembling shards of glass that had to be crushed, usually in a limestone mortar and pestle. Inch-sized bits would be stored in an air-tight jar till they were needed, when a bit of the spice was dissolved in a few teaspoons of water, and then the milky liquid was sprinkled on the ingredient being sautéed. However, as many a hobby cook has learnt, the best way to do this is off the fire, or on a very low heat. Adding water to sizzling oil can be a recipe for disaster. And whereas Indian cooking is all about approximate measures, asafoetida is a hard taskmaster. It will not allow itself to be used in anything more than minute quantities, or else the dish will turn bitter and become inedible.

And the volume of asafoetida used in this cuisine is formidable, too. For comparison, while most people in metropolitan cities buy packets of up to 50 grams at a time, most Kashmiri families that I know would not buy less than 250 grams at a time. They rue the fact that the pure asafoetida they used to use in Kashmir cannot be found for love or money elsewhere, and they have to make do with what is available.

Interestingly, nowhere is the phrase 'one man's meat is another man's poison' better illustrated than with the use of asafoetida in the Kashmir valley. Consider this example: My husband Hafeez, a Muslim from Kashmir, had never tasted asafoetida while growing up. One day, his Kashmiri Pandit friend offered him a biscuit that he had just bought from a baker in the old city of Srinagar. Hafeez was ravenous, as teenagers usually are, and took a generous bite. In a trice, his face contorted. Torn between the desire to spit it out yet not wanting to offend his childhood buddy, he stood by the side of the road, until his friend told him to spit it out if he didn't like it. And then there was a Kashmiri Pandit friend of mine, Sanjay, who told me of the time when, at the age of

12, he was on his way to school in Srinagar and spied a man distributing taheri, the yellow rice that both communities – Pandits and Muslims – cook. Sanjay was given a handful, as is usually the case, and he enthusiastically shovelled a large portion of it into his mouth, only to spit it out immediately, because of the unfamiliarity of the flavour of fried onions!

To each his own.

While most meat-eaters, as a very general rule, fall back on onions and garlic to cut out the heaviness of pulses, a few, like the Bunts of Mangalore use both in the same preparation. Mensakai, a South Kannada vegetable or fruit dish with a trademark sweet-sour taste, is cooked differently by the various communities of Mangalore and its surrounding towns. The Bunt community (of which Aishwariya Rai Bachchan is the most famous example) has a much-loved pineapple mensakai that includes chopped garlic as well as a touch of asafoetida.

In Bengal, one of the main uses of asafoetida is in the delightful hinger kochuri, a puri with a filling of industrial quantities of asafoetida. Every sweet shop in Kolkata makes it to accompany a spicy potato curry as a tea-time snack. For a community that is big on pungent flavours, hinger kochuris are a spectacular treat.

But as far as sheer quality and strength of asafoetida go, no other community is as particular as Tamil Brahmins. Their sambar is flavoured with but four spices: asafoetida, fenugreek, coriander and red chilli. Visit just about any corner shop or supermarket in the state and you'll encounter a plethora of brands of asafoetida on the shelves, whether it's in Chennai, Coimbatore or Madurai.

You can tell a surprising amount about the use of a particular spice in the cuisine of a region by looking at the size of the packaging. The packets of asafoetida are at least 100 grams in size, as opposed to, say, the 10-gram packets in North India. Plus, there are a slew of brand names that are never seen outside Tamil Nadu. LG may be the oldest, most venerable, best loved of all, but there are others like TT, PC and Chakra, each offering a choice between pure asafoetida and compound. By comparison, other states have tiny packets of the spice, and that too, available only under one or two brand names. In the north, although asafoetida is technically one of the substances allowed to be eaten in the strict Navratri fasts that occur twice a year, in practice, most orthodox observers of the fast do not use it because of the flour in it, and flour – as indeed any type of grain – is not allowed for these nine days.

When I came away from Bhatia's office-cum-godown in Khari Baoli, I brought back a fistful of his best grade of Iranian and Afghani hing that cost me a small fortune. In contrast, the stuff that is sold in the supermarket is about one-tenth the price, but also one-tenth the potency. While Afghani asafoetida is what we all are familiar with, the product of Iran is milder, with a faintly lemony aroma. But it takes a seasoned dealer like Bhatia to be able to discern the difference with just one sniff. At first, our household help couldn't figure out that only a tenth of the normal amount had to be used, and several dinners turned out to be inedible. Now, all she uses is a single grain, as small as a grain of sugar, and a vegetable dish for four persons becomes perfumed with the signature flavour that I have come to love.

KASHMIRI DUM ALOO

Without a doubt, Rajni Jinsi is the finest cook of Kashmiri food in the National Capital Region. She has magic in her hands. Most of the dishes cooked by her have the aroma of asafoetida, because she – indeed the entire Pandit community of Kashmir – uses no onions or garlic, so asafoetida plays a vital role in the cuisine.

INGREDIENTS

- 1 kg potatoes, medium-sized
- Mustard oil, for frying (approx. 350 ml)
- 4 cloves
- 3 tsp (heaped) Kashmiri chilli powder, mixed in 2½ tbsp thick yogurt to form a paste
- Kashmiri garam masala (one pinch each of cardamom powder, cumin powder and cinnamon powder)
- 2-inch cinnamon stick
- 1 tsp ginger powder
- 2½ tsp fennel powder
- 4 whole black cardamoms, crushed
- A generous pinch of asafoetida, dissolved in one tbsp of warm water
- A pinch of sugar
- Salt, to taste

METHOD

- Boil potatoes with the skin on till tender but not completely cooked. Cool them but do not put them under tap water (they tend to become stiff if you do). Peel them. Prick potatoes with a thin knitting needle. See that it goes all the way through. Prick each potato 10 times.

- Heat mustard oil in a kadhai until smoking hot. Slightly lower the flame and add potatoes, a few at a time, taking care not to crowd the kadhai. Give them space, so that they fry evenly. Slowly increase the flame, and keep turning, until the potatoes turn a dark golden brown. Keep repeating this step with each batch, till all the potatoes are fried evenly and are uniformly brown.
- Next, in a heavy-bottomed pan, put around 4½ tablespoons of the oil in which the potatoes were fried. Add the cloves, cardamom and cinnamon, all coarsely crushed, along with the asafoetida water and chilli powder mixed with yogurt.
- Keep stirring till the paste turns red and the yogurt is fully mixed in. Add a pinch of sugar.
- Add 3 cups of water, salt, fennel powder and ginger powder. Stir well, and add the potatoes to this mixture.
- Let the gravy simmer till the oil floats on the top. The colour should be bright red. For testing, break one potato to see if it is red on the inside. If not, add some more water and boil the potatoes till fully done.
- Finally add the Kashmiri garam masala, cover and simmer for 1–2 minutes before serving.

ATUL SIKAND'S MANGO AND HING PICKLE

INGREDIENTS

- 1 kg raw mangoes
- 1 tbsp asafoetida
- 4 tsp salt
- 3 tbsp red chilli powder (optional)
- 120 ml mustard oil

METHOD

- Peel and grate the mangoes. Do this with your grater set to coarse – you do not want a finely grated mush. Add salt. Spread in two large thalis (plates), cover with muslin cloth and keep out in the sun for two days.
- At the end of the second day, add all the other ingredients and your pickle is ready. Give it a day in the sun for all flavours to infuse.

Note: Unless your supply of asafoetida is exceptionally pure and hence strong, do not decrease the quantity in the pickle: When ground to a coarse powder, it will have a soft granular texture in the pickle.

KALPASI

Kalpasi is a mystery spice if there ever was one. Known by several names all over the country, its aroma is deep, dark and mysterious, and its flavour is as earthy as truffles. It is never, but never, displayed proudly in spice jars, no matter where in the country you go for reasons that eludes me completely.

This is the one spice that has eluded me for years. The first time I heard of it was in the early days of my career as a food writer. I had been sent on assignment to do a story on an ongoing Chettinad food festival at a hotel. The young chef, who was from Madurai, and I spoke about Chettinad ingredients for far longer than it took me to sample everything he sent out from his kitchen. I remember him telling me how long he had spent at the University of Chennai library poring over old texts trying to find the English name for kalpasi, but without success. A few years later, when I started to research this spice, the same feeling of helplessness took root in me. It is a challenge to find out more about this elusive spice when all I knew was its Tamil name. This was in the early days of Google searches, when most searches in regional languages came up empty.

I knew that a mysterious black flower was indispensable in Maharashtrian 'goda' masala – a special spice blend – so I walked up and down the Lalbaug Spice Market in Mumbai asking each and every dealer – and there are dozens – for 'black flower', but none of them knew what I was talking about because it's known as dagad phool in Maharashtra.

But that still didn't explain how I didn't see it as I peered into every last spice shop at Lalbaug, and spied every other spice except the one I was looking for! That's what I never understand: If people use it, why don't shops have a bit of it displayed prominently?

And that's not the only mystery surrounding kalpasi or dagad phool. There are several others. For one, its provenance is unknown to most dealers and chefs; for another, it doesn't have much in the way of a distinctive taste but rather a flavour whose perfume transforms a cooked dish without affecting the actual flavour profile of the dish to any great extent. In 2004, I was in a spice factory on the outskirts of Ahmedabad and saw a modest-sized bag of kalpasi. So what spice mix did they use it for, I asked them. Whereupon the senior management began to shift uncomfortably from one foot to the other, looking away sheepishly. It turned out that the spice cannot be declared to be free from inclusions, dust, etc. given the fact that it cannot be air-cleaned without damaging the delicate, papery tendrils. So the factory resorted to the simple expedient of using it in their garam masala but not mentioning it in the ingredients!

It's hardly known to the cooking public at large, but this rare spice has several names. It is a form of lichen but it's variously called stone flower and black stone flower in English. In Maharashtra, as I discovered, it is called dagad phool, kalahu in Kannada, riham karmani in Urdu, pathar phool in Hindi, kallupachi in Telugu and shaileyam in Sanskrit.

I'll start with Kalpasi because that is its Tamil name and its most 'famous' use is in Chettinad chicken. The inexplicable part about the spice is that most people are blissfully unaware of its existence, though they may be using it in a spice mix (like those who use the mix made in the Ahmedabad factory I visited). I even started carrying around a piece in my handbag which I'd show to people when they didn't seem to know what I was talking about. Many people would shake their heads uncomprehendingly, though it would finally transpire that they had used it in Maharashtrian goda masala, potli masala or eaten it in Chettinad chicken.

For the longest time, I tried to find out where exactly kalpasi came from. Spice sellers and chefs all had their own theories. The general consensus was that kalpasi formed spontaneously in the presence of a certain amount of moisture. From that point on, however, there was little agreement. One Delhi restaurateur told me that it was scraped from the sides of wells in Uttar Pradesh, and now that wells were not used very much, kalpasi was in danger of becoming extinct. A prominent spice dealer in Coimbatore told me that it was also called sea stone flower because it grew on partially submerged rocks in the sea. The effect of low tide followed by high tide, followed again by low tide, caused this flower to form. The only problem to this theory was that sniff as I might, there was no trace of iodine or salt in my kalpasi, which it most certainly would have if it had originated from the sea.

An interesting perspective was given to me by Kaveri G. Ahuja, an army wife who has travelled the length and breadth of the country due to various postings. When I gave her my tiny jar to identify, she took a deep sniff and exclaimed, 'It smells like a Ladakhi monastery!' Once she pointed it out, I took another sniff and realized she was right. So, of course, I went and collected samples of fragrant powders that are used in family altars and monasteries in Ladakh. The only problem was, that it was just that: fine powder, and it is difficult to say whether or not kalpasi is one of the ingredients. Shopkeepers in Leh willingly disclosed the ingredients of this powder, but all the names were local: sandalwood powder and nagkesar (oil extracted from the seeds of the *Mesua ferrea* tree) were all that I was able to translate. Havan samagri – the mixture of naturally scented herbs that are used to fuel the fire that is lit during a North-Indian puja to purify the air – uses kalpasi, which is why a Delhi-based spice dealer claims that the spice is not used in food in Delhi or Punjab. His theory is that nothing that is burnt in a sacred fire is suitable for using in food.

After months of hunting for the origins of kalpasi; or indeed any more verifiable information on it, I met Dr S.K. Subramanian, reader in the Department of Botany, Madurai Kamaraj University, who has actually done his doctorate on algae that includes, among other things, lichens.

He told me that there are three kinds of lichens: those that hang and are called pendant, those that grow on stone and those that grow on tree trunks.Like mushrooms, only some lichens are edible; others are poisonous and still others are neither edible nor poisonous. Reindeer and musk ox, for instance, consume the fleshy pendant lichens that grow in the Arctic region that are called *Cladonia rangiferina*. What's more, lichens grow spontaneously, and cannot be cultivated. Not unlike truffles, lichens too require very precise habitats for growth: they grow spontaneously in the presence of precise conditions. They grow only in pollution-free atmospheres, at an altitude of 4,000 feet above sea level, in cool climes where plenty of moisture is present. They form spontaneously on the trunks of trees and the sides of buildings, but not on rocks that jut out of the sea! Indeed, according to Dr Subramanian, European governments study the trees that grow on the sides of highways and the presence of lichens confirms that the air is unpolluted. No growth of lichens means that the government has to swing into action to supply cleaner fuel or to legislate more rigorous anti-pollution measures for vehicles. Subsequently, whenever I have seen forests where lichens grow, they have been far away from roads with vehicular traffic and can be said to be free from pollution.

Parmotrema, the genus that *Parmotrema perlatum* or kalpasi belongs to, is usually flat, leaf-like, lobed, and attached to bark of trees and rocks. Lichens are capable of storing a starch-like carbohydrate that makes it useful for human food, though most of them are highly unpalatable. You cannot, for instance, pluck kalpasi off the tree and pop it into the cooking pot. They have to be neutralized of their acid content, by soaking in a weak solution of sodium or potassium, before being dried. In Tamil Nadu alone, lichen grows in the forests around Ooty, Yercaud and Kodaikanal: all upland regions. In Kerala, it is picked from the forest of Thekkady, and in Maharashtra, the forests of the Western Ghats yield rich pickings. I'm sure many other states that have optimum conditions for their growth have their own source of this spice. It is said to be collected by the tribals who live in these forests, who then sell it to a middle-man from where it makes its way to the market. Perhaps one reason for the mystery surrounding kalpasi is because, along with a fistful of other spices, the commercial use of it often does not pass muster with the Prevention of Food Adulteration Department, since it does not lend itself to the kind of cleaning that is required for a ISO 9001 certification.

To match its mysterious origins, kalpasi, dagad phool or patthar ka phool, whatever one may call it, is mysterious even when being in food. It is the ultimate secret weapon of the traditional cook. Add a pinch of it in a meat or chicken dish and you'll get a deep, undefinable flavour. But, be warned: add too much and the dish will be bitter and the smell too overpowering for enjoyment. It is known that kalpasi is warming to the system, releases its aroma slowly and can also cause food to turn black, which is why it is sometimes used in conjunction with roasted and powdered chana dal. This trick is a favourite of caterers and cooks in Hyderabad and is especially used in shorba and nihari.

The most famous use for this spice is undoubtedly Chettinad chicken, the one dish of the Chettiar community that has catapulted the entire cuisine to fame. There are distressingly few clues about why this spice has become so integral to Chettinad cuisine, but I personally feel that the male members of the community probably saw the use of star anise and kalpasi from their extended travels in South-East Asia. Travel around Chennai and keep your eyes peeled for local restaurants, and you'll notice that a high proportion of them will advertise that they serve Chettinad cuisine. Most don't, but the very name strikes a certain amount of awe in passers-by. The cuisine is a masterful blend of Tamil culinary traditions, overlaid with influences of those Asian countries like Burma (now Myanmar) and Sri Lanka where the menfolk went to trade for centuries. Unlike many other cuisines found in pockets of Tamil Nadu, this one is proudly meat and poultry based. Many restaurants that do serve Chettinad cuisine manage to botch it up by using fists full of chillies and little else. However, many believe that the key ingredient which gives Chettinad chicken its characteristic dark, forest-like taste is kalpasi.

Dr Subramanian tells me that packets of chicken or mutton masala, sold at modest rates in markets in Madurai, contain a teaspoon of poppy seeds, a couple of cloves, a stick or two of cinnamon and a pinch of kalpasi. The common man buys it for his Sunday curry. It is not the exact spicing of a Chettinad pepper chicken, but because Madurai is close enough to the Chettinad region, it's the one city in the state whose cuisine has a distinct resemblance to Chettinad flavours.

However, acclaimed author Meenakshi Meyyappan, a Chettiar herself, stoutly denies that Chettinad chicken calls for the addition of kalpasi. At least, in her rather famous hostelry, The Bangala, in Karaikudi, one of the many villages in the Chettinad region, she has neither seen nor used the spice. The Bangala is so renowned for its cuisine, which is somewhere between catered and home-style food, that tourists often make a special detour to the village just for it. The truth seems to be something akin to the relationship between Punjabi food as cooked in people's homes and that served by restaurants throughout the country. Few residents of Amritsar or Ludhiana would cook butter chicken or dal makhni in their homes and even fewer restaurants would serve baingan bharta and aloo parathas to their diners. It is the same with Chettinad food: The home-style version is a world apart from what you get to sample at restaurants.

Kalpasi is also used in Hyderabadi cookery. The most

famous dish in the repertoire that uses kalpasi is chakna – a stew of animal entrails that is a specialty of Hyderabadi Muslims. Kalpasi is the distinctive flavour in the stew that is described as 'a poor man's treat' – strongly spiced, and often washed down with arrack, the local country liquor that rickshaw-pullers favour. In fact, chakna is made extra spicy by arrack sellers to make their customers thirsty and thus drink more: the oldest trick in the book. Kalpasi has the specific purpose of cancelling some of the sharp tastes of the organ meats in this dish and is the single top-note of spice in chakna.

Then there's the goda masala, a common ingredient of Maharashtrian cuisine. It is the only recorded use of kalpasi that I've come across to go into a distinctly vegetarian spice blend. Goda masala is typically used by Maharashtra's Brahmin community in amtis or dals and vegetables cooked in a gravy. The mix contains finely grated dried coconut, sesame seeds, bay leaf, whole red chillies, dagad phool, cumin, coriander, cinnamon, nagkesar and peppercorns – all lightly toasted and pounded together. In Pune, being a Maharashtrian Brahmin stronghold, I knew I would find goda masala in some of the signature dishes, but even I was staggered at the sheer amount of dagad phool in the amti at ordinary wayside eateries. One, in particular, specializes in Brahmin thalis and claims that their version of goda masala is made on the premises, in quantities that would suffice for a year.

Goda masala is ubiquitous in the spice shops in Pune. The now separate PY Vaidya and RP Vaidya – venerable spice shops with branches at prominent locations – Pravin Masala and K-Pra all sell goda masala, but the Pune Brahmin community is nothing if not fastidious about quality and takes pride in grinding it at home. One friend, now getting on in years, buys the ingredients herself, and gently broils them while her son rolls out the family mortar and pestle, an all-iron monster, far too heavy to lift off the ground. It is pressed into service just once a year, and that too, just for goda masala, so it is important to the cuisine. Another friend is content to grind the components in her Moulinex mixer and a third friend sends the family retainer to the mill to grind sacks of rice, flour, chillies alongside the goda masala. In true Maharashtrian fashion, it is done in summer, just before the monsoon, and stored for the rest of the year.

In Lucknow, potli masala would be incomplete without a tiny pinch of kalpasi, but ask any true-blue chef from Lucknow, and he'll deftly change the subject. Potli masala is arguably India's most complex spice blend, using approximately 20 spices in varying quantities. Chef Ashfaque Qureshi, son of the legendary chef, Imtiaz Qureshi, tells me that there is no single recipe for potli masala, but every serious cook has his own formula. Usually, it is a mix of such obscure spices as nausadar, pan ki jadh, khus ki jadh, kebab chini, sandalwood powder, rose petals, star khatai, jarakus and hadh in addition to cloves, black and green cardamom, peppercorns, cumin, coriander, fennel, dry ginger, black cumin, stone flower, cinnamon, fenugreek, sweet attar, dry coconut, bay leaf and saffron.

The reason why the story of spice is such a fascinating one is because of the varied pattern of usage of many spices. Kalpasi is a prime example. It is used, on the one hand, to moderate the rather overpowering odours of organ meats in Hyderabadi chakna, as a defining flavour in Chettinad chicken (though that is debatable), as an infinitesimal speck in potli masala, and also sneaks its way into the cuisine of an avowedly Brahmin community, where it is used, quite prominently, to add a bold note to something as bland as dal. While, all the time, staying resolutely out of sight of people: they may have tasted it or even cooked with it but would not be able to recognize it or identify it in a market!

CHETTINAD PEPPER CHICKEN

Lata Aachi is the finest home cook I know. She is an expert in many of the regional cuisines of Tamil Nadu, as well as Andhra Pradesh and Karnataka. This is her 'showpiece' recipe when guests need to be wowed.

INGREDIENTS

- 3½ tbsp sesame oil
- 3–4 green cardamoms
- 4–5 cloves
- 1–2 pcs kalpasi
- 1 star anise
- 1-inch cinnamon stick
- 1½ tbsp black pepper, freshly crushed
- 400 g onions, chopped
- 3½ tbsp ginger-garlic paste
- 400 g tomatoes, chopped
- 2 tsp red chilli powder
- 2 tbsp coriander powder
- 1 tsp turmeric powder
- 10–12 curry leaves
- 2 tbsp ghee
- 800 g chicken

- Coriander leaves, to garnish
- Salt, to taste

METHOD

- Heat sesame oil in a heavy-bottomed pan. Add whole spices and sauté for a few seconds.
- Add chopped onion and cook until golden brown.
- Add ginger-garlic paste and cook until the raw aroma is gone.
- Add tomatoes, chilli powder, coriander powder, turmeric powder and salt. Cook until oil rises to the top.
- Add chicken and stir-fry until almost cooked. Add water for desired consistency. Mix and cook until chicken is completely cooked.
- Check seasoning. Finish with ghee and fresh coriander leaves. Serve hot.

SEED SPICES

Fenugreek

I once spent a day in Athens, showing a little stash of fenugreek seeds to shop owners in the main market. Though there were plenty of cinnamon sticks and other aromatic spices, I drew a blank with the seeds that I had carefully carried along from home. (It is far easier, in my opinion, to say, 'Do you have this?' in sign language rather than to attempt to converse with people with whom you don't share a common tongue.) My little collection drew surprise and even admiration, but nobody had ever seen anything like fenugreek seeds. I was surprised. After all, my research said that the spice originated in Greece several centuries ago. But today, it seems to have vanished altogether from the country.

This is a common problem when you embark on tracing the origins of a spice. Most of the agricultural plants we are familiar with today have been in existence for millennia, though not as cultivated plants, but as wild ones. Today, all we can do is guess the approximate geographical area where the earliest plant of a particular genus might have been found. It is a fascinating 'hunt the slipper' sort of puzzle, in which, among a set of clues, one or two are designed to throw you off track. In the case of fenugreek or *Trigonella foenum-graecum*, to give it its Latin name, it appears to be the very name that is misleading. In the Greek language, *fenu* means hay and *greek*, one would presume, means that the earliest strains of the plant were found in Greece. But, as I recently discovered, all traces of the spice appear to have vanished from that country. What is more likely is, that being a wild, uncultivated plant, it was fed to horses and cattle along with hay – a use that the Romans continued once they brought it back from Greece. In fact, it does not seem to have ever been considered as food for humans in Greece; that connection seems to have been made once it travelled out of the country.

The best any biologist can say with certainty is that fenugreek first made its appearance in the Eastern Mediterranean. The earliest evidence of fenugreek seeds was found at an archaeological site in Iraq. The finds were carbon dated to 4000 BCE. Much later, fenugreek seeds were found in the tomb of Tutankhamun, in Egypt, which dates back to 1323 BCE. However, like all spices, indeed, all agricultural products, it is easy to grow them elsewhere, and so, today, India is the world's leading producer of this spice, with just Rajasthan weighing in with three-quarters of the country's crop. Early on in my quest of discovering spices, I encountered a curious laddoo in a well-known shop in Jaipur made with equal parts of methi seed (fenugreek's Hindi name) and powdered almonds alongside the divine ghewar, peda and barfi. When I asked the shopkeeper about it, he informed me that particular this confection was usually bought for nursing mothers, as fenugreek seeds are one of nature's galactagogues – a substance that increases breast milk production. That was my very first encounter with a spice used as an ingredient in a mithai, though it was far from being the last. I must say that the rather rank appeal of the confection was lost on me. It will be a long time before I can be persuaded to try another fenugreek laddoo.

There actually is a way of cooking with fenugreek seeds, so that there is no bitterness. The secret comes from

Rajasthan, the origin of most of India's crop, and the state that uses the spice in everything from mutton to vegetables, dal dumplings (*mangodis*), papads, pickles and mathris. Apparently, when a handful of the seeds are soaked prior to cooking, a layer of mucus forms around them. If you use your imagination a bit, you could possibly refer to it as a mucilaginous sac. Well, according to microbiologist Sangeeta Khanna, the Rajasthanis call it a stomach! According to their ancient wisdom, as long as you don't 'rupture the stomach' of the fenugreek, but take care to pour it out carefully into the cooking pot, the bitterness of the endosperm will be absorbed by the mucilaginous seed coat as long as it is not ruptured during cooking.

But fenugreek, or methi, is not just popular in Rajasthan; it is one of the most commonly used spices in Indian cuisine, right after the Big Four, and owes much of its importance to its medicinal value. In fact, after turmeric, fenugreek seeds have the highest medicinal effect of all the commonly used spices. It is used as a digestive; it has the near-magical ability to control blood sugar, since it's hypoglycaemic in nature. The seeds are also used as a kitchen remedy to control phlegm in the respiratory tract, to help increase milk production in lactating mothers because of their high calcium content (as much as 40 per cent), to cure cough, and even to increase potency.

In our family, we go through industrial quantities of powdered fenugreek seeds. I take it powdered first thing in the morning to control my cholesterol and blood sugar; my husband takes it because he suffers from sinusitis, my son takes it when he's been making too many trips to the chaat shop and needs something to soothe his stomach and my daughter soaks the powder in yogurt and uses it in her hair. About the only thing we don't do with this panacea is cook with it as a spice, because it is not widely used in Kashmiri food. But, of course, we ingest it when we eat pickles, because no matter what part of the country you belong to, pickles always, but always, use fenugreek.

Our family is hardly unique. I have Tamil Brahmin friends who soak the seeds overnight in milk, add a drop of curd to it, and consume this first thing in the morning. Others soak the seeds in water and drink the water with the seeds. Still others sprout fenugreek seeds and either eat them first thing in the morning or piecemeal throughout the day, in salads or as a vegetable. In Ayurveda, it is believed that fenugreek plays a part in reducing the *vata* element in the body that produces symptoms like joint pains and heaviness in the digestive tract. In fact, had fenugreek been marketed as well as, say, aloe vera, I have no doubt it would also have been on your dressing table, among the pots of cream and lotion, because it does wonders for one's hair too.

Like coriander, fenugreek is a seed spice, and like coriander, its foliage too is used widely in our cooking. Fresh fenugreek leaves are used as a vegetable and when dry, they are used for flavouring curries.

In fact, fenugreek is so versatile that its multifarious uses vary drastically from cuisine to cuisine within the country. Take the Muslim community of UP, especially Lucknow, for instance, who cannot imagine cooking fish without fenugreek seeds. The seeds are first soaked in water and the water is then used to prepare a paste with ginger and garlic. Coriander powder, turmeric and chilli powder are added and aamchur is used at the end as a souring agent.

And as for dried fenugreek leaves, most Indians use what is branded as 'Kasuri methi' as a flavouring agent.What they usually don't know is the interesting story behind why fenugreek is marketed under that name. There is a town called Kasur 55 kilometres south-east of Lahore. Besides being the burial place of poet-philosopher Bulleh Shah, its claim to fame is that the world's best fenugreek comes from there. So when we're buying Kasuri methi at our local supermarket, are we actually buying leaves from Kasur? Of course not. Like 'Multani mitti', another misnomer, what is being acknowledged on those 'Kasuri methi' packets is the excellence of the spice from Kasur. Perhaps the finest use of dried fenugreek leaves is in Kashmir, where they are combined with the chopped stomach and intestine of sheep in a fabulous dish called methi maaz. While cooking it, the strong smell of the intestines and the sheer labour of preparing them for the table (I won't divulge more – none of it is particularly pleasant) hardly prepares you for the moment when dried fenugreek leaves are sprinkled over the organ meats over a low flame. In a trice, what was a most unpleasant smelling dish is transformed completely. The expression 'marriage made in heaven' was probably invented with this combination in mind!

Occasionally, a pinch of dried fenugreek leaves are crushed between thumb and forefinger and sprinkled on an almost finished dish of rogan josh, chicken, potatoes or tomato chutney in the valley. The principle is the same as sprinkling fresh coriander leaves atop a finished dish, but it is nowhere as classic or as distinctive as in methi maaz, where fenugreek is the single most important seasoning.

Sometimes, the bitterness of fenugreek seeds is used to counteract the sweetness of a vegetable. Most Punjabis will cook pumpkin (kaddu) with no other spice except fenugreek in addition to turmeric and chilli powder, to cut through the sweetness of the vegetable. It's the same in Bihar as well, yet in UP, the thought of anything but cumin and coriander powder in combination with pumpkin is anathema. I myself am partial to pumpkin soured with tomatoes and spiced with cumin, coriander, turmeric and chilli powder. For me, the inherent sweetness of the vegetable is offset by the sourness of the tomatoes, even without the addition of methi.

In Karnataka, the Kodava version of pumpkin curry, too, uses fenugreek seeds instead of cumin, but it uses two sweet ingredients – coconut and jaggery – in addition to turmeric. Fenugreek seeds are also a vital part of kadhi, the curd-based gravy that is eaten with rice as a light, easy-to-digest meal in the north, especially on Tuesdays when many in North India observe a no-meat day. In Punjab, there is no pickle that is made without fenugreek, which is always in combination with carom seeds and fennel. And in Bihar, Odisha and Bengal, there are different versions of panch phoron (or five-spice), but the one spice that goes into each of them is fenugreek.

In the cooking of Tamil Nadu, on the other hand, fenugreek seeds are used in conjunction with mustard seeds and asafoetida for all dishes that have a tamarind base, of which sambar is the most common example. Fenugreek seeds are used in conjunction with curd as well, as I've seen in the simple, home-style preparation that is called moru kachiyathu in Kerala. Here, fenugreek seeds are sautéed with green chillies, cumin, turmeric and mustard seeds. Beaten curd is added and is cooked on the slowest possible flame, stirring all the time. It is very like the North Indian kadhi, but the only difference is that kadhi uses gram flour as a thickening agent, while moru kachiyathu uses long, slow cooking. Each tiny variation in spicing of Kerala's fish curries is known by a different name – meen manga curry, vattichathu, vevichathu, pollichathu, varutharacha, mullagattada and so on. Meen vevichathu, a deep carmine curry, soured with tamarind, makes use of fenugreek seeds, turmeric and chillies. In the Syrian Christian community of Kerala, where this fish dish originates, it is believed that the methi holds the fillets of fish together and prevents them from flaking.

At the other end of the country, the minuscule Muslim population of Shimla and its surrounding areas makes a fenugreek pulao. They soak 250 grams of methi seeds overnight, fry them in ghee and combine this with rice: an unusual preparation that I haven't come across anywhere else. But a similar use of it is in Coorg, where the iconic pandhi curry – Coorg's famous pork preparation – is eaten with balls of coarsely ground rice to which powdered fenugreek seeds are sometimes added. Idiyappam – those large idlis seemingly made of metres and metres of thread – too have methi seeds added to them in a very fixed, immutable proportion.

Another country, besides India, that uses fenugreek

perhaps as much as we do is Iran. There is not a market or shopping centre in that country that does not have a whiff of fenugreek. The reason is not far to seek: khoresh or stew, roughly analogous to our curry, and rice is the mainstay of an Iranian meal. And one of the best-loved varieties is the one that features ghormeh sabzi: a mixture of greens such as spring onion tops, parsley, coriander and, above all, fenugreek leaves. All the leaves are coarsely chopped and cooked with some onions and a bit of mutton and then served with rice. The fragrance is unmistakable and always reminds me of home.

ANUPAMA MICHAEL'S SPROUTED FENUGREEK SEED RECIPE

Anupama Michael is a hobby cook who keeps her eyes peeled for healthy, nutritious recipes that are tasty and easy to cook as well.

INGREDIENTS

- 330 g sprouted fenugreek seeds (rinsed and drained)
- ½ tsp mustard seeds
- 2 pinches of asafoetida powder
- Curry leaves, to taste
- 1 big onion, finely chopped
- 1-inch ginger, finely chopped
- 1 tsp red chilli powder
- ½ tsp turmeric powder
- 1 tsp jaggery powder
- Salt, to taste
- 2–3 tsp coconut, grated

- Juice of ½ lemon
- Coriander leaves, for garnish

METHOD

- In a non-stick kadai, take a tsp of oil (I normally use sesame oil). Add mustard seeds.
- After they splutter, add asafoetida, curry leaves, finely chopped onion and sauté on low flame till the onions turn pink.
- Add the chopped ginger and sauté for a minute or so.
- Add the sprouted fenugreek seeds, red chilli powder, turmeric powder, jaggery powder, salt and mix well. Cover and allow to cook in its steam for 10–15 minutes while stirring occasionally (else the jaggery may stick to the pan).
- When done, add grated coconut and coriander leaves, cook for 2 more minutes. Turn off the gas and add lemon juice and mix well. Serve hot.

RUKIYA MUKADAM'S METHI PORRIDGE

In the vast Reshi clan, the cousin that I am closest to, is married into a family from Ratnagiri. This is how they start their fast before sunrise, during the month of Ramadan. Fenugreek seeds are said to have low glycaemic index, so one does not feel too hungry early in the day – an important consideration while you fast.

INGREDIENTS

- 2 tbsp fenugreek seeds, pounded
- ½ cup semolina
- ½ cup milk
- 1 cup water
- Jaggery, to taste (1–2 tbsp)
- 1 tbsp ghee

METHOD

- Heat ghee, add semolina and braise over low heat till it becomes pale brown.
- Add pounded fenugreek, water, milk and jaggery and cook till the liquid is absorbed.
- To make every grain of semolina dry, put the covered cooking pot on a tawa on the lowest heat for 15 minutes.

DANA METHI MURGH

Before he became the executive chef of the Intercontinental Hotel, Chennai, Chef Manpreet travelled widely around Rajasthan, picking up as much as he could about Rajasthani food from private homes, villages, roadside eateries and wherever else he could. The one dish that struck him was this one, in which fenugreek is used in generous quantities, making it very healthy. The other spices are bit players on the stage, but fenugreek is the hero, undoubtedly.

INGREDIENTS

- 4 tbsp fenugreek seeds (soaked for 30 minutes)
- 500 g chicken
- 2 tbsp oil
- ½ tsp asafoetida
- 10–12 long green chillies (chopped)
- 2 tsp red chilli powder
- ¾ tsp turmeric powder
- Salt, to taste
- ½ tsp fennel
- 100 ml yogurt
- 2 tsp coriander powder
- 1 tsp aamchur powder
- Onion, chopped
- Garlic, minced

METHOD

- Boil fenugreek seeds for 5 minutes.
- Heat oil in a pan, add asafoetida to it.
- Add in the green chillies and remaining dry spices to it.
- Cook for 2 minutes.
- Add boiled fenugreek seeds to the pan and cook until the oil separates.
- In separate pan, heat oil, temper fennel, add onions sauté till golden brown.
- Add chopped garlic, and sauté, add spices and chicken, simmer for a while, till the chicken gets cooked.
- Add yogurt and mix the cooked fenugreek seeds and the chicken.
- Simmer till chicken is done.
- Garnish with fresh coriander leaves.

CHEF RANVEER BRAR'S FENUGREEK YOGURT PANNA COTTA

INGREDIENTS

- 170 g fresh cream
- 100 g yogurt
- 3 tbsp honey
- ½ tsp gelatin
- 1 tsp fenugreek seeds

METHOD

- Lightly toast the fenugreek seeds till they smell nutty.
- Boil the cream with the fenugreek and add honey towards the end.
- Strain the fenugreek seeds out and then add the yogurt.
- Soften the gelatin and after melting it add it to the yogurt mixture.
- Pour into glasses and serve as desired.

SALMOLI MUKERJI'S MASOOR DAL WITH METHI

Salmoli is a hobby cook, communications advisor, frequent flyer and publisher, and the one thing she suffers from is a lack of time. However, when she does enter her kitchen, it is to cook dishes which have a Bengali sensibility, yet are quick and fuss-free.

INGREDIENTS

- 250 g masoor dal (pink gram)
- 1 tsp vegetable oil
- 1 tsp fenugreek seeds
- 2 whole dry red chillies
- Green chillies, slit, to taste
- 1 tsp ghee
- Salt and sugar, to taste
- 3 cups water

METHOD

- Boil dal in a big pot with 3 cups of water and salt to taste for about 15–20 minutes till soft and well cooked. Set aside.
- In a pan, heat oil and add the fenugreek seeds and two whole red chillies till they start smelling aromatic.
- Pour into the boiled dal and mix well, add salt to taste and a little sugar and bring it to a boil again.
- Just before switching off the heat, add the ghee and slit green chillies to taste.

Mustard

If there was ever an award for the most secular of spices, mustard would have a strong case going for it. It is one of those rare spices that has been referred to in the scriptures of almost every major religion. Gautam Buddha asked a grieving mother to bring him a handful of mustard seeds from the house where nobody had ever died, to show her the folly of crying over a dead son in a world where every household has seen death. The Quran assures us that even the equivalent of a mustard seed will be accounted for on the Day of Judgement. The Torah compares the knowable universe to the size of a mustard seed and there are no fewer than five different instances in the New Testament where mustard seeds are referred to.

And, while all spices have their origins in antiquity, mustard is thought to be one of the oldest, having been found at pre-historic sites ranging from Europe to China. Pythagoras (570–495 BCE) used a poultice of mustard seeds as a cure for scorpion bites, while Hippocrates (460–370 BCE) praised the efficacy of mustard paste in healing aches and pains.

According to K.T. Achaya, author of the monumental *A Historical Dictionary of Indian Food*, *Brassica juncea* (brown Indian mustard) was found carbonized at the site of Chanhudaro, a part of the Indus Civilization, and can be dated to 1500 BCE. Early Sanskrit literature also mentions it, though for written references of mustard oil pressed in India, we have to turn to the *Arthashastra*, written around 500 BCE.

Even the name mustard has origins in the ancient world. The term does not have anything to do with the genus of the plant, Brassica, which includes cauliflower, broccoli, turnips and cabbage. Instead, the name is derived from the preparation that has been made in Europe since Roman times by the addition of freshly fermented wine (*mustum*) to the pungent (*ardens*) seeds, which leads one to wonder what the plant was called before that time.

In India, mustard is hardly the most assertive of spices as far as cooking is concerned in most parts of the country, unlike the West where, next to black or white pepper, it is the second most widely used spice, mainly as a condiment. The world's largest producer of mustard is Canada; other countries include USA, Germany, Czech Republic, Nepal, Russia and Ukraine, with India, Pakistan and Bangladesh producing relatively small amounts, and using it more as a cooking oil than a spice. Mustard is characterized by that peculiar nose-tingling pungency that is quite different from the pungency of chillies and black pepper, but more akin to horseradish and wasabi.

Mustard comes in three colours – yellow, brown and black – and is graded by pungency according to colour: yellow being the least pungent, black the most. Each colour has its own characteristic size, with black being the largest and brown the smallest. Interestingly enough, mustard seeds have little aroma when whole or even ground. The spice releases its trademark pungency when its two components – myrosinase and sinigrin – come into contact with a liquid: water, vinegar, wine or even beer! It takes 15 minutes for the full flavour of soaked mustard to develop, so if you want instant results, add milk, not water, and never hot water. Hot water retards the potency of mustard, so adding cold water is mandatory if you want the full punch of flavour. After 15 minutes or so, however, the pungency starts to decline. This can be delayed by adding an acidic element, which is why the French add vinegar to their Dijon mustard .

If there's one community in India that is inextricably linked to mustard, it's the Bengalis. According to Chef Sharad Dewan of The Park, Kolkata, Bengalis are the only Indian community to eat mustard in both its forms – as a spice as well as a condiment, not to mention cooking almost everything they eat in mustard oil. They eat the whole seed as shorshe bata, where the seed is ground till it becomes a fine paste as well as kashundi – a pounded paste to which a bit of vinegar has been added: The Bengali version of the French Dijon mustard and just as addictive, especially alongside breaded, fried fish.

All over Bengal, mustard is pounded before being added to the cooking pot, whereas in most other states, it is used whole as a tempering. So elemental is shorshe bata to the cuisine that a couple of enterprising local brands like Cookme package it to make life easier. However, old habits in Bengal really do die hard, as I learn quickly. For Salmoli Mukerji and her husband – a young, thirty-something power couple based in Kolkata – like most young working professionals these days, coming home from work at 11 p.m. is not uncommon. You would think that they would be sitting ducks for every household shortcut known to man, but even to them using ready-powdered mustard seeds is unthinkable. They only buy whole seeds – part of which they use in that signature Bengali five-spice mix, panch phoron –

and have them ground on the shil nora, Bengal's version of the sil batta, or batan. They assure me that they are hardly unique in their city: The average home-cook, no matter how harried, considers five minutes of grinding mustard well worth the value addition it makes to fish curries.

On the other hand, kashundi, an accompaniment to snacks, is almost always store-bought. In Kolkata, there at least three different brands of kashundi including Elmac, Druk and Tai. However, it is the unbranded ones that are preferred. There is one that is sold in half-litre brandy bottles that you'll see on most dining tables in private homes.

But surprisingly, for a community that loves its mustard, the leaves of the plant are rarely consumed in West Bengal. In contrast, mustard leaves (sarson ka saag) is the ultimate Punjabi winter treat. North India, as a whole, does not use mustard in cooking to any significant extent, except for rai, the smaller, brown version of mustard seeds. The larger, dark mustard seeds are preferred in Bengal, Maharashtra, Assam, Odisha, and most of South India. Even then, rai is used mostly in modest quantities, usually only for tempering. In Gujarat, dhokla is always sprinkled over with rai; in UP, patod, a besan dish, also has rai sprinkled over it. Patod, a dish made with colocasia leaves and besan, can be found in most Indian cuisines albeit with slightly different names. While the names may vary, along with the main ingredients depending upon the community and the geographical area, surprisingly, the dish is always cooked with the same spicing. Besan, according to ancient wisdom, is a heavy ingredient and needs a digestive agent to balance it out and this is where mustard comes into the picture. Since it's an extremely good digestive agent, it is always an integral part of patod.

In Kashmir, rai, known as javed, is used exclusively for pickles, in combination with ajwain, known as asur.Referred to in the same breath as javed-asur, about a teaspoon is used by the average Kashmiri in the entire year, and that too, only if they make their own pickles, so far is it from the cuisine. There is one theory in the valley that fish dishes can be given a hint of sourness by sprinkling raw rai over the almost finished dish, bringing it to the boil, and then taking it off the fire. My sister-in-law, Shafiqa, the best cook in the Reshi clan, swears that this is her secret ingredient, but I myself have never heard of this being a general practice.

Unlike North India and Maharashtra, black mustard seeds are used ubiquitously in the five South Indian states: Telangana, Andhra Pradesh, Kerala, Tamil Nadu and Karnataka, to temper each and every single dish except biryani.

Tamil Brahmin Chitra Narayanan uses mustard seeds in conjunction with methi seeds and hing for all her tamarind-based dishes. She makes a pachadi (which I can only describe as a Tamil Nadu raita) with curd as its base, to which she adds coconut and a generous quantity of mustard seeds that have been ground in an electric grinder. This is the only instance I've encountered where uncooked mustard seeds have made their way into a dish, besides the kashundi of Bengal.

The ultra simple moru kachiyathu or mor kuzhambu, depending whether you are speaking in Malayalam or Tamil, also has curd as its base, though this version is cooked the way kadhi is cooked. Mustard seeds go into this one too, accompanied by methi, zeera and haldi. And while sambar has mustard seeds in a tempering along with a whole red chilli and methi powder, rasam uses mustard seeds too, though along with zeera, black pepper and chillies. The other way mustard seed is consumed across the country is of course, through mustard oil: The cold pressed, strongly-flavoured oil that has never been marketed as successfully as its Western cousin, olive oil. Its strong, distinctive taste stands up to Indian spices and its ability to withstand high heat makes it ideal for Indian cooking. Apart from Bengal, only Kashmir and Himachal Pradesh have a pronounced use of mustard oil. In my home in Kashmir, we typically heat the oil to smoking point once a week, and then store it for later use. Without this smoking process, mustard oil has a rather bitter edge, and tends to catch the back of one's throat. While no self-respecting Kashmiri would use mustard oil without bringing it to smoking point, there are several dishes in Bengal that rely on the pungency of 'raw' mustard oil for their appeal. One such is posto bata – ground poppy seeds flavoured with pungent mustard oil and occasionally, green chillies. As marriages go, this one is an exceptionally fiery one!

But the prize for the most eye-watering mustard preparation, in my opinion, goes to the Dogras of Jammu. Jyoti Singh, artist, sculptor and daughter of Maharajah Karan Singh of the erstwhile Jammu and Kashmir princely state, served me a stunning potatoes-and-curd-based dish in her villa that overlooks the Dal Lake in Srinagar. The colour was a sunny custard yellow, to which mustard seeds, crushed in a mortar and pestle or a food processor, had been added. The curd itself had been kept out in the sun for a couple of hours so that its pungency had increased exponentially. This sour, fermented appeal reminded me of Korean food.

While all spices are ancient, mustard seems to be so steeped in antiquity that no scientist is sure exactly which country it originated in. All we know is that besides being mentioned in the world's religious books, a feat it doesn't share with too many kitchen ingredients, it grows in every continent, is used as a spice, a medicine, an oil and a condiment and has a large number of 'relatives' like turnip and radish.

The last word on mustard has to be my friend Sangeeta Khanna's: 'Mustard is used all over the world because of its ability to increase digestion. So strong is the action of these tiny seeds that even grinding them and using them in a poultice on the skin can increase your metabolic rate. How many other kitchen ingredients can do that?'

CHEF VINEET BHATIA'S MUSTARD INFUSED CHICKEN TIKKA

Michelin-starred Chef Vineet Bhatia's legendary reputation precedes him. This is his signature mustard infused chicken tikka recipe.

INGREDIENTS

- 8 pcs of 40 g chicken tikka, cut from the boneless breast

1st Marinade:

- ½ tbsp ginger paste
- ½ tbsp garlic paste
- 1 tsp lemon juice
- Salt, to taste

2nd Marinade:

- 4 tbsp thick yogurt
- 1 tbsp vegetable oil
- 1 tsp mustard seeds
- 1 sprig curry leaves
- 1 tsp turmeric powder
- 1 tsp green chillies, chopped
- 1 tbsp grainy mustard paste
- Salt, to taste

METHOD

- In a bowl, marinate the chicken with the first marinade. Allow it to rest for 20 minutes.
- In a pan, heat the vegetable oil and add the mustard seeds. As they begin to pop, add the curry leaves, turmeric powder and chopped green chillies. Sauté for 30 seconds and pour this oil on to the chicken.
- Rub this flavoured oil into the chicken.
- Spoon the thick yogurt and the grainy mustard paste on to the chicken, mix them together. Check the seasoning and leave in the refrigerator for 6 hours to marinate.
- Thread the chicken on to skewers and roast in a preheated oven at 190°C for 12 minutes.
- Baste with left over marinade.
- Remove from the oven, rest for 2 minutes and serve.

CHEF SOUMYA GOSWAMI'S SHORSHE BATA MAACH

This recipe is ideally for rohu fish, but any fish can be used. It takes about 20 minutes or so to cook.

INGREDIENTS

- 800 g fish, ideally rohu, cut into medium-sized pieces
- 3 tbsp mustard seeds

- 2 tsp turmeric powder
- 2 green chillies
- Mustard oil to fry the fish plus 2 tbsp for making the gravy
- 2 to 3 cups of water
- Salt, to taste

Preparing the fish:

- Ask your fishmonger to cut darnes of a rohu around 1.2 kilogram in weight. If the fish pieces are too big they will break while frying or cooking, so make sure the pieces are not too big.
- Also make sure the fish scales are trimmed. Fishmongers usually trim the scales and leave the skin on the fish.

METHOD

- Soak the black mustard seeds in warm water for 2 hours.
- After the mustard seeds are swollen and soft, add the green chillies and use a sheel nora, Bengali stone grinder, to make a paste. Add a generous pinch of salt and about 3 tablespoons of water and grind it to a smooth paste. Keep the paste aside for future use.
- After washing the fish and getting rid of any lingering scales, pat dry with a kitchen towel.
- Sprinkle about a tablespoon of turmeric powder and equal amount of salt and coat each fish piece.
- In a pan, heat some mustard oil and once the oil is smoking hot, sprinkle in a pinch of salt. This will help the oil remain calm when the fish pieces are added.
- Fry the fishes till light brown and remove them.
- Drain away the extra oil, leaving about 2 tablespoons in the pan, add back the fish pieces. Add 3 to 4 cups of water, completely submerging the fish pieces.
- Cover the pan and let it come to a boil.

- Once the water starts to boil, add a broken green chilli and then add the masala paste and let the fish cook for about 10 minutes.
- Keep checking in between to make sure that the water has not dried. If the water dries, add some more. This way you can control the amount of gravy.
- Once the excess water has evaporated you will be left with a thick gravy with well-cooked pieces of fish.

SALMOLI MUKERJI'S CHINGRI AND LAL SAAGER CHECHKI

INGREDIENTS

- 1 bundle or 250 g laal saag (red amaranth)
- 50 g small shrimp
- 2 tsp whole black mustard
- 1 tsp vegetable oil
- Salt and sugar, to taste
- A pinch of turmeric powder
- Slit green chillies, to taste

METHOD

- Wash the laal saag thoroughly and chop them. Keep aside.
- Clean shrimp. Add a pinch of turmeric and salt and keep aside. In a hot kadhai, add hot oil and temper with black mustard seeds till spluttering.
- Add shrimp and stir till cooked.
- Add the leafy mass. Mix well and cover. Cook for 5–10 minutes till the leaves are blended and well cooked.
- Add splashes of water only if too dry.
- Add salt and sugar to taste.
- Add slit or chopped green chillies just before turning off the heat.
- Serve hot with steamed rice.

Poppy

I have a friend whose father-in-law reacts hysterically at the mention of Coca-Cola. Why? Because he is convinced, through some convolution of logic, that the drink contains cocaine. When someone tries to tell him otherwise, he says obstinately: why would the company name it Coke unless it contains traces of cocaine? A logic impossible to argue with.

What does this have to do with poppy seeds, you might ask. Well, poppy seeds are banned by countries like the UAE, Singapore, Taiwan and Saudi Arabia simply because it is presumed that they contain trace amounts of opium and will be addictive merely because they come from the poppy plant, from which opium is also derived.

A friend once had the alarming experience of trying to trace the Man Friday of his Dubai-based cousin. My friend had seen him off at the Delhi airport, but his cousin rang up a few hours later to say that he had mysteriously disappeared. Before long, the story unfolded. The poor guy was caught at the Dubai airport with a jar of suspicious-looking contents: poppy seeds. No amount of reasoning with the drug enforcement department at the Dubai airport could convince them that it was a harmless spice, fairly commonly used in Indian kitchens.

Many Bengali families, who have relatives in Western countries, too have quasi-horror stories to relate about carrying poppy seeds in the folds of their saris in suitcases to avoid detection. American airport security, for example, is convinced that anything that comes from the poppy plant must be extremely addictive. Indeed, until the 1990s, you could be jailed for failing a urine test after consuming two bagels, but the US authorities have since re-looked at the parameters of opiates.

Despite all the fear-mongering, most poppies have nothing to do with opium. There are 11 kinds of poppies and most of them are ornamental garden varieties. They produce neither the opiates nor the poppy seeds. It is only the white poppy (*Papaver somniferum*) that produces both poppy seeds as well as six types of opiates: morphine, codeine, thebaine, papaverine, noscapine and oripavine. They are extracted from the latex of the white poppy pod while it is still green. Once the pod is completely dry and begins to rattle when shaken, it indicates that the poppy seeds within are mature and can be extracted.

Because of the opiates, valuable for medical purposes, the Government of India strictly controls the crop: both the geographical region where it is cultivated as well as the exact size of each farm. Any deviation, however slight, and the grower's license is cancelled. Large-scale deviations and the licence of the entire area is withdrawn. This is why Barabanki near Lucknow and Ghazipur in eastern UP, near the Bihar border, does not grow poppies any longer, as I discovered on a trip to Lucknow, when I went to see how poppy grows in the field. By the time I went, however, the entire crop had been moved away from Barabanki. To find out why, I went to meet the friend of a friend. He was initially hesitant to talk about a subject that is as explosive as a minefield, but agreed on the condition of anonymity.

Since morphine, codeine and the other opiates are needed in the medical industry, there's no question of banning poppy cultivation out of hand. My source told me that, in order to control the cultivation, the Narcotics Commission hands out permits to those farmers who have a certain amount of land in the poppy-growing belt. Not only that, the commission also strictly monitors exactly how much land each farmer has under poppy cultivation, carefully measuring it and stating the exact area in the permit.

But, of course, there are ways to get around this. Farmers have their fields measured, but then grow poppy plants at the margins of the fields as well. My source painted a bleak picture of a bunch of agriculturists – prepared to take desperate measures for a fast buck – who would often sell off the clothes of the field workers: After all, at the end of a working day, there'd be some sap clinging to the fabric and skilled experts knew how to extract most of it. Unsuprisingly, addiction was a raging problem in Barabanki, which was why my source had escaped to Lucknow with his wife and teenage children. He'd seen too many teenagers growing up with stooped shoulders and vacant eyes.

Today, Neemuch in MP is the only place where poppies are cultivated for the production of opium in India. Now, Tasmania, in Australia, is the world's largest producer of opium poppies and is responsible for nearly 50 per cent of the world's production.

Nowhere in India is the use of poppy seeds, called posto in Bengali, as common as it is in Bengal. Depending on which side of the border they hail from, Bengalis either use it for a couple of dishes like potatoes and ridge gourd (aloo posto and jhinge posto respectively) or obsessively in every meal. People whose ancestors hailed from East Bengal (Bangals, as they are called) are partial to spicy food. Poppy seeds have a taste that veers towards mild and nutty, so they use posto, in fewer dishes. People who owe their ancestry to West Bengal (the Ghotis), on the other hand, are partial to sweetness in their food and use it almost obsessively. To them, a meal without posto is no meal at all. My neighbour, who is a Bangal, buys barely a hundred grams of poppy seeds that last her family of four through the month. Her sister, on the contrary, who has married a Ghoti, also with a family of four, goes through an entire kilo of poppy seeds in a month! Posto bata is one of the most popular ways to eat posto in Bengali communities. It's a chutney made with ground poppy seeds and flavoured with raw mustard oil. Aficionados like to eat it with slightly overcooked rice. Lal masoor bodis is another popular dish: quenelles made with skinned masoor dal that has been pounded and mixed with poppy and nigella seeds to impart texture and taste respectively, before being sun-dried. But the most intense use of poppy seeds – actually I'd say of any spice in the whole panoply of Indian cooking – is in posto boras or fried morsels. Cups full of the spice are coarsely ground, seasoned, mixed with sliced onions, and half-roasted, half-fried on a griddle, like a kebab. It's enough to send a Ghoti to heaven!

In the Bengali kitchen, poppy seeds are invariably ground before being used, but it is a challenge in a food processor and is difficult unless you soak the poppy seeds beforehand. (Hungarians, other substantial users of poppy seeds, have a mincing machine with ultra fine blades to do the job.)

But while Bengali cuisine uses poppy seeds mostly in vegetarian preparations, Lucknow cooks use it to thicken meat gravies and for its nutty texture, often in conjunction with chironji (*Buchanania lanzan*), cashew paste and grated dried coconut. In Hyderabad, pulverized poppy seeds together with sesame seeds, peanuts and grated dried coconut form the base of several gravy dishes like dum ka keema and dum ka murgh and a few types of halwa. In the case of sweets, the poppy seeds are kept whole; in the case of meat dishes, they are finely ground with other ingredients like peanuts and chironji. The Chettiars too have a similar use for poppy seeds. They use it to thicken vegetable kormas.

Kashmiris use it atop kulchas – those soft, buttery biscuits eaten with tea – and on phirni made with semolina and milk. In that respect, they follow the more Western usage of poppy seeds where they are sprinkled on breads and biscuits for a mildly nutty bite.

In Shimla, Yatish and Minu Sud are the owners of The Chalets Naldehra. On a recent trip to their place, they tell me about siddus from the apple-growing region of Himachal Pradesh: Kotgarh, Kotkhai and Jubbal. They are puris made with yeast and stuffed with poppy seeds. Baked – traditionally in hay rather than in an oven – they are dipped in ghee and eaten. Although Yatish does suggest going off to the interiors of the state to sample some siddus, I reluctantly decline, as I have work to finish. I do, however, go down to the Gunj, the lowest level of Shimla's bustling market, where in the area between the Krishna temple and the Ram temple, there are shops that sell spices, pulses and grains. Every other spice is visible except poppy seeds, because, as one dealer explains, the price has sky-rocketed and so it is kept safely inside the shop, not spilling across the passageway in sacks, as all the other spices are.

The Sud community has its roots in Kangra. Now spread

to many parts of the state, indeed, the world, they have their own cuisine within the tiny state of Himachal Pradesh. Yatish tells me about his all-time favourite: hafeem dana halwa. Apparently, this is one of the uses to which they put poppy seeds. It sounds kind of illegal, but that is the name the Sud community has given poppy seeds. Minu outlines the process to me. After the poppy seeds have been cleaned and soaked in water, they are ground on a stone tablet. Next, plenty of ghee is added and the mixture is slowly sautéed. In Himachal Pradesh, poppy seeds are considered very drying, and the only way to eat them is with tons of ghee. Sugar is added when the mixture turns pale brown. Because the whole process is so laborious and takes an age to complete, today hafeem dana halwa is today only made twice a year: on Shivratri and on Janmashtami.

Despite the many concerns over the addictive qualities of poppy seeds, records all across the world show that poppy seeds have been in use for centuries for a large variety of uses. The use of poppy seeds in cuisine have been known for at least 3,000 years, by the Egyptians (the Ebers Papyrus dating to 1550 BCE mentions their sedative use), the Minoans, the Bronze Age civilization on the Greek island of Crete, who used poppy seeds as a sedative for cranky babies, and the Sumerians of present day Southern Iraq, an agricultural community that dates far back as 2700-1450 BCE, who also cultivated poppy plants for its seeds. In India, it has been mentioned in writings that date back to the 8th century CE.

So no matter the many challenges in producing, transporting and even cooking this controversial spice, we can safely say that the poppy seed is here to stay for centuries more to come.

POPPY SEED HALWA

Part of Sangeeta Khanna's family is from the district of Ghazipur, once an important poppy-growing district between UP and Bihar. This halwa was a popular pudding in the family. You don't need to soak the poppy seeds unless you are going to attempt this on a grinding stone; in an electric grinder, the sheer quantity will make it easier if it is dry.

INGREDIENTS

- 200 g poppy seeds
- 4 tbsp ghee
- 100 grams sugar
- 100 ml water

METHOD

- Grind the poppy seeds in an electric grinder till they form a lump.
- Add about 100 ml water and continue to grind, till you get a thin milky paste.
- Pour in the ghee into a heavy-bottomed kadhai and tip in the poppy seed paste.
- Stir constantly while maintaining a medium heat, scraping the bottom if necessary.
- Once the colour darkens slightly, but the paste is still moist, add the sugar and stir slowly till all the sugar is incorporated and the sugar dissolves.
- Once the sugar is dissolved, turn the halwa into serving bowls. The appeal of this lies in its simplicity and the inherent sweetness of the poppy seeds. It is not recommended to garnish it nor flavour it with essence.

Other Seed Spices

RADHUNI

Radhuni is the dark horse of Indian spices as not many people know about it. It is only used in panch phoron, the five-spice blend that is a signature component of the cooking of Bengal. (Though Odisha, Bihar and eastern UP too have their versions of panch phoron, they do not contain radhuni.) I suspect that radhuni is indeed not known outside West and East Bengal. Even in Bengal, many people are unaware that so much of their food contains radhuni. I have several Bengali friends who had absolutely no idea that the panch phoron that seasoned so much of their food contained radhuni till I had a conversation with them about it.

Radhuni comes from the plant *Trachyspermum roxburghianum*, from the umbelliferae family that mostly consists of aromatic flowering plants and is commonly known as the celery, carrot or parsley family. It is akin to wild celery, and its appearance is not unlike carom (ajwain), though in taste it is closer to fenugreek. The Hindi name for radhuni is ajmod, derived from the same Sanskrit word as ajwain: *ajamodika*. Technically, it would be called a fruit, but then, chillies are called fruits too by botanists.

I must say that I am extremely partial to this somewhat obscure spice. Its fragrance is not heady and intoxicating – you have to have a fairly sharp sense of smell to perceive its fragrance at all. But, to me, it tastes like a combination of celery and caraway, with a mild, fleeting flavour when used in the correct quantity.

The primary source of the spice is Bangladesh, where the bulk of the crop grows; but ironically, radhuni in Bengali cuisine is primarily a staple of the Ghotis, that is, the people who are native to West Bengal as opposed to the Bangals who came in from East Bengal. They are also the only ones who use radhuni on its own, though even that is becoming increasingly rare in modern households. However, the one dish that always uses a tempering of radhuni alone is shukto: the signature Bengali vegetable stew. Light years apart from the assertive, bitter dish that the Bangals favour, the Ghoti shukto is mild with a combination of five homely vegetables cut into chunks, sweetened with milk, ghee, a dash of sugar and tempered with radhuni. You can also cook mustard leaves and masoor dal and temper them with just radhuni. But be careful: Only very small quantities of this spice are required. It is easy to overpower a dish using this spice that is content to remain firmly under the radar.

Radhuni also has a certain amount of medicinal properties. It is helpful in the treatment of colic, asthma, kidney disorders and diseases of the digestive tract. Indeed, some digestive churans in Ayurvedic medicine include radhuni.

SHUKTO

Our maid Jaya is a true-blue Bangal, originally from Bangladesh. I prefer her version of shukto to that of the fancy restaurants where I have sampled it.

INGREDIENTS

- 1 medium sized aubergine

- 2 bitter gourds (karela)
- 100 g pumpkin
- 2 raw plantains
- 1 large white radish
- 2 large dal bodis (lentil nuggets)
- ½ tsp fennel
- 1 tsp poppy seeds
- ½-inch piece of fresh ginger
- 1 tsp radhuni
- 1 whole red chilli
- 2 tbsp ghee

METHOD

- Make a paste of the poppy seeds, ginger and fennel. (Jaya does this on our grinding stone, but you could use an electric grinder.)
- Cut all the vegetables into even-sized chunks: long rather than broad. That is the traditional shape of shukto vegetables.
- Add the oil in a wok and gently fry the bodis.
- Remove from wok; add bitter gourd and sauté.
- Take off from heat and add the paste.
- Sauté it, then add all the vegetables and bodis with enough water to make a thick gravy after the vegetables have cooked through.
- In a small vessel, heat the ghee and fry the red chilli and the radhuni.
- As soon as the fragrance arises, pour over the vegetables in the wok, cook for half a minute. Serve hot.

CAROM

Another spice from the umbelliferae family that has an uncompromisingly Indian appeal is ajwain or carom, also called bishop's weed. These tiny little seeds (which are, technically, fruits) grow from plants that are cultivated in Punjab, Bengal and in south Deccan within India, as well as in Egypt, Afghanistan, Iran and Pakistan. The flavour of the seeds has a piercing quality, not unlike thyme, but with a peppery appeal. In fact, in one of nature's mysteries, one third of the volatile oil in ajwain is thymol, and the only other plant that yields this oil is the herb thyme. Yet there is no taxonomic connection between thyme and ajwain! The mystery continues. Though the leaves resemble celery leaves and ajwain used to be called celery seed in cookbooks written during the Raj, there is no resemblance between the two plants either. There's just one more thing: the matter of its origin. While most authorities attribute it to the Indian subcontinent, historian Andrew Dalby points out that its Sanskrit name 'yavani' means 'the Greek spice' suggesting that its provenance was one of the Greek kingdoms of the Middle East.

Ajwain packs a huge punch, and is as much a part of our kitchen cabinets as our medicine chest. Every grandmother in the country will rush to prepare a teaspoon of ajwain with black salt and asafoetida for any sufferer of a gastric disorder, whether its indigestion, bloating or the other ills that befall overeaters.

Not surprisingly, given its digestive properties, it makes its way into the cooking of many communities.

It finds its place in the panch phoron (five-spice mix) that is used in Bengal, Odisha, parts of Bihar and Assam. In Bengal, radhuni often takes the place of ajwain, since both spices have notes of pine, more developed in the case of radhuni, and a cool, camphor-like, refreshing aftertaste.

In Gujarat, ajwain is one of the cuisine's defining spices, used for cooking arbi or colocasia leaves (called patra), root vegetables, green beans and even a simple onion and tomato gravy.

Matthis – tea-time savouries made with white flour, a dash of shortening and water, and deep-fried – usually include a pinch of ajwain seeds in them. Perhaps it is because the spice has a great affinity for starch. For the same reason, you'll find a combination of ajwain, salt and chilli powder being used as a stuffing for parathas: the ultimate comfort food for anyone from Punjab. Across North India, commercial bakeries in every neighbourhood churn out vast quantities of plain biscuits with a little ajwain, salt and sugar: a staple to offer with tea to unexpected guests. Whoever first hit on the formula was clearly a genius. Then there's paneer pakora, which is nearly impossible to make without a dash of ajwain.

And it's not only North India that has stumbled on to this winning combination of flour/starch and ajwain. Try the greasy yet irresistible bhajjis sold on Chennai's Marina Beach that have ajwain lurking in the spicy gram flour batter, and you'll definitely be coming back for more. Chef Srinath Sambandan formerly of The Park, Vishakapatnam, tells me that all masala puris in Andhra Pradesh use ajwain.

The other place where ajwain invariably makes an appearance is in Amritsari fish. You'll know winter is just around the corner when roadside stalls make their appearance all over Delhi and Punjab. Generous fillets of fish are marinaded in a paste which contains chilli powder, turmeric and ajwain, and then fried in a kadai or baked in the tandoor, depending on how sophisticated the stall is. Here, the presence of ajwain is needed not so much as a digestive as to take away the odour of the fish. (There seems to be the firm belief in Punjab and many northern states that all seafood has an inherent smell that won't go away unless it comes into contact with the wonder spice: ajwain!)

It also goes without saying that ajwain is the ultimate pickling spice. Nobody throughout the length and breadth of the country would dream of making a pickle without ajwain. Such is its brand equity as being a digestive spice! In fact, in Tamil Nadu, I've come across a drink called paanagam or panakam, which is used to welcome guests, made with tamarind and jaggery for a sweet and sour taste, and flavoured with dried ginger and powdered ajwain. It not only refreshes you and quenches your thirst, but because of the presence of ajwain, it has the added effect of making you feel hungry.

When it comes to medicinal properties, ajwain is not just used for digestive ailments. When my children were young, protecting them from colds and coughs was a preoccupation every winter. Then one day, a neighbour gave me a gift. It was a bottle of mustard oil that had been heated to smoking point, with a teaspoon of ajwain added to it before taking it off the fire. The resultant decoction had been left out in the sun until it became a dark amber colour. My kindly old neighbour told me to rub the oil on to the soles of my children's feet and their chests every night after tucking them into bed. Every winter since, I have made the oil myself, and even gifted it to friends and family over the years. And if you have a bad cold or blocked nose, boil a teaspoon of ajwain in water and inhale the steam. It works wonders!

If a girl is suffering from menstrual cramps, just boil a litre of water, put in a heaped tablespoon of ajwain seeds and boil steadily till about half the water has evaporated. Now, wait till the water is warm but not boiling hot, pour it into a glass bottle (such as a jam jar) and place it on the lower abdomen of the sufferer. I was extremely sceptical of this at first when I heard it, but since then, I've lost count of the number of sufferers whom I have converted with this home remedy.

MATTHI

- 1 cup flour
- 1 tbsp semolina
- ½ tsp carom seeds
- Salt, to taste
- Refined oil for frying and dough-making

METHOD

- Mix all the ingredients together to make a firm dough. Add 1 tbsp oil to the dough while mixing to make it moist and soft. Let it rest for 10 minutes.
- Flatten out the dough into a sheet, a little thicker than a chapatti. Prick the entire sheet with a fork. Cut out small rounds or diamonds or any other shape you want.
- Heat the oil in a kadhai and fry them on low heat until they are golden brown. Cool and serve. These keep well in an air-tight container.

FENNEL

When I first went to my in-laws' house, I figured that I would have to make several adjustments. More than a quarter of a century later, I've overcome most of them. But one that I still grapple with is the use of fennel, or saunf. Before I was married, like most people who lived in North India and ate the cuisine that a series of maids cooked – not a rare occurrence, I'm sure – cumin and coriander went into well-nigh everything. In Kashmir, the first culture shock was to learn how little cumin and coriander were used in this cuisine. Instead, there was fennel in practically every dish.

There are many variations of this spice, but the two broad variations are the darker hued, delicate fennel that comes from around Lucknow, and the fat variety, much lighter in colour, that grows in parts of Rajasthan and Gujarat. It is only the latter variety that is used in the kitchen. The darker, slimmer kind, considered the more refined sort, is used mostly as a mouth freshener.

Because two types of fennel grow wild in the Mediterranean region – the annual sweet fennel that is used in the kitchen as well as the perennial wild variety that is bitter and not used for culinary purposes – it is assumed that fennel is native to southern Europe and the countries of the Mediterranean. However, it has been around since antiquity in Indian and Chinese cuisines. The Italian make the most intensive usage of the entire plant: The edible variety of fennel has been called Florence fennel and its bulb is used as a vegetable, and the pollen is collected painstakingly and sprinkled over cooked dishes. Even the tender leaves are chopped finely and used to flavour pies and sauces.

It is easy to see why fennel is such an important spice: It has the ability to provide sweet as well as spicy notes simultaneously, the only seed spice to do so. All other seed spices are overwhelming savoury, with little in the way of sweetness. The sweetness is due to the presence of the compound trans-anethole that also exists in aniseed and star anise.

The very first spice that I remember tasting was, in fact, fennel, because of gripe water, a slightly sweet, extremely pleasant clear liquid that I used to be given from time to time as a baby for treating colicky symptoms. When my children were born, my mother-in-law would boil a little fennel in half-a-cup of water and the resultant decoction was cooled and stored till the babies let out a loud yell indicating their need for a sip or three of gripe water.

That fennel is an excellent remedy for ailments of the digestive tract is well known. There is a theory that the use of fennel in food is primarily because of it being settler of stomachs. It is precisely because of this that it makes an appearance in Indian restaurants, where it is served in bowls at the conclusion of a meal.

Fennel is always used in North-Indian pickles in conjunction with fenugreek, kalonji and ajwain. It is also used for those savoury preparations that have a sweet tinge, which is, after all, the flavour profile of the spice. Thus, in Kangra, where celebratory menus have a clearly defined sweet, salty as well as sour component, melon seeds (char magaz) and fennel are combined with a thin sugar syrup and eaten with rice as one course. Rentha, as it is known, is served with a plethora of other dishes, all either spicy or sour, as an antidote to its sweetness.

In West Bengal, the single usage of the spice is after it is browned gently, pounded and then sprinkled over the deluxe version of tomato chutney. This version of the chutney has tiny bits of raw mango to perk things up, raisins to add sweetness, and, among other spices, fennel to make it recognizably grand. The other usage of fennel is of course in panch phoron, to temper a dish of dry vegetables called chochchori as well as a couple of types of dal. Considering that most Bengali families eat either one or the other dish at least four times a week, a considerable amount of fennel is used, but that is nowhere near the quantities used by other communities.

As I mentioned before, fennel plays a crucial part in Kashmiri wazwan. A few dishes are flavoured with no other spice except fennel, and the only ready powdered version of this spice that I have ever encountered across the length and breadth of the country is in the valley. Wazas use powdered fennel in yakhni, the mild, curd-based gravy while aab gosht, or mutton curry made with milk, uses whole fennel seeds. Aab gosht translates into 'water meat' and refers to the fact that the milk keeps its natural colour: no chillies to redden the gravy and no turmeric to add the trademark golden hue.

Besides Kashmir, the only other community that uses fennel in any significant amount is the Chettiars. Meenakshi Meyyapan, the gracious owner ofThe Bangala, a heritage hotel in the heart of the Chettinad region in Tamil Nadu, holds an informal workshop on the cooking of her beloved community for those of her guests who are interested. And plenty of them are.

Meenakshi Aachi (or Aunty as she is called) tells us that sweet spices like poppy seeds, cloves, cinnamon and fennel are to be combined with cumin, coriander seeds, coconut and chillies. When all the ingredients have been sautéed separately on low heat, they are ground on a flat basalt rock that every kitchen in the Chettinad region has. This mixture is, quite frequently, added to vegetables or chicken preparations. I can vouch for the fact that it takes me back to my trip to Karaikudi. The typically Chettinad combination of fennel and cumin is what makes the flavours of this cuisine so unique.

The Tamil-Muslim community of Uthamapalayam and Madurai also uses quite a bit of fennel in their cooking. No kozhambu – the Tamil word for curry – is complete without powdered saunf, which also goes into lamb mince, koftas, biryani and their signature mutton curry, called thakkadi. In the West, fennel often refers to the tuber root of the plant, which is eaten as a vegetable – stir-fried, baked or raw and the feathery leaves are used to garnish a salad. Fennel is an ingredient of a famous liqueur too: Absinthe is made with wormwood, fennel and a few other ingredients. In India, however, it is more or less confined to the spice rack.

RASHMI SOOD'S MEETHA

My college friend Rashmi Sood was a great cook even in the days when a heater and a saucepan was all that our hostel 'kitchen' consisted of! Here's her recipe of a meetha that exemplifies the sweet-savoury taste of fennel.

INGREDIENTS

- 2 tbsp ghee
- 1 tsp fennel
- 1 tsp magaz (melon seeds)
- 10–12 dried coconut slivers
- 1 cup raw papaya, cubed

- ¾ cup sugar
- 1 cup water

METHOD

- In a heavy-bottomed pan, heat ghee. Add fennel and magaz. Cook till golden brown.
- Add papaya and cover till papaya softens.
- Add sugar and water and stir till sugar dissolves. Cook till it thickens to the consistency you like. Add coconut slivers. Serve hot over steamed white rice.

KASHMIRI STYLE TURNIPS

Meat-loving Kashmiris would never dream of serving this rather homely dish when visitors are over, but it is precisely because there is no lamb in this version that you can taste the sweetness of the fennel.

INGREDIENTS

- 500 g turnips, washed and peeled
- ½ cup mustard oil
- 1 onion, finely sliced
- 5 cloves garlic, finely minced
- 1 tsp chilli powder
- 1 tsp turmeric powder
- ½ tsp fennel powder
- Salt and sugar, to taste

METHOD

- Cut each turnip into three thick slices horizontally (i.e. one slice will be the top, one the middle and the other the bottom).
- Heat the mustard to smoking point, let it cool. On medium heat, fry the turnips a few at a time, till they are translucent but not brown. In the same oil, fry the onion and garlic.

- Take the vessel off the fire and put in the chilli, turmeric and fennel powder.
- Stir for a few seconds on a very low flame. (Kashmiris do not sauté their spices and the colour of burnt spices is very unattractive to them.)
- Add the turnips, hot water, sugar (start with half-a-teaspoon) and salt.
- Cook till done. The sugar will just about cut out the pungency of the oil; it will not be perceived as such in the finished dish. It will also accentuate the natural sweetness of the fennel.

RASHMI SOOD'S DAHI TAMATAR PANEER

INGREDIENTS

- 300 g paneer, cubed
- 50 g paneer, mashed
- 5–6 tomatoes large, chopped finely
- 2 cups thick yogurt, churned
- 1 cup makhana (fox nuts)
- 1 cup cashews, halved
- 1 tsp ginger, finely grated
- 2 tbsps refined oil
- 1 tsp black cumin (shah zeera)
- 3–4 broken green cardamon
- Red chilli powder, to taste
- 3 tsp fennel powder
- ½ tsp turmeric powder
- Salt, to taste

METHOD

- In a heavy-bottomed pan, heat refined oil, gently sauté cardamom and black cumin.

- Put in the tomatoes and grated ginger and fry till the oil forms a layer on the top.
- Spoon in all the dry spices and sauté.
- Add yogurt, keep stirring till it boils and cook till the oil is visible on the sides of the pan.
- Put in the crushed paneer, cashews, makhana and fry.
- Add paneer cubes and mix well.
- Now add enough water to make gravy and cook for 10 minutes. Add salt to taste and simmer till it thickens.
- Garnish with coriander leaves.

DRIED GINGER

Chef Saneesh Varghese, of The Oberoi Group, cannot ever eat something with the flavour of dried ginger, without remembering Maundy Thursday, the day before Good Friday. That's because many Christian communities of Kerala drink milk that has been flavoured with dried ginger powder and cardamom on that day. When I asked him why, he couldn't give a specific reason. Even though the reasons have been lost over time, the tradition, and its flavour, continues.

It's exactly the same with me. Walk into the kitchen of the average householder of the Goan Catholic community and you'll never find dried ginger powder, because it's just not on the culinary radar. However, in Goa, the festival of every saint in heaven is celebrated with the same gusto that is present in all other spheres of life in this coastal paradise. The church or chapel in question gets a whitewash. An army of furniture makers and purveyors of women's and children's apparel set up camp for a week on the grounds around the church. The sweet sellers appear out of nowhere. The sweets are not particularly good, or even particularly popular, but one of them, kadeo bodeo, a homely, fat pretzel with a layer of dried sugar syrup forming the crust, has a strong flavour of dried ginger powder. I, too, cannot rid myself of the association between saunth and church festivals because I have grown up eating kadeo bodeo at church festivals.

While ginger, a cousin of galangal, is used in every kitchen in India, dried ginger powder, or saunth, is less common. Ginger is thought to be native to India as the largest number of genetic variations of the plant (as accurate a barometer as any) exists in the country, and India is the largest producer of ginger in the world, producing a third of the world's crop. Most of the essential oils of ginger are present in the skin of the plant, so once ginger is dried with the skin removed, the final product has a markedly altered flavour profile. As a result, a number of ways of drying ginger have evolved. Each is practised by one region or another, and the taste is identical, no matter what the method: With the skin intact, with it bruised in parts, with the skin removed by peeling and with the skin removed after being scalded in boiling water. Once ginger has been dried, it loses 80 to 85 per cent of its weight. Throughout the world, ginger is available in three forms: fresh, dried (and usually powdered) and preserved in sugar. As in the case of turmeric and mango, both of which are used in their fresh as well as dry forms, these two versions are not interchangeable. In the Western world, ginger beer and gingerbread make use of dried ginger whereas in Chinese, Japanese and Indian food, a full meal without fresh ginger is practically unthinkable.

In Goa, the Hindu community too makes plentiful use of dried ginger powder. Whether it is dried Bombay duck or red pumpkin, saunth is used to lend a spicy, warm note to many

Goan dishes. It is the same in Kashmir: while Muslims use it too, the Hindu Pandits use it far more liberally, sprinkling it in almost every dish. In fact, it is one of the defining flavours of the cuisine, together with asafoetida.

My own perception of dried ginger is based on the fact that it is extremely heating to the system. It is probably why it is used in many dishes in Kashmir, as a kind of antidote to the cold. Even during the summer in Srinagar, any ingredient that is considered cooling enough to give you a cold – tomatoes and gourd are two examples – are never cooked without half a teaspoon of powdered, dried ginger, just to crank up the heat factor.

Surprisingly, nowhere else in the country is dried ginger powder used as much as it is in Tamil Nadu, particularly in the Kongunadu community of the eponymous region whose largest city is Coimbatore. The region is well-known for turmeric. The ancient cuisine of Tamil Nadu, researchers tell us, used dried ginger powder as the only spice in their food. At that time (3rd to 16th century CE), there was no chilli, so dry ginger and black pepper provided the spice quotient. In *Ettuthogai*, the classical Tamil poetic work written in the 4th century CE, the author gives us a vivid picture of the culture of the people at that time, describing 'the mountains of dried ginger root [that] could be seen for sale in the markets'.

Today, the most prominent communities of Tamil Nadu seem to be the Iyers and Iyengars, but they only make up 10 to 15 per cent of the population. Other regions of the state – Chettinad, Kunkunad, Nanjilnad, North Arcot and a host of others – each have a distinctive cuisine. It is these cuisines that have been researched painstakingly by food historians of the state. But the Kunkunad region, which coincidentally consists the turmeric-growing belt of Mettupalayam, Coimbatore and Erode, has a cuisine that is not even particularly well-known within the state. However, by all accounts, dried ginger powder is one of the elemental spices of the region. It is used in a plethora of masala powders by the community, most notably along with black sesame, groundnuts and turmeric. The region's most well-known spice blend – Pallipalayam masala, named after the eponymous town – too contains copious amounts of saunth.

DEEBA RAJPAL'S GINGERBREAD CAKE

Deeba Rajpal, one of the most prominent home bakers in the capital whose blog is called *Passionate About Baking*, tries to bring her passion for food styling and her love of wholesome ingredients together in her baked goods. This is one of her trademark cakes.

INGREDIENTS

- 100 g unsalted butter, softened
- 135 g jaggery granules or finely chopped jaggery
- 3 tbsp golden syrup or honey
- 2 tbsp water
- 1 tsp dried ginger powder
- ½ tsp cinnamon powder
- Zest of 1 orange (or ½ tsp orange extract)
- 1 tsp baking powder
- ½ tsp baking soda
- 2 eggs
- 175 g whole-wheat flour

- Demerara sugar for sprinkling
- ½ tsp vanilla extract

METHOD

- Preheat oven to 180°C. Line a baking sheet with parchment and lightly grease a 6–7-inch round baking tin.
- Place the jaggery, butter, honey and water in a heatproof bowl. Heat in microwave for a minute, until the butter has melted. Whisk well with a balloon whisk until the jaggery and butter are combined.
- Add the ginger powder, cinnamon powder, orange zest, vanilla extract, baking powder and baking soda. Whisk well to mix.
- Whisk in the eggs one by one. Now fold in the whole-wheat flour gently.
- Ladle into the prepared tin and sprinkle over demerara sugar. Bake for approximately 20–25 minutes until risen and light golden brown (adjust the temperature according to your oven). Use tester to check if done.
- Allow to cool in pan for 10 minutes, then gently loosen sides to remove. Serve warm as is, or with a drizzle of unsweetened single (low-fat) cream.

SESAME

Every year, as winter approaches, there are a couple of things that I look forward to. First of all, sellers of boiled eggs make their appearance all over Delhi's roads. They position their carts near bus-stops on the roadside and the sight of them warms my heart. Eating a boiled egg on the side of the road is a pleasure that I've never been tempted to partake of – so far, at any rate. I welcome their appearance chiefly because I can herald the start of my favourite season. But it's the other beginning-of-winter phenomenon that really gladdens my heart: It's the arrival of rewri and gajak in the market. While rewri is a rather simplistic sweet fit for the nursery, it is gajak that is stupendous. Made with either sugar or jaggery and sesame (til), gajak is available all through winter, and with very good reason too. Ayurveda deems that sesame is warming to the system. Ditto for jaggery. That makes eating gajak practically a necessity during the cold months, usually from right after Diwali till the end of February. It is just as well, because sesame is only harvested around Diwali in UP, Rajasthan, Maharashtra and Punjab where it is grown as a kharif (summer) crop. In Andhra Pradesh, Odisha and Tamil Nadu, it is grown as a rabi (winter) crop.

At my insistence, Atul Choudhury, a Delhi-based photographer, takes me on a day's trip to Meerut – home to some of the most famous gajak in the country – sometime after Diwali. Though Atul has made Delhi his home, his roots are in Meerut, so in the few hours we spent there, I got to see every single shop selling gajak, and there are dozens of them.

At Kansal Shudh Mishthan Bhandar, Sri Kishan Kansal, the fourth-generation owner of the famous sweets shop, waxes eloquent about the quality of sesame called Ganga Sagar. What is particularly notable about it is the almost complete absence of black grains of sesame, which would ruin the appearance of the sweet.

Kansal runs me through the recipe: For every kilogram of gajak, you need 750 grams of sesame and 250 grams of jaggery. While every mithai shop in town sells quantities as large as 50 kilos of gajak a day or more, nobody actually hires the skilled labour that is needed: They rent out workers by the day because the gajak season lasts a mere three months of the year. Kansal says he only uses about one sack of til a day during the rest of the year as compared to a humongous 20 sacks a day used in the peak season, with each sack containing roughly 50 kilos. The artisans work out of fairly primitive surroundings: They are all barefoot because the gajak will be tossed on to the floor and kneaded and pulled. It is as fascinating as watching noodles being made in the Chinese-speaking world. After visiting Kansal, Atul and I stroll down a road where over a dozen tiny shops all sell nothing but gajak. Each shop sells a few varieties of gajak and every winter, a couple more are added to the ever-growing list. These are usually variations on the texture and shape of the basic form.

What is remarkable is that far from being alone in the rewri and gajak sweepstakes, Meerut has Agra and Gwalior for company. Each one has a distinctly different style of making the delicacy – I'd hate to fuel the burning controversy about which is the best. However, each town probably uses 2,25,000 kilograms of til in a season, which lasts for two or three months. Although one associates spice with cooking food, in this case, spice in vast quantities is used for a sweet. What makes gajak great as opposed to merely good is the technique that causes it to become brittle, like mille-feuille. That, and the whiff of ghee. Ghee is also what is used in lavish quantities in bhugga – an earthy mixture of sugar, khoya and til pounded together: the Punjabi cousin of gajak.

Tilkut is a somewhat similar winter speciality of Gaya in Bihar. Sesame seeds are pounded with great force with a wooden hammer on the floor with a quantity of jaggery. The heat of the pounding causes the gur to partially melt and fuse with the sesame seeds, most of which become pounded to a coarse powder.

Sesame is also used to coat a fried morsel made from pounded rice flour, filled with grated desiccated coconut. Called andarse ki goli, they are very slightly sweet because of the coconut and are highly seasonal: They are made during the monsoon months in Haryana, Punjab, UP, Bihar, Jharkhand and some traditional markets in Delhi. Though this rather dense doughy ball is coated with a few grains of sesame seeds, it is considered suitable for eating in the rainy season, a time when, before climate change, temperatures actually dropped significantly after summer.

While in North India, sesame seeds are used as a spice, though not in great quantities, what is almost never used is sesame oil. In South India, on the other hand, til oil is so highly rated that in Tamil it is known simply as 'nallenai', which, translated, means good oil. (If, however, you are preparing Chinese food and need a few drops of sesame oil, resist the temptation of substituting the produce of Tamil Nadu: The flavour profiles are as different as they can be. The sesame oil that is used all over South India is made from raw sesame seeds, and does not have a strong smell. On the other hand, the Chinese variety is made from toasted sesame seeds for the precise purpose of being strongly aromatic.) In Kerala and Tamil Nadu, til oil, also called gingelly oil, is used to make pickles, whether of shrimp, mango or large lemons. Vegetarians consider this oil indispensable for tempering sambar: no other oil will do. Fish eaters across Tamil Nadu will never use any other oil for fish curry.

Sesame is the one spice that has that has the distinction of being grown on every continent, because of its ease of growing, whether for oil or for use as a spice. Considered the oldest oilseed known to man, the earliest references to it were in the Greek comedies of the 3rd and 4th centuries BCE, according to Jack Turner's book *Spice, the History of a Temptation*. It is considered native to sub-Saharan Africa as well as to India (although the two cultivars are distinct from each other). There is evidence of a 4,000-year-old drawing on the walls of a tomb in Egypt depicting a baker adding sesame seeds to dough, which dates its use as a spice to around four millennia ago. Look in virtually every part of the world, and you will see this ancient spice. Take for example, tahini, which the countries of the Middle East use as an ingredient in many preparations, notably hummus and other cold mezze. In addition, sesame seeds themselves, whole or pounded, find their way into a number of sweets in the region as well as in Turkey. Japanese food has a pronounced usage of sesame seeds, sesame sauce and sesame oil. Every South-East Asian restaurant in Indian metropolitan cities serves goma-ae – a super simple, extremely tasty and healthy cold salad featuring steamed whole spinach leaves with a dressing whose defining flavour is sesame seeds. It serves as a reminder of how spices don't need to overpower to be effective. But the prize for using the most amount of sesame seeds goes to McDonald's, which buys three-quarters of the entire crop of Mexico for use on its buns!

Microbiologist Sangeeta Khanna does not believe that sesame seeds are a spice. Her opinion is that they are oilseeds, rather like mustard. According to her, sesame seeds have no spice note whatsoever. My own opinion is that leaving out sesame seeds from a list of spices has never been done by any author, Indian or Western. To omit any mention of them here would be tantamount to attempting to reinvent the wheel!

SANGEETA KHANNA'S SESAME BRITTLE

This recipe is courtesy Sangeeta Khanna's *Banaras Ka Khana* blog, where she chronicles heirloom recipes of eastern UP and Varanasi.

INGREDIENTS

- 500 g white sesame
- 200–250 g jaggery (I use 200 gm or even less)
- 2–3 tbsp fresh ginger, finely grated
- 1 tbsp water
- Ghee, to grease the baking tray or plate

METHOD

- Dry roast the sesame in a pan on low heat, stirring all the while. It will be ready in about 10 minutes or as soon as a nutty aroma starts emanating and the colour turns golden brown.
- Now mix the grated or curled (using a paring knife) jaggery and grated ginger in a heavy pan or kadhai. If the jaggery is in small pieces it can be used directly.
- Heat these ingredients on high flame with a tbsp of water and watch the melting of jaggery. The jaggery and ginger mix will cook together, first melting to make a syrup and then bubbling to become a frothy mass.
- Tip in all the roasted sesame to it and mix quickly so every grain of sesame is coated with the sticky syrup of jaggery.
- Grease a baking tray with ghee and spread the mixture over it evenly. Press the mixture firmly and smoothen

it using a cold, greased knife. Let the brittle cool down completely, invert on a work surface, cut in desired shapes.

NIGELLA SEEDS

Kairouan in Tunisia is a charming little town whose Mosque of Uqba attracts many tourists from around the world. The old, walled part of the town, where the Mosque stands, is fascinating, especially for someone as food-obsessed as I am, with shops selling rudimentary kitchen implements that would not be out of place in a village market in India, alongside coffee houses and a bakery. It's the aroma wafting from the bakery that makes me take my place at the end of a long line of customers at 4 o'clock one afternoon. The large bun-shaped bread I choose is good enough, but it is the sprinkling of spices on top that remains fresh in my memory even after all these years. Warm, nutty nigella seeds, slightly sweet fennel and whole cumin. Try as I might though, I was unable to spot the nigella seeds in any of the stalls, though the big four – turmeric, chilli powder, cumin and coriander were present – all ground and arranged in neat piles on wheeled carts.

Back home in India, restaurants sprinkle nigella seeds (kalonji) on naans. Quite why, nobody really knows. What's fascinating, to me at least, is that no other Indian bread is topped with this little black triangular seed. Not tandoori roti, and certainly not griddle-fried breads like paratha or deep-fried ones like puris. The only theory I've come across that comes close to explaining this curious phenomenon is this: Prophet Muhammad has been credited with the saying, 'Black granules are the cure for everything except death.' It is assumed that black granules referred to here are kalonji, which is why they are called *habbatul baraka* in Arabic, which translates to 'blessed seed'. There is a hypothesis that the action of sprinkling nigella seeds on the flatbread in the Middle East mimics the action of bestowing blessings. If true, it would explain why in India, wholly indigenous breads like parathas are not sprinkled with the spice. It would also explain how the bread in Kairouan was sprinkled with nigella seeds, though the presence of the other spices remains a mystery. Warm and nutty are the first two flavours that explode on your palate when you bite into a nigella seed. And its fragrance is powerful indeed – pass any kitchen where it is being broiled or fried and the aroma will envelop you.

Though it is believed to be native to South-West Asia, there is no conclusive proof of its provenance. However, all the earliest archaeological evidence points to Egypt, where it was found in Tutenkhamen's tomb and to Turkey, where it was present in a flask that dates back to the 2nd millennium BCE. In India, it is grown primarily in three states: in MP, near Neemuch, in UP between Lucknow and Kanpur and in West Bengal, in a smaller amount. From the wholesale markets, most of the crop, which is harvested in April, goes to North India for use in pickles and East India for use in panch phoron and as tempering in curries. Unlike other crops that have several grades, nigella has but one quality, but after processing, it can be divided into average, machine-cleaned and sorted. These are grades that do not concern the average consumer: they are buzzwords for traders who are asked for particular specifications.

The highest use of the spice is probably in West Bengal where it is used in panch phoron. Bengalis who trace their origins back to East Bengal make more use of kalonji (called kalo jeere in Bengali) than anyone else in the country. Machher jhol, the classic Bengali fish curry, is made with a tempering of nigella seeds, as is masoor dal. Bodis, little sun-dried dumplings made from masoor dal, also contain kalonji in addition to posto.

While nigella is famously used on naans in North India, it is also an important pickling spice and so is used in those vegetable dishes where a pickle-like flavour needs to be recreated, like achari aloo. Many sweet chutneys are made with kalonji, and some people use it as a tempering spice in kadhi. In UP, kalonji is often used to stuff karelas, along with a few other spices, namely fennel, coarsely pounded red chilli, coriander seeds and aamchur.

Despite its less-than-spectacular usage in Indian cuisine, kalonji is the hottest selling item in any Unani medicine shop and is credited with the ability to cure diabetes, obesity, asthma, falling hair, kidney stones, arthritis and even paralysis. Drinking half a teaspoon of kalonji oil in half a cup of boiling water once a day, Unani doctors will tell you, can vanquish most of your chronic ailments. While nigella seeds are known to have radical scavenging properties and are a known antioxidant, research in several Middle-Eastern universities like Egypt, Riyadh and Jeddah, is on to verify exactly how miraculous these little black seeds really are.

Until then, I am quite content to smell the warm, toasty smell of nigella seeds atop freshly baked challah bread, German pumpernickel, Iranian barbari or Turkish pitta bread.

SALMOLI MUKERJI'S KALO JEERE DIYE ILISH

INGREDIENTS

- 500 g ilish (hilsa fish), cut into pieces
- 1 tsp nigella seeds
- 2–3 green chillies (slit lengthwise)
- 1 tsp vegetable oil
- Turmeric, just a pinch, for colour
- Salt, to taste

METHOD

- No thorough washing under running water for hilsa, lest its fragrance be washed away. The fresh fish should be just dipped in bowl of water and drained quickly. Put a little salt and turmeric on the raw fish and set aside.
- In a kadhai heat vegetable oil to smoking point, put in the nigella seeds and the slit chillies till they splutter, lower heat and put in water – 2 to 3 cups for 4 to 6 pieces of fish.
- Add a pinch of turmeric and salt to taste, stir, cover and boil. When water is bubbling, put in the fish, cover and cook till the fish is cooked through. Flip fish over to cook well.
- Serve with extra green chillies to taste and steamed rice.

SPICE GRINDERS

Where there is spice, there are kitchen implements to grind them. The flat grinding stone with the hand-held stone tablet is one end of a continuum that metamorphosed into the mortar and pestle that is most commonly used today. In between the two, there are a welter of designs that change slightly depending on which part of the world they are used in.

Depending on the job, all spice grinders have different shapes and are variously made of limestone, granite, lava rock, betel wood, brass, bronze, apple wood, clay or porcelain. Their great advantage over the food processor is that the texture of the ingredients is not bludgeoned into nothingness.

The flat tablet that you'll find in many traditional homes across the country is used to grind mainly dry ingredients that need to be moistened with the addition of a few drops of water, or a single ingredient that contains moisture like ginger and/or garlic. In Bengal, almost every home I've been to uses the shil nora to grind mustard seeds, whole turmeric root, cumin, poppy seeds or ginger every single day. Most Kolkata-based families have a succession of part-time maids, at least one of whom is co-opted into grinding the spices for the day. I even have a bachelor friend, a drummer in a band with keeps madly irregular hours, who insists on grinding his spices on a shil nora himself, even at the improbable hour of 3 a.m. – rather than use a food processor to do the job – since it teases out the flavours of the spices better than any food processor.

In Goa, you'll find two models, fathor (which means stone) and rogdo, in every traditional kitchen. Fathor, the tablet, is used for cumin, peppercorns and green chillies that are ground together for a variety of fish curries. Powdered haldi is often added to the other spices on the stone: a throwback to the time when haldi root would be pounded on the flat stone to make a coarse turmeric paste.

The mortar and pestle – called rogdo – is usually cemented into place in a corner of the kitchen. You never actually have to lift the pestle, instead you slide red chillies, grated coconut and the other spices into the well of the pestle, sit on a low stool, and work the pestle round and round in a constant motion. After over half an hour, the coconut starts to become almost silky smooth. You continue till you have the consistency you want. Interestingly, back in the olden days, aristocratic families – who were also landowners – had so many coconut trees that they didn't have to grind coconut. They'd just grate it and add it to hot water, extracting the milk and discarding the rest. Families of more modest means could not afford to waste the coconut, and so, were obliged to grind it.

More or less the same principle is used further down the west coast, in Kerala, where home-cooks use the rotary mortar and pestle for coconut-based mixes, as well as for puttu, idli and dosa batters, while more or less dry spices with just one or two 'wet' ingredients, like green chillies or ginger, are ground on the stone tablet.

I've seen many variations on the theme of grinding stones across the country. In Chettiar homes, the flat tablet comes with a smaller stone shaped exactly like a chapatti-making belan. In Kashmir, the nyeum tchota, a piece of limestone that is shaped like a well, is an instrument used to pound, as opposed to grind, spices. The pestle is a stout wooden stick made of apple wood or cedar. It is usually used to make chutneys or to pound lamb mince finely; spices get pulverized almost incidentally. But if you wanted to pound whole spices for a single dish, you would use a miniature mortar and pestle, also made out of limestone. On the other hand, if you were pounding the annual supply of whole chillies into powder, you would use a kanz-moohul, so large a pounding instrument that it is left year-round in the courtyard and never brought indoors. The kanz, too, is made of limestone.

Pantha Chowk, just outside Srinagar, has a large limestone quarry next to it, and so, ipso facto, has metamorphosed into Kashmir's centre for the crafting of mortars of all sizes. Drive by the little town and your ears will be assaulted by the flinty noise of hundreds of workers chipping away at limestone blocks so that someone can pound spice in them. Limestone mortars and pestles are popular in other parts too. In Solan, Himachal Pradesh, I spied a row of shops selling limestone mortars and pestles of identical design. And in the Goa-Maharashtra belt, certain roads have permanent markets selling household accessories, of which limestone mortars and pestles are an integral part, often being chipped into shape on the road itself.

In Lucknow, a metal hamam dasta does the job of pounding dry spices, but every roadside cart all over the country has a few marble, marble-dust or ceramic miniatures that look too toy-like to actually be of much use. I once saw a larger, more robust version of it in a Pune household, made of solid iron. Though the bowl was no more than a foot high, it was impossible to lift it off the ground. At best, you could drag it a few feet.

In the Chettinad region of Tamil Nadu, all households

have the stone tablet on which they place the spices to be ground. But the smaller stone is in the shape of a rolling pin, albeit one made of stone. The speed and efficiency with which spices can be ground on this are far more superior to any other implement that I have seen.

I myself have a host of tiny grinding stones, made variously of limestone, betel-nut wood, olive-tree wood, Jaisalmer stone and brass. They each have different depths and widths: the deepest does not allow cumin seeds to come flying back out, the widest is useful for pounding crisply-fried onions, but the one that I use most often is the limestone one, because of the way the spices become more fragrant once they've been in contact with it rather than a more porous material like wood or porcelain.

In Indonesia, grinders usually have to do the job of bruising spices, herbs and candlenuts together, so the mortar is shaped with a twist at the end, the better to do the job. Thai mortars and pestles for spice (as opposed to those for bruising salad ingredients like raw papaya and dried shrimp), too, are made in sizes and materials that look good on restaurant tables, to give guests the experience of 'preparing' their own ingredients.

Outside of Asia, spice-pounding implements *are* used, although they are not as common as they are here. One implement that you'll never find in traditional Indian kitchens is the nutmeg grater of the Western world. Even kitchens in India that use nutmeg would be likely to have an alternative arrangement for pounding nutmeg. Nutmeg graters are tiny and look quite unlike the mostly large, heavy duty, no-nonsense implements used to pound or grind spices in India.

In Mexico, I've come across two instruments: one for grinding and another for pounding. The metate is an almost flat tablet that is primarily used for spices and is confined to the kitchen. The molcajete is a wide-mouthed stone bowl with a pestle, usually used to bruise avocados and tomatoes for salsas. Surprisingly, I came across the metate in a very different form in the unlikeliest of places: Paris! That's when I realized that the metate is also used to grind cacao nibs. In fact, the logo of the famous French chain of chocolates, La Maison du Chocolat, is a stylized metate.

I think of mortars and pestles at the end of a continuum that begins with powdered spices. Once you have graduated in the kitchen to adding freshly-ground spices to your dish of the day, you will be able to tell the difference between pouring out powder from a packet and controlling the exact grind of your cumin or fenugreek, even while your kitchen is enveloped in a swirl of enticing smells.

SPICE MIXES

KASHMIRI VER

God alone knows when the average Kashmiri family pounds this spice paste, because not only will you never catch anyone in the act, you'll never even hear anyone admitting to making it lest the closely-guarded secret of its ingredients is somehow sniffed out by the neighbours. Yet, practically every family does make it. It requires specialized equipment: an enormous well-shaped mortar and pestle called kanz-moohul. The kanz is too large to be brought indoors, so it stays out in the family courtyard, and is pressed into service once a year. It is too heavy even to be tipped over on its side, being made of limestone. All you can do is stand next to it, grasp the giant pestle firmly and pound like mad. My mother-in-law tells me that in the 1950s, her mother-in-law used to insist that the kanz-moohul be used at least once a week; especially by pregnant daughters-in-law – normal deliveries were guaranteed!

The objective of ver is to add a spicy note in a cooked dish that already contains some chilli, which is to say, most of Kashmiri cooking with the notable exception of yakhni. Ver, a spice cake, is shaped like a doughnut, with a hole in the middle. Home-made ver is smooth, has an oily appearance and is of uneven shape. That which is available in the market is grainy in texture, has no surface oil and has cookie-cutter precision. There's another difference: Most of the ver you find in markets outside the state has no garlic or shallots because it is usually made by the Pandit community. Within Kashmir, the majority of ver has both shallots and garlic, being made by Muslim families.

In our house, equal quantities of garlic, shallots or praan and whole red chillies are pounded till they lose their texture. This is the base, to which black cardamom seeds, dried ginger, cloves, black pepper, fennel, coriander seeds and salt are added. When you are left with a stiff paste, doughnut-shaped patties are formed, the central hole helping air to circulate freely. The patties are left to dry under the eaves that most old houses have: Sun-drying would result in blackening the patties and Kashmiris are extremely particular about not blackening their spices, while drying or while cooking.

Ver is used in a few dishes throughout the year. To my father-in-law, it is comfort food, plain and simple. When he's feeling under the weather, we make him a teaspoon full of ver fried well and eaten like a chutney with rice and the dish of the day. There's a sliced potato preparation that is a specialty of our family, in which ver is the only spice used. It is commonly used by popping a teaspoon of it into a finished dish during the last five minutes of cooking.

GARAM MASALA

From North to South India, there's only one consensus about garam masala, and that is how useless branded ones are in comparison to what is made at home. That's about the only thing that most people agree on, because the defining factor about this key spice blend is how it differs not only from one state to another, but also from family to family.

It is completely impossible to give a 'standard' recipe for garam masala. One man's ambrosia is another's anathema. In our family, we use equal quantities of green cardamom, cloves and cinnamon and use this in tiny pinches that we sprinkle over dishes that we want to jazz up with aroma. Others would use different proportions of the same spices, still others would include cumin in garam masala; to me that's a travesty.

Gunjan Goela, researcher of the cuisine of her Vaish community, tells me that typically garam masala in a Bania household would consist of black and green cardamom, bay leaves, cinnamon, nutmeg, mace, cloves, black pepper, cumin and sometimes saffron.

A caterer friend who hails from Lucknow uses his own variation of a family-held recipe that includes cloves, black and green cardamom, cinnamon, nutmeg, coriander, cumin, fennel, bay leaf, rose petals, kababchini or tailed pepper, black pepper and kalpasi. A chef who was born in Bareilly, has an ultra simple recipe that he reserves for sprinkling over biryanis, mutton with lentils, korma and stew: Green cardamom and mace. He uses more cardamom than mace, since it gives an aromatic finish.

Serious cooks make a distinction between domestic garam masala and the commercial kitchen variant. They also say that in commercial kitchens there is one sort for curries and another variety for kebabs. The latter usually contains shah zeera and other lighter spices, so that the flavour of the main ingredient – the meat – can come through.

POTLI MASALA

Lucknow's potli masala is arguably the most sophisticated spice mix on Indian shores, which makes it one of the finest blends in the world. A member of Lucknow's Qureshi clan of chefs had once given me a list of the spices that went into its making. (Lucknow's cooks are famously secretive about their spice mixes and are loathe to relinquish what they perceive as their unique selling point, so I considered myself quite lucky!) But since potli masala is an art that has been passed on from father to son for generations and involves minutely measured spices combined at the right time at the right temperature, I am aware that merely possessing the list of spices is not going to help me much.

Nevertheless, the ingredients are, in no particular order: cloves, black and green cardamom, peppercorns, cumin, jarakus, star khatai, coriander, fennel, dry ginger, black cumin, kalpasi, rose petals, cinnamon, fenugreek, sweet attar, dry coconut, bay leaf, saffron and hadh.

By contrast, Hyderabad also has a potli masala, the ingredients for which include rose petals, vetiver root, betel root, sandalwood, bay leaf, black and green cardamom, cloves, kalpasi, coriander seeds, cumin, poppy seeds, lajwanti, peppercorn and wheat kernels. The friend who gave me this recipe, maintains that the potli masalas of the two erstwhile princely states, Lucknow and Hyderabad, sum up the difference between two approaches to cuisine. That of Lucknow is sweeter and milder while that of Hyderabad is more forceful and aromatic.

PANCH PHORON

Bengali panch phoron may be the most famous of the spice mixes used in the east of the country, but Odisha and Assam too have their own versions. In her book *Purba: Feasts from the East: Oriya Cuisine from Eastern India*, New York-based IT professional, Laxmi Parida writes about panch phutana, the Oriya equivalent of panch phoran. When she needs a break from her day job at IBM, Laxmi cooks meals from her native Odisha. The only downside to being from this particular state is that there's no ethnic market for Oriya ingredients in the Big Apple, so Laxmi has to scour stores like Dean & Deluca and Balducci's where she buys a tiny stash for the price of gold dust. Twenty-five dollars for 25 grams is an awful lot, but it's not too much for a homesick girl who wants to recreate the tastes and flavours of her grandmother's kitchen.

Laxmi's recipe of panch phutana consists of whole cumin, black mustard seeds, fennel, fenugreek and dry red chilli seeds. If panch phoron is made in West Bengal, it would use radhuni, mustard seeds, fenugreek, fennel and kalonji. Together, the spices have an aroma that defines Bengali and Oriya cooking.

Panch phoron is only used in leafy-green vegetable dishes which have their own juice as gravy. The most iconic dish that uses panch phoron has got to be chochori – mixed vegetables that are traditionally made with vegetable leavings like stems and skins. In addition, some dals and all jhols – the light, thin, watery curries that can be made out of either fish or vegetables - use panch phoron. The blend is never used for meat. It changes form from a tempering in dals to the base spice in jhols – something it does not share in common with other spice blends that are always used in either one form or the other.

GODA MASALA

Perhaps the most famous spice blend of Maharashtrian cuisine is the goda masala, usually associated with the Brahmin community. While Mirchi Galli in Lalbaug has ready-made goda masala, it is a generally acknowledged fact that the best version comes from the Brahmins of Pune. Alaka Hudlikar, a resident of Pune and an expert of sorts on the matter, educates me on the intricacies. She shows me the ancient iron mortar and pestle in which the family pounds the ingredients for goda masala. Her kitchen is quite as packed with mortars and pestles as mine, each one for a precise use. I immediately feel that I have met a kindred soul.

Alaka's goda masala contains coriander seeds, red chillies, cumin, sesame, peppercorns, cinnamon, bay leaves, dagad phool or kalpasi, black cardamom, green cardamom, shah zeera, nutmeg, mace, cloves, fresh turmeric, nagkesar, salt and asafoetida. Minimal oil is used to roast the ingredients, the better to darken them: goda masala has a typically dark brown colour and a sweetish taste. Alaka uses it to make amti, the Spartan dal that is eaten each and every day around Maharashtra. Made with the rather bland toor dal, or pigeon pea, it is the perfect vehicle for the dark, earthy flavour of goda masala. She also uses goda masala for vangi bhath, the iconic dish of rice with aubergines, masala bhath and as a stuffing for vegetables. The more dagad phool in the blend, the more assertive goda masala becomes. Interestingly, the Hudlikars themselves do not refer to goda masala as such. They call it, instead, garam masala, and indeed that is what it is: an extremely unusual garam masala for a Brahmin community. Alaka does not add grated, roasted dry coconut to her goda masala because it keeps the mix from turning rancid in the last few months of the year, but most commercial blends do contain coconut.

The flavour profile of goda masala is a culinary puzzle. Some of its constituents – dry coconut that has been roasted, sesame and coriander – are reminiscent of neighbouring Andhra Pradesh, except that in Andhra, the combination is used by the Hyderabadi-Muslim community, while Pune has traditionally been a Maharashtrian-Brahmin stronghold. However, Alaka Hudlikar tells me that in the days before the states were re-organized, a part of Maharashtra – around Aurangabad primarily – was part of the royal state of Hyderabad. Till today, there is a striking similarity in the spice mixes of the two neighbouring regions.

There's something else that stands out in Mumbai in terms of spice mixes, brought about by the sheer pressure of its population and the famously inventive nature of its people: It's what I think of as the 'half brand'. Let me hasten to add that this is my own terminology, and is in no way meant to be condescending. But there are some particular features that I've noticed among these 'half brands', like Jaffson in Bandra, makers of a variety of spice blends for kormas and kebabs, Ashok Khamkar of Lalbaug, Mumbai, and PY Vaidya of Pune, whose whole spices and blends are a byword for quality in their respective cities. They depend on word of mouth to get publicized and there's rarely any advertising or marketing, which means that one poor product and their reputation comes crumbling down. Their packaging is invariably plastic, with either a sticker on it or a piece of paper with a name, address and telephone number. I have a whole stack of spice blends on my kitchen shelves which lack even basic information about what exactly the product is and how it is to be used.

Typically, it works like this: Imagine a Mrs Deshpande in Parel who is known for her cooking skills. Her goda masala is the go-to among the neighbours. And because most of her neighbours are working women, they don't have the time to put in the effort that goda masala requires. Hence, the natural corollary is to ask her to roast a larger quantity of spices and have them ground and then buy a pre-determined amount from her. Over the next couple of years, news spreads like wildfire in the neighbourhood that Mrs Deshpande has started taking orders for her goda masala. It is essentially a circle of people who are known to Mrs Deshpande, people who know that she can be trusted not to cut corners. Outsiders need to know about her through one of her customers, because on the face of it, the masala is not sold at a store. This sort of thing happens with far more frequency in Mumbai than it does anywhere else in the country. The clearest and most public example of it is in the area of Lalbaug: The long line of spice shops there sell whole spices, most visibly byadagi chillies from neighbouring Karnataka as well as a few aromatic spices, coriander seeds and whole cumin. Just behind the spice market is a smaller, more difficult to find road that has a related specialty: grinding spices. I have never seen this particular method of pounding elsewhere. It consists of a series of brass pistons that have a pounding motion as soon as the electricity is switched on. The great advantage is that the spices do not heat up at all in the process, which is optimal, because heating causes them to lose some of the essential oils.

Because of Mumbai's torrential monsoon, families tend to prepare their dry stores so that they don't have to venture out for spice shopping during the rains. So they buy the ingredients for their spice mixes well before the rainy season and dry them on a terrace or verandah. Chef

Prakash Pawaskar of The Trident, Mumbai, says that the enduring memory of his childhood was spending every day of his summer holidays guarding the family stash of chillies, coriander seeds and sesame as it lay on mats on the terrace of his house. Chef Pawaskar figures that most children in the Lalbaug-Shivaji Park area of Mumbai did the same, spending most of their summer holidays guarding spices from crows, neighbours and unexpected rains.

BHAKAR

Bhakar, the name given to the combination of roasted, grated dry coconut, sesame and chironji, makes its appearance in a number of surprising and unrelated places. Families from Nagpur typically call in Brahmin cooks from Telangana for a wedding feast. The most popular dish on their menu is one in which chunks of red pumpkin have been cooked with a light spicing and sprinkled over with bhakar. In both Maharashtra and Gujarat, bhakar is used as a stuffing for the deep-fried bhakarwadi – a mouth-watering crunchy snack in which flour has been spread with bhakar, rolled like a Swiss roll, cut into inch-thick pieces and fried. The vehicle could not be more different: a vegetable in one case and a tea-time snack in another, but the spices are identical.

KARI MASALA

I would never have known exactly how difficult it was to break into another community's spice blends had it not been for a Khoja friend who told me about kari masala, the signature spice blend of the Khojas and Bohras. They are two sub-sects of Shia Muslims who only exist in a few parts of the world. Mumbai is a stronghold, though Gujarat is also home to some of them. There's not much interaction between the two groups, but their food does have some commonalities.

I was told I could buy kari masala on the road leading from Null Bazar to Bhendi Bazaar, so, of course, I went to try my luck, knowing not much else except the general direction of the shop. The entire area is Muslim dominated, but Sunni Muslim shopkeepers looked bemused when I asked them about kari masala – not one of them had even heard about it. Then, one kindly old man selling gleaming aluminium vessels quizzed me about exactly what it was that I wanted. When I told him, he told me to try the Bohri Mohalla, which was in the very next street. Sure enough, solicitous shopkeepers in the Bohri Mohalla directed me straight to the very shop where kari masala is sold.

Abdul Husain Dosaji Sakerwala sold not only kari masala, but a host of other spice mixes, all specific to the Bohra community. He claimed that his kari masala was famous throughout the world, and reached all corners of the globe, but his quality was not in the same league as the Khoja housewife from Bandra my friend introduced me to. Farida Virani operated out of a laughably small kitchen, but her kari masala was spectacular. Pale lemon in colour, it contained ground cashew, ground peanut, pounded sesame and poppy seeds, besan and cardamom.

BOTTLE MASALA

While few Bohra and Khoja Muslim families would grind their own kari masala, it being considered a task for specialists, 50 per cent of East-Indian Catholic families in Mumbai still make bottle masala in their own home once a year. Hardly anyone outside Mumbai knows about this community, but they are said to be the original inhabitants of the city. They are entirely Roman Catholic and used to live in Vasai, though pockets in Bandra, Dadar and Girgaum also have an East-Indian population.

The spice mix of this community is the famous 'bottle masala', so called because the blend was always packed in one-litre bottles tinted brown or green. Usually made once a year in the summer, two or three bottles can last a family 12 months. Every housewife has her own tightly guarded recipe, and those families who do not grind their own bottle masala tend to buy it from a relative or neighbour. Judeline D'Souza, a housewife from Marol, tells me how it works. No member of the community would dream of procuring this all-important spice blend from an unauthenticated source. After all, it is the basis of their cuisine for the next several months – too serious a matter to be left to the devices of any old shop.

Judeline's own family recipe for bottle masala contains the following: Kashmiri chillies, Madras chillies, resham patti chillies, coriander, turmeric, cumin, khus-khus, til, rai, pepper, cinnamon, cardamom, cloves, nutmeg, mace, kabab chini (tailed pepper), nagkesar, fennel, teflem, shah zeera, asafoetida, sambal paan, maipatri (mugwort), chana (chickpea) and wheat.

I have repeated the exact terminology of Judeline's family recipe, but if you were to ask me what some of the ingredients are, I honestly don't know. After they had been bought, the spices would then be carefully picked over, sunned for a couple of days and then lightly roasted in a terracotta vessel. It was only then that they were pounded.

Twenty years ago, women from the Koli community would go from house to house, pounding all the spices. It was done with suitable ceremony. The Kolis would work in groups of five, and would take turns, two at a time, to pound the spices in a large mortar and pestle that they would carry with them from house to house. One would sieve the blend from time to time, so that the larger flakes of spice could be pounded until they had reached powder consistency.

Today, in the age of nuclear families, the pounding ladies have vanished, though spice traders still come door to door to the houses of their old customers. Because they visit so many East-Indian families with never-failing regularity, they virtually know the entire recipe of bottle masala. Judeline tells me that even if the recipe is wiped out of the collective memory of the community, it will still live on in the largely Muslim spice-trading community.

My own mother used to buy one bottle of masala every year from a Mrs Baptista and use it in her fish curry. My aunt, on the other hand, couldn't understand what was so special about the Baptista bottle masala; she used to procure hers from a Mrs Nazareth. From my early teens, I remember how long and detailed the arguments used to be in favour of the products of either Mrs Baptista or Mrs Nazareth: one of my most endearing memories about growing up in a household as obsessed with spices as I would later become.

Other communities too have bottle masalas. The Maharashtrian one usually has two types of dry red chillies – resham patti and sankeshwari is a typical mix for colour and hotness. The other ingredients are coriander seeds, sesame, turmeric, cumin, cinnamon, black pepper, cloves, cardamom, bay leaves and asafoetida. All the ingredients are bought whole, even the turmeric. They are ground on a stone or in the neighbourhood pounding machine until they become a fine powder and then are stored for the year. Traditionally, a lump of asafoetida is put on the powder to prevent it from spoiling.

KARI VADAGAM

I confess I fell in love with the name as soon as I heard it, such was the musical cadence that the word had. Though I first heard it being enunciated by Chef Praveen Anand of ITC Hotels, Chennai, it is not, believe me, a five -star mix. It is, in fact, on the opposite end of the spectrum, being more closely associated with the fisherfolk of rural Tamil Nadu. Of all the spice mixes I've come across, I guess you could say that this one has the taste of the 'real India' imprinted in its DNA. It doesn't even have its own well-defined recipe. Chef Anand tells me that every district of coastal Tamil Nadu, if not every family, makes kari vadagam to their own specification.

You start with mustard seeds, cumin, fenugreek, red chillies, curry leaves and shallots. That much is certain. You could add salt, fennel, black pepper, coriander and/or garlic and coarsely grind all the dry ingredients. Last of all you pound the shallots, curry leaves and garlic. Then you get a straw mat and some manpower. The mat will hold all the balls of kari vadagam that you roll between your palms. To be sure, it will be messy work. The juice from the onions will run all over the place. That's what the manpower is for: Someone has to shoo crows away, keep flies from settling on the kari vadagam, and roll and re-roll the balls throughout the day, for as many days as it takes for them to firm up.

The strong sunlight will cause the juice in the onions, garlic and curry leaves to ooze, yet the juice is precisely the point of kari vadagam. Once it blends inextricably with the spices, you have a spice mixture that, with the help of a drop or two of castor oil, can be kept in an earthen vessel through the year.

Chef Anand makes it a point to have lunch with all the chefs in his team. They all eat together in the kitchen, and everybody's lunch is everybody else's property. He maintains that it is the most expeditious way to delve into all the regional cuisines of Tamil Nadu. He does have a point. It is how he found out about kari vadagam, after all. One of his team members, who hails from a coastal village, had brought a fish curry with an earthy flavour. One morsel of it, and Chef Anand didn't stop following the spice trail till he saw it being made!

NADAR 'CORIANDER POWDER'

I had never heard of the Nadar community of Tamil Nadu till I met the late Chef Jacob, restaurant consultant, TV show host and researcher of the ancient cuisine of Tamil Nadu. He himself was from the Nadar community, said to be associated with owning small grocery stores in the Nanjilnad region of the state. The Nadars use the term 'coriander powder' rather loosely. What they call coriander powder is actually a spice blend consisting of coriander seeds roasted till they are very dark along with curry leaves, dry ginger, urad dal, asafoetida and fenugreek.

There is a Nadar-owned shop in Chennai's delightful T. Nagar. Amidst shops of gaudy plastic flowers spilling onto the road and stuffed blue dogs displayed atop cars in the parking lot, there is a shop in one of the side lanes. It has no name as far as I can tell, but sells a variety of podis, pappadams and packets of this 'coriander powder'. Chef Jacob had nothing but scorn for it, but for an outsider like me, it was better than not trying any at all.

PODIS

To the average North Indian, the four southern states might seem to have much the same cuisine. However, there's not even an ounce of truth in that statement. Even podi – that marvelous, dry spice mix that just needs to be poured from a jar on your kitchen shelf to your plate and eaten like a chutney with rice, idlis, dosas or other snacks – changes dramatically from state to state. The Iyers and Iyengars of Tamil Nadu claim that they have the best range of podis in the region, but that's only because they haven't been up close and personal with those of Andhra Pradesh. Chef C.B. Shankaran of Dakshin, Hotel Sheraton, New Delhi, tells me about a couple of quintessentially Andhra podis. Nalla karam podi is a mixture of Bengal gram and black gram, rice, whole tamarind, red chilli, curry leaves, coriander seeds, cumin, garlic and salt. As with all podis, you dry roast all the ingredients except the salt and tamarind, grind it, add the other two ingredients and store in an air-tight container. Verusenga podi contains ingredients that are vital to the state: peanuts and sesame seeds. These are roasted with cumin, coriander seeds, asafoetida powder, red chilli, seasoned with salt and ground to a powder.

Andhra Pradesh does indeed have a plethora of podis, pickles and chutneys – the most famous among the four southern states. Next are those of the Brahmin communities of Tamil Nadu. Karuveppilai Podi is the most famous of them, and is marked by the signature fragrance of curry leaves. The leaves have to be separately roasted till they lose most of their moisture and then combined with Bengal gram, black gram, rice, red chilli, black peppercorn and asafoetida, all roasted together and seasoned with salt.

Kerala has one famous podi called chammanthi podi that contains grated dry coconut which is different from most other podis, and this combination of dal(s) and spices roasted and then ground to a fine powder will transform plain rice into a meal fit for a king.

CHURAN

No account of spice blends can afford to ignore one particularly Indian invention which is churan. Its roots are almost certainly in Ayurveda. You take a spice or spices, add salt and/or sugar, form them into globules and consume them after meals. In India, they are sold at roadside stalls in almost any market worth the name. Ajwain golis contain carom seeds in their midst and are coated with a mouth-puckering layer of sour and salty powder, while hing ki goli is a sweet-sour ball with the trademark punch of asafoetida. The most famous of all are zeera golis, in deference to their reputation as a digestive. Churans are – or should be – far from simplistic. The tastiest of them, anardana churan, has a long line of ingredients: pomegranate seed extract, cumin, black pepper, dry ginger, dry mango, dry rose petals, long pepper, extract of lime, black salt and sugar. Churan brings out the art of blending spices that we Indians have perfected over the years, and is a testament to how spices have moved past our meals and become so inexorably linked to our culture.

SPICES ABROAD

You've probably tasted asafoetida in an English recipe without even realizing it. I certainly hadn't, and could scarcely believe it when I was told that England's much-beloved Worcestershire sauce contained the spice. The story goes that an Englishman, who was later knighted for his services to the Crown, returned from India where he served the East India Company for many years. While in India, he had developed a fondness for Indian food and asked his cook to give him the recipe for a spice blend or a chutney that he could douse on his meals in England. The cook obligingly gave him a recipe. The nobleman went to a couple of chemists in the neighbourhood (he lived in the city of Worcester) to make a sauce using the cook's recipe. The chemists, whose names were John Wheeley Lea and William Henry Perrins, attempted to make the sauce, but when they followed the recipe, the result was so unpalatable that the chemists consigned the barrel to the basement where it lay forgotten. A few years later, when Messrs Lea and Perrins were making space in their basement, they caught sight of the barrel and opened it cautiously. To their surprise, the mixture had mellowed and tasted quite delicious. And that is the story of Worcestershire sauce.

We are so used to thinking about spices vis-à-vis Indian cuisine that we often forget that countries across the world have an intricate relationship with these magic ingredients. The Western world, of course, has an ancient connection with spices. Once upon a time, pepper and all the other aromatic spices like cinnamon, cloves, cardamom, nutmeg and mace were used in industrial quantities by western European countries as status symbols, preservatives and sometimes, as flavour enhancers. However, a few centuries later, most of Europe has lost its feel for the usage of spices entirely, except, perhaps, for pepper. In fact, the spice that is most commonly used across the world is black pepper. Cinnamon is also used to some extent, almost exclusively in baking and in sweets; nutmeg and mace are used as a top-note in a few sauces and the astringency of cloves can be felt in certain stews. Hungary, the world leader in paprika – a particularly mild pepper with a fruity fragrance – uses it most famously in goulash, a ratatouille-like stew. The south Italian states of Calabria and Puglia are known throughout the country for the hotness of their food, courtesy of the chillies that grow there.

The belt that uses spices that are most familiar to Indians extends over most of Asia and right into North Africa, although the ways in which they are used are surprisingly different. Ras el hanout is a classic spice blend of the North-African triumvirate of Morocco, Tunisia and Algeria. It is not unlike our own garam masala, where everybody and his uncle has their own recipe. In the Levant, every shopkeeper grinds his own blend that he firmly believes is the best combination around. Ras el hanout, which literally means 'top of the shop', could contain pepper, cardamom, mace and cinnamon as well as nigella, cumin and coriander in combination with dried flowers like rose petals and lavender. The whole objective of the spice merchant is to pack in as many flavours in his version of ras el hanout as possible, but in combinations that are completely alien to the Indian sensibility. A mélange of tree and seed spices with flower petals thrown in – unthinkable in India!

Another difference with Indian cuisine is that the food of this region depends heavily on condiments for its flavours:

like olives and preserved lemons. Chilli makes its presence known in North-African food only in the most incidental way. Side dishes for the famous couscous tend to be stewed onions with soaked raisins, turmeric-based condiment, steamed chickpeas or garbanzo and pounded chillies. These pounded chillies have the consistency of a thick sauce and are called harissa. Almost never used in the kitchen for cooking, harissa is added by the diner at the table, according to personal preference.

In Lebanon, spices are used in conjunction with a variety of ingredients, with a completely different result. Here, as in the rest of the spice-using countries of the Middle East, they use herbs and spices together in the same dish: Thyme is combined with cumin. Similarly, at a Turkish dinner, I have tasted roast beef that was thinly sliced and sprinkled over with toasted, powdered cumin, marjoram and chilli powder. Curiously, the first thought that occurred to me was how strangely the flavour of cumin sat upon the palate. At a similar meal featuring Indian food, the cumin would have never been a single note. Instead, it would have formed a network with other spices and their flavours.

Closer to home, the Middle-Eastern baharat, used in everything from soups and chutneys to marinades, consists of paprika, pepper, coriander, cumin, cinnamon, allspice, cardamom, cloves and nutmeg. The underlying theory is that aromatic spices dominate, while paprika and pepper are used to pep up the spicy quotient and coriander is a neutral background.

There is also some similarity in the spices that are consumed all across South America and Mexico – where aromatic spices were brought in by the Spanish – with those we're familiar with here in India. Already into the spice trade, they propagated the use of cinnamon and cloves besides black pepper throughout Mexico, and parts of South America. Cumin is also used in cooking all over Mexico, while coriander leaves are considered an important herb, although the seed is used only occasionally. Mexican cumin, however, is nowhere near as fragrant as its Indian counterpart, as every visiting chef learns. Proportions have to be adjusted sharply downward in India.

However, despite the familiarity, there are differences. Take for instance the Mexican chilli. We don't have anything approaching the range of chillies used in Mexican cuisine. In fact, the average Indian will have to be hospitalized if he consumes the habanero chilli, routinely consumed in Mexican cuisine. But perhaps this is a testament to the fact that Mexico has been using chillies for 2,000 years now and Indians for a mere 400 years.

In general, Mexico, in common with much of the Western world, uses cinnamon for desserts rather than savoury dishes. The one exception is the mole – the chicken 'curry' that uses cinnamon, cloves, ancho and guajillo chillies, sesame, fennel, coriander seeds and cumin in combination with sugar, almonds, prunes and chocolate! It has to be the most bizarre combination in the world, and legend tends to corroborate that. According to one story, an impoverished convent was about to be visited by none other than the archbishop of the diocese. After feverish brainstorming, they made use of whatever they had in their meagre store and cooked them with a turkey from the convent's own poultry farm (it was a common enough way of being self-sufficient). Though the combination of the ingredients was unorthodox to say the least, the archbishop was impressed enough to ask for the name of the dish. 'Mole,' blurted out one nun – the ancient word for 'mix' – and since then, the name has stuck for this type of sauce served with cooked turkey or any other meat.

In South-East Asia, curries form an important component of the cuisine and, like their Indian neighbours, they use one or all of the big four spices in almost all of these curries. For instance, Malaysian and Indonesian rendang use turmeric, chillies, cumin and coriander, and in Thailand, red, green and massaman curries use turmeric, chillies, cumin and coriander.

The one Asian country whose use of spices is rather unusual, compared to the rest of its South-East-Asian cousins, is Japan. It's not a country well-known for its use of spice, but they do use a spice mix called shichimi, that is made of white sesame, chilli powder, black sesame, aonori (a kind of seaweed), ginger powder, poppy seeds and pepper. Also called the seven-spice powder, it is incendiary by Japanese standards, though Indians could probably consume it by the kilo without noticing the chilli content.

There's also something called Japanese curry, popular across the country, which contains the familiar aroma of turmeric and cumin besides a mélange of other flavours. It's usually made from instant curry powder or blocks, sold in packets everywhere. What prevents Japanese curry from tasting more like its Indian counterpart is the presence of emulsifying agents and wheat flour, which are never used in Indian masala mixes. The spices mentioned on the packet are mostly simply listed as 'curry powder' which suggests that the mix is imported, already blended, from elsewhere.

It is the same with curries from other countries of South-East Asia. Why don't their curries taste like their Indian counterparts? It is because of the variety of other ingredients that are used: cilantro root, lime leaf, candlenut, galangal, lemongrass and, of course, dried shrimp (often fermented) as well as fish sauce in the case of Vietnam and Thailand. From the cuisine point of view, this is interesting. It means that the spices that you use do have a bearing on the final product, but they are not the only factor in the reckoning. The method and the other ingredients used are just as important.

You might not think automatically of spices when you think of Hong Kong – the place is more famous for its silk fabric and dried seafood than for spices – but I once bought an enormous piece of cinnamon bark from Hong Kong's Des Voeux Central area which is 17-inches long and 18-inches wide and looks like a piece of driftwood. I bought it in a shop that sold dried lizards and seven types of ginseng used in Chinese medicine. The shop would not break the bark into pieces for me, so obviously large quantities of cinnamon have their place in Chinese medicine. (My cinnamon bark today adorns my living room in much the same way as driftwood is used as a decoration.) I have also bought packets of Sichuan pepper, dried ginger powder, cumin powder and the Chinese version of black cardamom, along with a blend of whole spices for chicken soup that contains bay leaves, aniseed, star anise, ginseng, cinnamon sticks and black pepper. No attempt has been made to make the packets look fancy: they are as homely as those you'd find in a corner store in India.

Mainland China, too, makes use of spices in certain provinces. All of us know about the lethal Sichuan pepper, but preserved chillies are also used copiously in the hot cuisine of Sichuan and its even more lethal neighbour, Hunan cuisine. (There is even a saying in China that the people of Guangdong fear spicy food, the people of Sichuan do not fear spicy food and the people of Hunan fear food that is not spicy!) Every Sichuan restaurant I've been to marks each dish with chillies. One chilli means that it will be as mild as Sichuan cuisine gets. Two means watch out – order this dish if you know what you are doing. And three means that you must have insides made of cast iron. It's only people who hail from Sichuan who order three chilli dishes, then call for the waiter and complain with a deadpan expression that the chef forgot to put the chillies in!

Five-spice powder is another common spice used all over the Chinese-speaking world, and contains any five of these spices: star anise, cinnamon, coriander seed, white pepper, clove, fennel and black cardamom. Apart from this, braised dishes contain star anise, which is a favourite in China. In fact, Chairman Mao's favourite dish, red braised pork, contains both star anise and cinnamon.

There's hardly any common ground between Chinese and Indian food. There is, however, one exception: the little-known region of Xinjiang, in the extreme west of China, whose population is overwhelmingly Muslim. Their braised clay-pot dishes contain spices like star anise, cinnamon, bay leaf, dried ginger and red chilli, making it quite close to an Indian curry, without turmeric, and with the addition of noodles. The people of Xinjiang have another trick up their sleeves that is closely related to our own mutton tikkas. Tiny tikkas of lamb (the Muslims of west China are the only ones in that country to eat mutton) are rubbed with salt, chilli powder and zeera powder in addition to a smidgeon of pounded sesame seed. They are then threaded on skewers and grilled on a charcoal fire that is strongly reminiscent of our very own bhatti. At every corner of Beijing, the sight of stalls run by Muslims from Xinjiang selling barbecued lamb is a familiar one. The boys who man the stalls wear white lace prayer caps, which makes them easy to spot. They are, in all likelihood, a feature of the Silk Route. How else do you explain the identical way in which the tikkas are yanked off the seekh, by wrapping them in a naan, in both Xinjiang and Kashmir?

As much as you'll find combinations of spices around the world that are unfamiliar to the Indian palate, you're just as likely to find the familiarity of Indian flavours across continents in unexpected nooks and crannies. I once discovered one such Indian connection in the unlikely precincts of Rue Tiquetonne, Paris, when I met Bruno, as typical a Parisian as you could ever hope to find. He had a gruelling job in the financial world and was fond of cooking so, whenever he could manage, he would cook for a small group of friends, usually within an hour of coming back from work. What he invariably noticed was that by using spices, he could cook something that was both interesting and expeditious. The more he explored cooking with spices from all over the world, the more fascinated he became, until one day, he decided to quit his job and start selling spices. His well-appointed boutique, not far from the old Paris market of Les Halles, is called L'Epicerie de Bruno, where each spice is packed neatly in 50-gram portions and wrapped in brown paper bags with a little cellophane window. The dainty shelves are artistically arranged with spices in jars, tins and brown paper packets. Bruno sources many of his spices from organic-spice farms in Kerala. Bruno's customers have the same profile as he does: They are mainly French and they cook Western – if not uncompromisingly French – food with a few spice accents.

Yet another Indian spice connection was revealed on a trip to Netherlands, where I was taken on the obligatory tour of a cheese-and-clogs factory in the area I was in, an hour's drive from Amsterdam. If you had stopped me at the door of the factory and asked me what the three things I would never expect in a cheese factory in the Netherlands were, I would have answered: machine guns, elephants and Indian spices. Fortunately for everyone concerned, the first two things were absent, but guess what was lurking in the cheese? Methi seeds!

In fact, there is scarcely a part of Europe where you do not see Indian spices in one form or another. Langenthal is a small town in the canton of Bern, Switzerland. I have friends from there who are uncompromisingly Swiss. They tell me that any European company who wants to test-market its products in Switzerland, does so in Langenthal, because of its entirely Swiss population. Neighbouring towns have some percentage of non-Swiss residents, but not Langenthal. But even in this quintessentially Swiss town, at the local Coop, there is an entire rack devoted to spices – Madras curry powder, Thai spice, individual spices like cumin and coriander – and, what's more, they are all clearly targeted at the Swiss customer as Coop is the leading supermarket of Switzerland, with stores in every city and town.

But if there's a single city that could be called the spice capital of the world, it would be London. The finest spices in the world make their way to it. Call it the lure of market forces, but I've never seen another city with so much spice for sale in the retail markets, and of such premium quality. By far and away the largest share of spices is sold out of Indian and Bangladeshi shops, but I suppose that's hardly surprising. Numerically, both communities have a huge presence in London, and Indians are hardly known to be slack businessmen! Dadoo's in Tooting is representative of the very best grocery stores that sell spices. Tooting itself is a supremely middle-class bastion of a cosmopolitan bunch of people, including that soon-to-become-a-minority – the British themselves! There are Jamaicans, Senegalese, Indians, Pakistanis, Bangladeshis and plenty more, but the best part about the riotous mix is that there is an English feel attached to the semi-detached villas and well-tended gardens.

Going sightseeing to all of London's ethnic areas in search of the best spices is something I have undertaken over the years with all the seriousness of an army general planning a military campaign. I have discovered that the three giant consolidators of spice here are TRS, Top-Op and NATCO: packaging and selling everything from the smallest 100-gram packets of cumin sold in Iraqi shops to the 5-kilo ones sold in a huge, hangar-like supermarket on Brick Lane. TRS, Top-Op and NATCO are so well-entrenched that I've seen them everywhere, whether it's an Arab, Greek, Syrian, Iranian or Jamaican store. If there is coriander, cumin, fenugreek seeds or turmeric being sold, it is packaged by one of these three giants.

The quality of the spices that you find in London, too, is remarkable, perhaps because of the strength of the pound sterling, which ensures that the average exporter makes more money if he sells to the UK than to, say, Brazil, or Indonesia. And the quality really does make a difference to your meal; it's why Indian food in London is of such a high quality in fine-dining establishments run by prominent chefs like Vineet Bhatia, Cyrus Todiwala and Vivek Singh.

I'm not a fan of eating Indian food when I'm outside the country, but I broke my cardinal rule at Chor Bizarre, Mayfair, and was I glad! The lamb forcemeat kebab really did have a hint of nutmeg in it and the whole potato was livened up with just a smidgeon of aamchur that was not only flavourful but fragrant too! Now this was a true marriage of food and spice.

From Xinjiang to Hong Kong, London to Mexico, hardly anything unites the world as much a shared history of spices. When an unsuspecting diner reaches for the French mustard in a restaurant, she has probably no idea that halfway across the globe, turmeric and mustard seeds are regularly ground into the Bengali kashundi. And when you stop to pick up some chicken tikka at a hole-in-the-wall in London, you might marvel at how, in only a few hundred years, Indian spices have travelled to practically every part of the globe, reminding you of home no matter where you are. For me, nothing tells me more about a place than the way they use their spices – in their food and in their culture – because, after all, the history of spices abroad is a microcosm of the history of the world.

EPILOGUE

A few years ago, a well-known US-based policy analyst of Indian descent asked a few of us food writers on Twitter how many recipes of dal (lentils) there would be all over India. At first, there was a dumbfounded silence. Then, after more prodding, each of us came up with our back-of-the-envelope calculations. After wildly random figures like 2,00,000 and 1,000 were bandied about somewhat half-heartedly, he finally pronounced that he was going to go with 10,738. As he rather cunningly put it, nobody would be able to counteract – or verify – that figure.

Substitute garam masala for dal and you will see where I am going with this. In the era before the Internet took over our lives, chronicling something as complex as spice mixes across the country was an impossible dream. Today, it is within the realm of possibility to tabulate the various ways of preparing garam masala, chai or biryani masala made around the country, and in Indian communities settled elsewhere around the world. It may not be an easy task, mind you, but it is not the staggeringly impossible task it would have been a few decades ago.

But the problem is, even with so many resources at hand, there is surprisingly little research, amateur or otherwise, that has been done on the subject. In fact, before I started researching this book, if you had asked me about spice blends – or, indeed, about spices themselves – I would have shrugged nonchalantly. This is because, in our world today, it's so easy to forget where our spices are coming from – or even what they look like – in the air-conditioned, uniformly-labelled convenience of supermarkets. Recipes, like the Lucknow chef's treasured spice blend for biryani, or the goda or sambar masala, passed on from generation to generation through home-cooks, are in serious danger of dying out. Give it another couple of decades, and branded spice mixes may well take over our lives and obliterate individual recipes, as more and more companies cater to customers who are satisfied enough with the results to not be tempted to try out grandma's recipe because of the laborious processes involved.

If there is one thing writing this book has taught me, it is how important it is for all of us to view – and taste – spice in a different light, because it is perhaps the single, most visible way to trace how India's culinary history has evolved through exchanges with the rest of the world and to celebrate the culinary differences that have evolved through each community's interaction with these ingredients. And now, more than ever, it is vital for us to remain hungry for traditional recipes, and the intricate stories behind their evolution: What spices are used, how they got to that region or community, the reasons for the use of one spice over another – or avoiding a spice altogether. Not because we will be entering the kitchen any time soon to slave over grinding stones and wood fires, but because unless we are aware of our culinary heritage – of which spices are central – we will, in a couple of generations, have dumbed down one of the world's greatest cuisines.

As I write this, I am on my way to Kashmir, where I will be taking a friend from overseas to see saffron fields. It is not quite the right time of the year for the fields to be in bloom, but we will, nevertheless, travel to Pampore and one of the dealers there has promised to show us kilos and kilos of saffron, the fallow fields and a corm or two. For me, there is no better way to learn about the spice – straight from the horse's mouth, so to speak – but for you, it might be by tasting different cuisines, talking to chefs, or even trying to conjure up your great-grandmother's spice mix at home. Whichever path you choose, I hope that after reading this book you, too, will set out on this journey for yourself and discover some of the fascinating stories and recipes behind these complex, magical, versatile and eternally enriching ingredients.

ACKNOWLEDGEMENTS

This book has changed my perspective on spices, as a commodity and an ingredient, dramatically. And for the writing of it, I owe a debt of gratitude to several people. Sangeeta Khanna, my microbiologist friend, who has spent hours giving me her perspective on the essential oils in spices; Sudha Kukreja, who has an unparalleled view on how spices are used in Indian, Indonesian and Thai cuisines, and can dig out the truth behind seemingly trivial old wives' tales; Harpreet Singh Chhabra of Baby Brand Saffron, who could probably fill an entire library with his knowledge of saffron; and biologist Rajesh Kumar, who could easily write an encyclopaedia or two on chilli-growing. I'd also like to thank chefs Sheikh Arif, Ranveer Brar, Arun Tyagi, Praveen Anand, Gaggan Anand, Bakshish Dean, Srinath Sambandan, Arun Kumar, Irshad Qureshi, Dirham ul Haque, Kaizad Patel, Laiju Jameson, Manish Mehrotra, Manjit Gill, Ravitej Nath, Rajdeep Kapoor, Urbano Rego and Raymond Sim. Then there are Yatish and Minu Sud of The Naldhera, Rashmi Sood of Delhi and Kangra, Niraamaya Resorts of Kumily and Kovalam, Sonali Sudarshan, K.T. Gyaltsen and his family in Gangtok, Benny of Green Park Ayurveda, Raju K.G. of Elephant Junction, Kaveri Ponnapa Kambiranda, Iram Rao, Rohit Aggarwal, Sanjeev Goswami, Maj. Umaid Singh Rathore, Jyoti Jasol, Hetal and Neha Dave and Madhvi Gargesh of Rasa Spices, Tarandeep Phull, Nadiyah Akram formerly of Colombo and Cinnamon Hotels, Sri Lanka, Nawabzada Raashid Ali of Bhopal, Chitra Narayanan, Vipin

Gulati, Kaveri Ganapathy Ahuja, Dr S.K. Subramanian, Vikram Doctor, Meenakshi Doctor, Meenakshi Meyyappan, Paresh Arya, Atul Choudhury and the late Jacob Sahaya Kumar.

There would have been no book had it not been for Diya Hazra who set the ball rolling, Thomas Abraham and Poulomi Chatterjee who breathed life into it and Sohini Pal who licked it into shape. Most of all, I'd like to thank my patient children, Amara and Asif, who must have longed to have a more normal mother, but never voiced it out loud.

BIBLIOGRAPHY

Achaya, K.T. *A Historical Dictionary of Indian Food*. Oxford, 2001.

Hemphill, Ian. *Spice Notes and Recipes*. Macmillan Australia, 2006.

Katzer, Gernot. *Gernot Katzer's Spice Pages*. http://gernot-katzers-spice-pages.com/engl/index.html, accessed 2017.

Swahn, J.O. *The Lore of Spices: Their History, nature and Uses Around the World*. Stoeger Publishing Company, 2001.

Turner, Jack. *Spice: The History of a Temptation*. HarperCollins, 2005.